OUTSTANDING DISSERTATIONS IN
LINGUISTICS

edited by
LAURENCE HORN
YALE UNIVERSITY

GRAMMATICAL CASE ASSIGNMENT IN FINNISH

DIANE CARLITA NELSON

Routledge
Taylor & Francis Group
LONDON AND NEW YORK

First published 1998 by Garland Publishing Inc.

2 Park Square, Milton Park, Abingdon, Oxon OX14 4RN
711 Third Avenue, New York, NY 10017, USA

*Routledge is an imprint of the Taylor & Francis Group,
an informa business*

First issued in paperback 2016

Copyright © 1998 Diane Carlita Nelson

All rights reserved. No part of this book may be reprinted or reproduced or utilised in any form or by any electronic, mechanical, or other means, now known or hereafter invented, including photocopying and recording, or in any information storage or retrieval system, without permission in writing from the publishers.

Notice:
Product or corporate names may be trademarks or registered trademarks, and are used only for identification and explanation without intent to infringe.

Library of Congress Cataloging-in-Publication Data

Nelson, Diane Carlita, 1968–
  Grammatical case assignment in Finnish / Diane Carlita Nelson.
    p.   cm. — (Outstanding dissertations in linguistics)
  A revision of the author's thesis (Ph. D.)—University of Edinburgh, 1996.
  Includes bibliographical references and index.
  ISBN 0-8153-3180-0 (alk. paper)
  1. Finnish language—case. I. Title. II. Series.
PH175.N45 1998
494'.5415—dc21

98-25645

ISBN 978-0-8153-3180-3 (hbk)
ISBN 978-1-138-97541-5 (pbk)

For Ruth

Contents

Preface	ix
List of Abbreviations	xi

1. Introduction	3
1.1 A brief overview of Finnish grammar and morphology	3
1.2 Functional categories and the structure of the Finnish IP	15
2. Grammatical Case Assignment in Finnish	39
2.1 Introduction	39
2.2 Subject and object case	40
2.3 Object case assignment and agreement in Finnish: Previous accounts	62
2.4 Conclusion	70
3. Patterns of Case Assignment	75
3.1 Introduction	75
3.2 Case and external arguments	77
3.3 Agreement morphology and case	89
3.4 Weak and strong AGR	93
3.5 The argument structure of imperatives	95
3.6 Split-S ergativity	98
3.7 Conclusion	105
4. Mechanisms of Case Assignment	111
4.1 Introduction	111
4.2 Finite clause structure	112
4.3 Mechanisms of case assignment	118

4.4 Nominative case assignment	122
4.5 Objective case assignment	130
4.6 Case assignment in transitive sentences	149
4.7 Double case marking: An account for Split-S ergativity	152
4.8 Case assignment and measure phrases	174
4.9 Conclusion	178
5. The Morphosyntax of Possessive Affixes	**185**
5.1 Introduction	185
5.2 The distribution of Pxes	186
5.3 Px morphology and phonology	192
5.4 Previous analyses of Finnish Pxes	200
5.5 The syntax of Pxes	203
5.6 Conclusion	226
6. Complex Predicates and Non-finite Clauses	**229**
6.1 Introduction	229
6.2 Case assignment and complex predicates	229
6.3 Gerundive clauses	241
6.4 Adverbial adjunct clauses	246
6.5 Conclusion	250
Bibliography	255
Index	263

Preface

This book is a revision of my 1995 University of Edinburgh dissertation entitled *X^0 Categories and Grammatical Case Assignment in Finnish*. In this work I provide a structural account for patterns of grammatical case in Finnish within the Principles and Parameters framework. The rich case and agreement morphology of Finnish make it an important language for testing hypotheses about the relationships between morphological case and abstract Case, and Case/case and agreement. In particular, several case 'splits' occur in Finnish which challenge standard theoretical accounts about the relationship between abstract and morphological case.

Data relevant to the analysis includes a particular set of environments where internal full DP arguments appear in nominative case but alternate with accusative pronouns. In the same contexts, internal arguments may also receive partitive case to encode features related to aspect or indefiniteness. Because these environments lack an external argument coindexed with agreement, the data is particularly relevant to predictions made by Burzio's Generalization. By testing Burzio's hypothesis systematically against a range of sentence types, I show that Finnish contains a split-S ergative subsystem within a nominative-accusative main system. The assignment of objective cases is linked with the licensing of aspectual roles at D-structure, and finite Tense is posited as a bi-unique Case assigner. I conclude that the case split arises as the result of two case features being assigned simultaneously to an internal argument where no external argument is available. Morphological spell-out rules for particular argument types are also proposed which determine the surface case realization of doubly-case assigned nominals.

In undertaking the original research for this book, I am deeply grateful first of all to my supervisor at Edinburgh, Ronnie Cann, for all his help and support despite being an overworked department head. I am eternally grateful to Maija McKinnon, Jussi Klemola and Simon Kirby for going over the final drafts; all errors in the data, typos and other errors are of course my own.

My interest in Finnish grammar developed at Columbia and was fuelled by the boundless enthusiasm and energy of Aili Flint. Thanks also to the Finnish Ministry of Culture for sponsoring well-organised summer language courses, and to Maija McKinnon in Edinburgh for language tuition, for interesting discussions on grammar and semantics. During the course of my PhD I was able to visit Helsinki and to work with Finnish student informants in Edinburgh. Thanks especially to Soili Turro, Ulla Tuomarla, Henna Makkonen, Hanna Taantsainen, Ilkka Kari, Liisa Laakso-Tammisto and Satu Manninen.

I've found the community of syntacticians working on Finnish to be consistently friendly and supportive, including Maria Vilkuna, also my external examiner; Arto Anttila; Joan Maling; Erika Mitchell; Hannu Reime; Elina Rigler; Susanna Shore; and Trond Trosterud. In particular, thanks to Anne Vainikka for editing *Finnsyntax* and for many helpful comments during the course of my research. In many ways this book is inspired by her work.

I am deeply indebted to linguists in Edinburgh and around the UK for providing stimulating shop talk, including Jim Miller; Bob Ladd and Ellen Bard, for bringing me Cheerios; Nagita; Dimitra Kolliakou; Ethel Jack; Jim Hurford, for his ability to have a conversation on any topic and for his kindness; Antonella Sorace; Robin Lickley; Catrin Rhys; Gillian Ramchand; and Anna Siewierska. Special thanks to Mary Tait; David Adger; and Caroline Heycock, for being my internal examiner and a good friend.

Without the love and support of my friends and family I would be lost. Thanks to everyone at CFA; Miriam Eckert; Louise Kelly and Catriona McPherson; Coffeetalk; Tanja Meurs; Amy Isard; Ian Armit; and Paul Foulkes, Bethan Davies and staff and students in Linguistics and Phonetics at Leeds. In particular, hugs to Simon Kirby, my grandmother Blanche, and my mother Ruth, to whom this book is dedicated.

List of Abbreviations

Nominal morphology

abess	abessive case
abl	ablative case
acc	accusative case
adess	adessive case
all	allative case
com	comitative case
ela	elative case
ess	essive case
gen	genitive case
ill	illative case
iness	inessive case
inst	instructive case
nom	nominative case
part	partitive case
trans	translative case
pl	plural
sg	singular
Px1s	first person singular possessive affix
Px2s	second person singular possessive affix
Px3	third person possessive affix
Px1p	first person plural possessive affix
Px2p	second person plural possessive affix

Verbal morphology

np	nonpast tense	
past	past tense	
cond	conditional mood	
imp	imperative	
MA	MA infinitive	
pass	impersonal passive	
pcp	participle	
pot	potential mood	
TA	TA infinitive	
1s	first person singular verbal agreement	
2s	second person singular verbal agreement	
3s	third person singular verbal agreement	
1p	first person plural verbal agreement	
2p	second person plural verbal agreement	
3p	third person plural verbal agreement	

Other abbreviations

comp	comparative
qu	question
cl	clitic
rel	relative clause marker
caus	causative

Grammatical Case
Assignment in Finnish

CHAPTER 1
Introduction

1.1 A BRIEF OVERVIEW OF FINNISH GRAMMAR & MORPHOLOGY

Finnish is a member of the Fennic branch of the Finno-Ugric language family, a group which includes Hungarian and Estonian as well as a number of related languages spoken by relatively small numbers of speakers in northern and western Russia and in the Baltic region. The Fennic group includes Estonian, Karelian, Veps, Votic, and Livonian; Ugric languages include Mansi (Vogul), Khanty (Ostyak), as well as Hungarian; and the Permic language group includes Komi and Udmurt. Mari and Mordvin are also related. Saami (Lapp) is also a member of this language group, but its genetic relation to Finnish and the Finno-Ugric family as a whole is obscure. The Finno-Ugric family is subsumed by the larger Uralic group, which includes the more distantly related Samoyed languages spoken in the far north of Russia. Language death and extinction are a pervasive problem throughout the Uralic family: Motor became extinct during the last century, while Livonian and Votic are currently spoken by only a handful of native speakers.
 Features common to the Uralic languages as a whole include agglutinative morphology, lack of grammatical gender, auxiliary negative verbs, vowel harmony, possessive affixes (Pxes) to mark nominal agreement, lack of articles, and a rich system of locative cases (Austerlitz 1989). Finnish has no morphological future tense but encodes a past/nonpast distinction.

The data examined in this dissertation is from written Finnish (*kirjakieli*) only. The grammar of spoken Finnish (*puhekieli*) differs in many respects from that of written Finnish. For instance, written Finnish allows pro-drop, has possessive agreement affixes, uses an extensive collection of nominalized clauses, has prenominal relative clauses, lacks articles and pleonastic subjects, and disallows subjects in impersonal passives. In spoken Finnish, pro-drop is disallowed (Vainikka 1989c), and possessive agreement affixes tend not to be used. Subordinate clauses tend to be formed with finite CPs with an overt complementizer rather than nominalizations, and relative clauses tend to be post(nom)inal. The inanimate pronouns *se* and *sitä* are appearing with increasing frequency as both articles and pleonastic subjects. Finally, the historically subjectless impersonal passive has replaced the first person plural paradigm slot in verbal agreement morphology. Despite these differences, unified analyses of both spoken and written Finnish have been attempted, most notably by Vainikka (1989c). The fundamental and systematic differences between the two, however (relative presence or absence of pro-drop, tendency to use prenominal or postnominal relatives, and the presence or absence of articles and pleonastics) suggest that spoken and written Finnish do not share a single grammar, and so require independent analyses. This dissertation will examine the data from written Finnish only, because of constraints of time and space, and because native speaker intuitions about written Finnish tend to be more robust and subject to less variation as a result of social and geographical factors. Standard Finnish orthography is used in the data.

1.1.1 Morphophonology

Word formation in Finnish is highly agglutinative and largely suffixing, typical of the morphological structure of the Uralic languages in general (Tauli 1966). Morphemic alternations are to a large extent conditioned by two major phenomena, vowel harmony and consonant gradation.

Vowel harmony is visible in most derivational and all inflectional word formation, but not in most compound words. The alternation between the vowels *a/ä* and *o/ö* (where the umlaut in standard

Introduction

orthography indicates a front vowel) is conditioned by the back- or front-harmonic properties of the stem:

1) a. Kari-lta   pöydä-ltä
   Kari-abl   table-abl
   'From Kari'   'from the table'

   b. sammu-ma-ton   selvittä-mä-tön
   extinguish(nom)-un clarify(nom)-un
   'unquenchable'   'unexplained'

   c. epä-onni
   un-luck
   'bad luck'

   d. herätys-kello
   awakening-clock
   'alarm clock'

The vowels *i* and *e* are neutral to vowel harmony (though a stem containing only neutral vowels triggers front harmony).

Consonant gradation 'weakens' the stem consonant when the syllable is closed with most types of affixal elements (e.g. geminate consonants degeminate, voiceless stops become voiced, k > ∅, nk > ng, and certain consonant clusters become geminates):

2) a. ranta   'shore'   b. aikoa 'to intend'
   rannalla 'on the shore'   aion   'I intend'

   c. helppo 'easy'
   helposti 'easily'

Stem vowels can be affected by several morphopohonological rules discussed by Nevis (1984:175), one of which raises *-e* to *-i*, another of which shortens *-ee* to *-e*, and the third of which deletes the stem-final vowel:

3) a. lumi 'snow' b. herne 'pea'
   lume-n 'of snow' hernee-n 'of the pea'

   c. vanhuus 'old age'
   vanhuu-den 'of old age'

1.1.2 Nominal morphology

In the nominal morphological template, derivational affixes occur closest to the nominal stem, internal to inflectional morphology. Inflectional morphology is exclusively suffixing and occurs in the following order: stem > comparative/superlative > plural > case > possessive affix. A nominal expression incorporating all of these types of element except Px agreement is exemplified below. For the sake of clarity the traditional distinction between derivational and inflectional morphemes is retained for the present, and indicated with = and - to mark the respective types of morpheme boundaries.

4) epätoivoisempina, 'as more desperate (pl)'

   epä= toivo(i)=se[1] -mp   -i   -na
   NEG=hope =ADJ-comparative-plural-essive

1.1.2.1 Comparative/superlative

The comparative marker is -*mpi* and the superlative marker is -*in*:

5) punainen   'red'
   punaise-mpi 'redder'
   punais-in   'reddest'

1.1.2.2 Number

Plural in Finnish is signalled by -*t* in nominative and accusative case, and by the suffix -*i* in all other environments:

6) marsu 'guinea pig'
   marsu-t 'guinea pigs' (nom/acc)
   marsu-i-ssa 'in the guinea pigs' (inessive)

1.1.2.3 Case

Finnish is typical of Finno-Ugric languages in its proliferation of morphologically distinct case markers. Finnish has four grammatical cases:

7) Case   Form

   Nominative (nom)   zero (lexical form), -*t* (plural)
   Accusative (acc)   -*n*, -*t*, or zero[2]
   Genitive (gen)   -*n*, -iTEN (plural)
   Partitive (part)   -*ta*, -*tä*, *a*, *ä*

Grammatical case endings show concord with the head noun receiving case:

8) Tanja   näk-i   piene-n   ruskea-n   linnu-n.
   Tanja(nom) see-past small-acc brown-acc bird-acc
   'Tanja saw a/the small brown bird'

One of the primary aims of this dissertation is to account for the distribution of these four cases; Chapter 2 is devoted to a description of the relevant data.

In addition to having four grammatical cases, Finnish has roughly eleven productive or semi-productive semantic cases:

9) Name   Form

   Inessive (iness)   -ssa, -ssä
   Adessive (adess)   -lla, -llä
   Allative (all)   -lle
   Illative (ill)   -Vn, -hVn, seen
   Elative (ela)   -sta, -stä
   Ablative (abl)   -lta, -ltä
   Translative (trans)   -ksi
   Essive (ess)   -na, -nä
   Abessive (abess)   -tta, -ttä
   Comitative (com)   -ine
   Instructive (inst)   -in

Modifiers of nouns marked for semantic case agree with the head:

10) iso-sta vihreä-stä laatiko-sta
    big-ela green-ela   box-ela
    'from within the big green box'

There is a general consensus in the literature (Hakulinen 1946/1964; Comrie 1976) that the semantic (or locative) cases in Finnish are mostly historically reduced postpositions.[3] Semantic cases in this dissertation are glossed as English prepositions when semantically transparent, otherwise with abbreviations for individual cases.

1.1.2.4 Possessive Affixes

Finnish, like other Uralic languages, has a separate paradigm of markers to signal nominal and possessive agreement (Pxes) in addition to the verbal agreement paradigm:

11) 1s: minun auto-ni   'my car'
    2s: sinun auto-si   'your (sg) car'
    3:   hänen/heidän auto-nsa   'her/his/their car'
    1p: meidän auto-mme   'our car'
    2p: teidän auto-nne   'you (pl) car'

Introduction

These elements occur affixed to nouns, postpositions, adjectives, and nominalized verbs. Possessive affixes, however, differ from most types of affix in that they do not trigger consonant gradation:

12) laukku   'bag'
    laukkunsa 'his/her bag'

This fact about possessive affixes is discussed further in Chapter 5, where it is argued that Pxes are structurally distinct from verbal agreement, cliticizing rather than affixing to the host.

1.1.3 Adpositions

Finnish is primarily postpositional, but also has a small number of prepositions. Postpositions co-occur with genitive pronouns (13a, b) and possessive affixes (13c):

13) a. laatiko-n takana / edessä / ympärillä
       box-gen   back   / in front / around
       'in back of/in front of/around the box'

    b. äidi-n   luokse
       mother-gen to
       'to mother'

    c. luokse-mme
       to-Px1p
       'to us'

Prepositions appear to assign partitive case to their complements; Vainikka (1989c:143) suggests that partitive case is the structural default case for the complement of category P.

14) a. ilman   sanakirja-a
       without dictionary-part
       'without a dictionary'

   b. vasten   puu-ta
      against tree-part
      'against the tree'

1.1.4 Verbal morphology

The verbal template is analysed in greater detail later in section 1.2.2 of this chapter, when the individual constituents of Finnish INFL are discussed and functional heads posited for a subset of inflectional affixes. In addition to negation and auxiliaries, which occur as separate words, the basic template for the verbal stem consists of nonvarying positions for derivational morphology, tense/mood morphs, and agreement:

15) uiskentelin   'I swam around'

     ui=   skentel-   i-   n
     swim= iterative- past- 1s

Tense, mood, and agreement markers are discussed in greater detail in the section below on the structure of the Finnish IP.

1.1.4.1 Pro-drop

Although verbal agreement morphology in written Finnish is rich, with a distinct morphological marker for each paradigm slot, the omission of coreferential personal pronouns is actually only allowed in the first and second person. Omission of third person pronouns while retaining a personal pronominal (i.e. non-generic) reading is generally ruled out:

16) a. Mene-n   nukku-ma-an.
       go-1s   sleep-MA-ill
       'I'm going to sleep'

    b. ??Mene-e   nukku-ma-an
       go-3s   sleep-MA-ill
       'S/he's going to sleep'

Certain verbs do allow the third person pronominal subject to be dropped, but the interpretation is generic rather than personal:

17) California-ssa   voi   surfa-ta
     California-in   can/3s   surf-TA
     'In California one can surf'

Written Finnish may therefore be classified as partially, but not exclusively, pro-drop.

1.1.5 Word order and configurationality

The configurational/non-configurational taxonomic distinction among languages traditionally considers a number of general linguistic features, including relative freedom of word order, possibility of pro-drop, the presence or absence of pleonastic NPs, overt NP-movement, discontinuous expressions, the relative richness of case systems, and the (morphosyntactic) complexity of verbs and auxiliaries (Hale 1982). According to these criteria, written Finnish appears to show several properties typical of non-configurational languages: generally free word order, a rich case system, a lack of pleonastic elements, and pro-drop is allowed. The rich case system and pro-drop in Finnish have already been discussed. Word order in Finnish is relatively free in that given a simple transitive sentence, all six word order permutations may be possible. Finnish word order facts are, however, quite complex: constituent order has been argued to be to a large extent discourse-conditioned (Vilkuna 1989) or constrained by licensing of certain positions (Vainikka 1989c). A general tendency to fill the preverbal 'subject' position (spec(IP) or T) with lexcial material has been noted by Vainikka (1989c) and Vilkuna (1989). Word order can also be quite restricted in non-finite constructions and complex predicates. These constructions are discussed in detail in Chapter 6. In most of the literature on Finnish, the basic, unmarked word order is taken to be SVO.

In addition to free word order, pro-drop and a rich case system, another typical property of non-configurational languages (Hale 1982) is a lack of pleonastic NPs. Unlike in English, Finnish inverted unaccusative verbs, weather verbs and raising verbs do not require pleonastic subjects:

18) a. Asema-lle saapu-i juna.
 station-to arrive-past/3s train(nom)
 'There arrived a train at the station'

 b. Sata-a lun-ta.
 Rain-3s snow-part
 'It's snowing'

 c. Näyttä-ä, että Olli-lla on uusi ystävä.
 seem-3s that Olli-adess is new friend
 'It seems that Olli has a new friend'

Van Steenbergen (1990) uses 5 tests to determine the status of Finnish as configurational or non-configurational. Assuming standard GB principles such as the Binding Theory and the existence of asymmetrical, hierarchical X-bar phrase structure, she adopts a syntactic model of non-configurational languages. In this model, the tree structure of non-configurational languages is not completely flat; subject-object asymmetries and c-command relations hold at Lexical Structure, or LS (as introduced by Hale 1983). The main difference between configurational and non-configurational languages, in this view, is that the Projection Principle applies to configurational languages and ensures that arguments present at LS are also present at PS: in non-configurational languages the Projection Principle is vacuous (Chomsky 1981:133-4), i.e. the principle holds at LS only. Furthermore, in a non-configurational language both c-command and precedence are relevant at PS for syntactic operations.

The first test used by van Steenbergen to determine whether or not Finnish shows subject-object asymmetries is a test for coreferential

Introduction

interpretation. The following sentences illustrate relevant binding facts involving third person Finnish Pxes (discussed in greater detail in Chapter 5). Van Steenbergen assumes that third person genitive pronouns can be dropped, leaving the possessive affix bound with pro. In the following pair, the possessive affix is coreferential with the main clause subject only when the genitive pronoun is omitted:

19) a. Anna$_i$ rakasta-a häne-n$_j$ kissa-a-nsa.
       Anna love-3s her-gen cat-part-Px3
       'Anna$_i$ loves her$_j$ cat'

   b. Anna$_i$ rakasta-a *pro$_i$* kissa-a-nsa.
       Anna love-3s pro cat-part-Px3
       'Anna$_i$ loves her$_i$ cat'

The sentences below, however, illustrate that the omission of the genitive pronoun is restricted to certain environments:

20) a. Häne-n$_i$ kissa-a-nsa Anna$_j$ rakasta-a.
       her-gen cat-part-Px3 Anna love-3s
       'Anna$_j$ loves her$_i$ cat'

   b. *pro$_i$* kissa-a-nsa Anna$_i$ rakasta-a.
       pro cat-part-Px3 Anna love-3s
       'Anna$_i$ loves her$_i$ cat'

   c. Häne-n$_i$ kissa-a-nsa rakasta-a Anna$_{i/j}$ (i = j or i ≠ j)
       her-gen cat-part-Px3 love-3s Anna
       'Her$_i$ cat loves Anna$_{i/j}$'

   d. **pro$_i$* kissa-nsa rakasta-a Anna-a$_j$
       pro cat -Px3 love-3s Anna-part
       'Her$_i$ cat loves Anna$_j$'

Within a Principles and Parameters-based approach, the data presented above is straightforwardly accounted for by assuming that third person pronouns are pronominal, and cannot be locally A-bound, while pro is an anaphor, and must be locally A-bound, a hypothesis consistent with the principles of the Binding Theory.

However, van Steenbergen argues that in a non-configurational approach, all of the relevant facts cannot be accounted for in a model where the relations of c-command and precedence hold at PS only. In an analysis of Finnish as a non-configurational language, it could be stipulated that the third person genitive pronoun must be free, and pro bound, at LS, where Binding Principles A and B hold; however, the following data causes problems for Binding Principle C in a non-configurational approach:

21) a. Anna-n$_i$ kissa rakasta-a hän-tä$_i$
    Anna-gen cat love-3s him/her-part
    'Anna's$_i$ cat loves her$_i$'

   b. Hän$_i$ rakasta-a Anna-n$_j$ kissa-a.
      s/he love-3s Anna-gen cat-part
      'S/he$_i$ loves Anna's$_j$ cat'

   c. Anna-n$_i$ kissa-a hän$_j$ rakasta-a.
      Anna-gen cat-part s/he love-3s
      'S/he$_j$ loves Anna's$_i$ cat'

In a non-configurational approach, both precedence and c-command hold at PS. (20a) and (20c) show that a coreferential pronoun may precede a proper noun, while in (21b) a coreferential pronoun also c-commands its proper noun antecedent. The only way to account for the data might be to restrict proper nouns from being both c-commanded and preceded. However, this hypothesis would fail to account for why *Annan* and *hän* are not coreferential in (21c); the proper noun is c-commanded but not preceded by the pronoun, so a coreferential interpretation should be possible. In a configurational approach, the data can be accounted for easily by appealing to Principle C. According to Principle C, *Annan* in (21a) is not c-commanded by *häntä*, and *häntä* is not locally A-bound by *Annan*, so a coreferential interpretation is possible. In (21b), the pronoun c-commands its antecedent, so a coreferential interpretation is ruled out.

Van Steenbergen employs four other tests of this type, including a test for bound variable interpretation involving data from WCO (Weak Crossover) and SCO (Strong Crossover); data from VP-idioms; tests for superiority in sentences with 2 wh-elements; and finally tests involving long wh-movement. In all cases, accounting for the data within a nonconfigurational approach proves difficult or impossible, while straightforward analyses are available within a configurational approach. Her conclusion, that Finnish should be analysed as a configurational language, is adopted as an underlying assumption about the grammar of Finnish in the current work.

1.2 FUNCTIONAL CATEGORIES AND THE STRUCTURE OF THE FINNISH IP

1.2.1 Properties of functional heads

Following Abney (1987), Baker (1988), Pollock (1989), and subsequent work, e.g. Ouhalla (1991), non-lexical elements (e.g. DET, TNS, AGR, NEG) are assumed to project in the syntax as functional heads, according to the principles of X-Bar Theory developed in Chomsky (1970):

22) $X'' \rightarrow \text{spec}; X'$
$X' \rightarrow X'; YP$
$X' \rightarrow X; YP$

Underlying this functional head hypothesis is the notion that inflectional morphological processes operate according to similar principles as syntactic processes. Bound morphs projecting in the syntax attach to a lexical stem host via Head Movement (Baker 1988) or via cliticization if the element projects in a specifier position; this process is described in greater detail in Chapter 5.
  This theoretical shift in focus to the syntactic properties of functional heads allows for accounts of cross-linguistic variation in terms of differences in the order of functional heads, the relative 'strength' of the inflectional features they encode, and their individual case-coding properties (Ouhalla 1991, Tait 1991). If variation is the result of parametrization within a relatively small set of functional categories, then fewer language-specific rules are required to account for various case and word order phenomena.

Another approach in which the number of syntactic principles and constraints specified by UG is reduced even further is a model developed by Cann and Tait (1989), Tait and Cann (1990), Tait (1991), and Cann (1993). The approach draws on aspects of the Principles and Parameters framework combined with theoretical proposals from Categorial Grammar and GPSG. Cann and Tait propose that all relevant categories, functional and contentive, in a given language may project according to the rules of X-bar. Furthermore, as this generalization extends to all bound as well as free morphs, the distinction between morphological affixation previously held to occur in the lexicon (as idiosyncratic, derivational morphological processes) and more productive, syntactic affixation such as passivization and causative derivation is eliminated. All structure dependencies are specified in the lexical entries of all morphemes in a given language, with syntactic structure projecting directly from the lexicon. This model contains no separate module for morphology, inflectional or derivational. Syntactic structure is determined by the properties of functional categories specifically.

Lexical entries encode c- (categorial) and m- (morphological) selectional properties which underlie syntactic structure. These relations may be represented schematically as lexical trees, following Tait (1991); trees can be simple or branching. Superscripted 0 indicates a zero-bar (lexical) level of representation:

23) a. N^0 b.

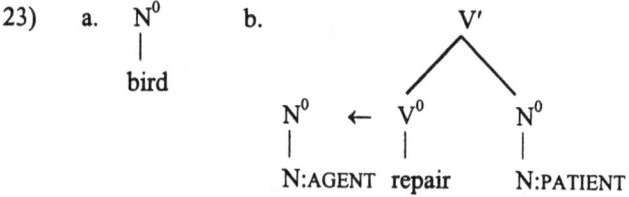

Argument structure is encoded at the lexical level,[4] and it is assumed that all categories display compositional semantics. Complements selected project directly from the lexicon as complements. Functional heads have the same relations specified in their lexical entry, providing a structural mechanism for the building of extended projections of contentive elements based on selection:

Introduction 17

24) a. 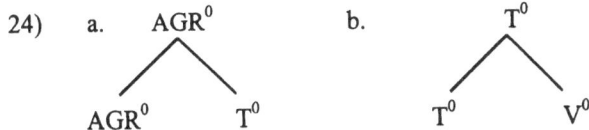 b.

Because the c-selectional properties of AGR and T(ense) in (24) are encoded lexically, no parameter-setting is required to regulate the ordering of inflectional morphemes in a given language. Cross-linguistic variation thus arises as the result of lexical variation, eliminating the need for a set of parameters specified within UG.

1.2.2 The structure of the Finnish IP

Since it is argued here that functional heads play a role in the assignment of case, it is necessary at this stage to make explicit the assumed structure of the Finnish IP. Two recent studies (Mitchell 1991a and Holmberg et al. 1993) have explored this area of research and have reached reassuringly similar conclusions; the agglutinative morphology of Finnish and the wide range of inflectional categories which appear overtly as affixes allow a relatively straightforward analysis, if proposals involving the syntactic projection of affixes such as those of Baker (1988), Pollock (1989) and Ouhalla (1991) are adopted.

The structure of INFL proposed by Mitchell (1991a) posits separate projections for the following functional categories: Agreement (AGR), Assertion (AST), Tense/ Mood, Aspect, and Voice, with the subject NP in spec(AGRP):

25)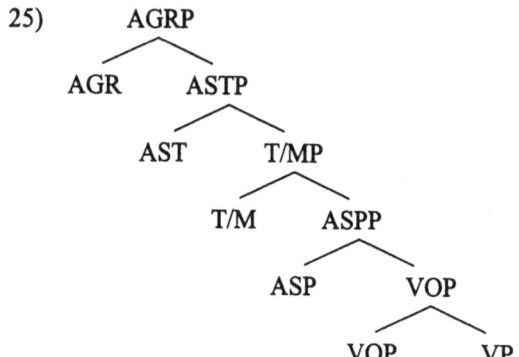

Mitchell (1991b) also proposes a slightly expanded version of the above phrase structure for Finnish, with the functional head Obligation (Obl), supported by the functional category Modal, projecting between AGR and Neg (equivalent to AST in Mitchell 1991b).

A similar configuration of functional heads for Finnish has been proposed by Holmberg et al. (1993). This paper assumes a constraint on representation, repeated below (Holmberg et al. 1993:178):

26) A head-chain must have overt morphological realization.

This restriction bars phonologically null instantiations of heads in the structure, and allows heads to be licensed by paradigmatically null elements as well as traces of moved elements, provided they are coindexed with phonologically realized material. A similar constraint, the PF-Licensing Principle, has been proposed by Cann and Tait (1989), Tait and Cann (1990), Tait (1991), and Cann (1993), and is discussed in greater detail in Chapter 4. Despite their requirement for the licensing of head-chains, Holmberg et al. propose a structure for Finnish INFL that contains one more functional head (AUX) than Mitchell's, who does not overtly assume such a constraint:

27)

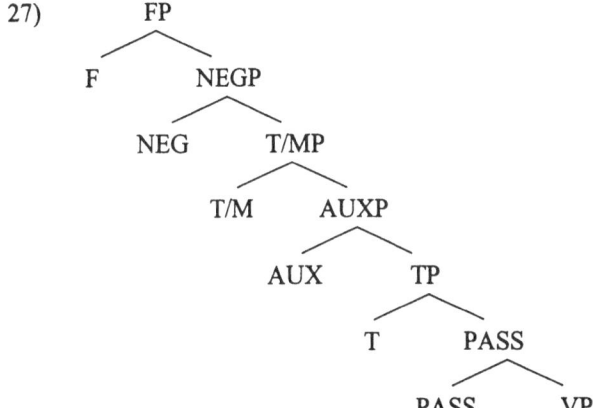

In their model, F represents Finiteness, T/M, Tense/Mood, AUX, Auxiliary verb, T, Tense (=perfect participles), and PASS, Passive. The terminology used in the two papers differs slightly, but the analyses are quite similar. The evidence from both papers for positing each of these functional heads is reviewed below, and a tree posited which adopts aspects of both hypotheses.

1.2.2.1 Agreement and Finiteness

Mitchell (1991a and 1991b) follows Pollock (1989) in proposing that AGR projects as a functional head in Finnish INFL. The morphological evidence from Finnish for a projection of AGR is straightforward: unlike in languages where agreement is nonovert (e.g. Swedish, Pidgin English), subject agreement in Finnish is overtly realized and comprises a paradigm of affixes signalling 6 permutations of person and number:

28) Verbal agreement paradigm of *laulaa*, 'to sing'

1s:	minä	laula	-n	'I sing'
2s:	sinä	laula	-t	'You (sing.) sing'
3s:	hän/se	laula	-a	's/he / it sings'
1p:	me	laula	-mme	'we sing'
2p:	te	laula	-tte	'you (pl.) sing'
3p:	he	laula	-vat	'they sing'

Mitchell notes that contrary to Pollock's analysis of the structure of IP for French and English, the morphology of Finnish provides evidence that AGR dominates Tense in the extended projection of V, rather than vice-versa:

29) minä   laulo-i-n[5]
    I(nom) sing-past-1s
    'I sang'

Holmberg et al. (1993) argue that finite clauses are dominated by F, Finiteness, which can be licensed by agreement features; they specifically do not posit AGR as a functional head. The motivation for this analysis comes from the Finnish data most relevant to the current work. In certain sentence types where 'zero-accusative' (nominative case-marked) objects appear, discussed in detail throughout this dissertation, the agreement marking on the verb is an invariant default third person singular form (-V in the paradigm above) or -Vn:

30) a. Peka-n   täyty-y myy-dä talo.
      Pekka-gen must-3s sell-TA house(nom)
      'Pekka must sell the house'

    b. Naapur-ien   täyty-y myy-dä talo.
      neighbor- gen/pl must-3s sell-TA house(nom)
      'The neighbors must sell the house'

These sentence types are described in greater detail in the next chapter. In Chapter 3 it is argued that the fact that the agreement morphology on the matrix verb fails to reflect the plural or singular number of the subject signals that AGR in these sentences may be present, but does not reflect a relation of coindexation between the verb and one of its arguments. Sentences like those in (30) above are, however, finite, taking tense and mood affixes:

31) Naapur-ien   täyty-i   myy-dä talo.
    neighbour-gen/pl must-past/3s sell-TA house(nom)
    'The neighbours had to sell the house'

Introduction

Holmberg et al. argue that Finiteness (F) is the highest functional head in the maximal projection of V, and that it can be licensed phonologically by either an agreement affix or by a verbal complex such as (30) and (31) above, inflected for tense or mood. Defective (default) third person agreement morphs in their model do not in themselves license Finiteness. AGR in Mitchell's analysis always projects, presumably licensed by these morphemes. Mitchell's terminology for verbal agreement (AGR) is adopted in the current analysis, and AGR posited as a functional head licensed by agreement features.

1.2.2.2 Negation and Assertion

Negation in Finnish in non-imperative sentences is realized by *e-*, a quasi-verbal element which hosts agreement affixes but not tense and mood affixes. In imperative sentences, negation is realized by *äl-*, which hosts a distinct paradigm of affixes signalling the person and number of the imperative addressee. Both Holmberg et al. (1993) and Mitchell (1991b) posit a functional head for negation, and both provide strong evidence that it intervenes between AGR and Tense/Mood (the node below Negation): in negated sentences, the verb appears as a bare stem form in nonpast tense or hosts tense and mood markers, and agreement is hosted by the negative element:

32) a. E-tte   nuku
     neg-2p sleep
     'You (pl) won't sleep'

   b. E-tte   nukku-neet[6]
     neg-2p sleep-pcp past/pl
     'You (pl) didn't sleep'

   c. Äl-kää   naura-ko!
     neg-2p laugh-imp
     'Don't laugh!' (plural addressee)

Holmberg et al. note also that adverbs which have sentential scope over FP (AGRP), e.g. *aina*, 'always,' must be adjoined to a position between Tense/MoodP and FinitenessP, given the word order in sentences such as (33) below (data from Holmberg et al. 1993:196):

33) Jussi   e-i   aina   ol-isi   valitta-nut   sii-tä.
    Jussi(nom) neg-3s always be-cond complain-pcp it-abl
    'Jussi wouldn't always have complained about it'

Because negation and the passive 'agreement' marker *-An* appear in complementary distribution, Mitchell (1991a) terms this projection "Assertion" and argues that it projects to signal assertion/negation polarity in all sentences:

34) a. Ikkuna   ava-ta-an
       window(nom)   open-pass-Vn
       'The window will be opened'

    b. Ikkuna-a   e-i   ava-ta
       window-part   neg-3s open-pass
       'The window will not be opened'

She concludes that *-An* in passives represents the non-negative polarity instantiation of the functional head Assertion. Furthermore, in Mitchell's analysis Assertion projects in all clauses, actives and passives.

However, diachronic evidence indicates that the -Vn element is historically a Possessive affix (Hakulinen 1946/1961:157), analysed in Chapter 5 as being category AGR. Considering this fact it is not surprising that *-An* occurs in complementary distribution with Negation, patterning like verbal AGR in this respect. An analysis of the *-An* element in passives as default third person agreement similar to defective markers in modal verbs such as *täytyä* (as in ex. 31 above) is also consistent with traditional grammars, but removes the motivation for positing a universally-occurring functional element Assertion. Holmberg et al.'s terminology (NEG) is therefore be adopted in the current work.

1.2.2.3 Tense and Mood

Mitchell (1991a and 1991b) and Holmberg et al. (1993) concur that Tense and Mood in Finnish conflate in a single functional head Tense/Mood (T/M), and they present similar arguments for positing this functional head. The morphological evidence is clear: preceding agreement in non-negated sentences is a slot in the morphology for the tense and mood markers, which cannot co-occur.

Past/Nonpast Indicative

The affix *-i* preceding agreement signals past tense. A zero morph in the same position signals nonpast tense:

35) a. Isoisä   syö[7]   kala-a.
    grandfather eat/3s fish-part
    'Grandfather is eating/will eat some fish'

    b. Isoisä   sö[8]-i   kala-a.
    grandfather eat-past/3s fish-part
    'Grandfather ate some fish'

The active participial morphemes -NUT and -VA (interpreted as future tense) are posited as allomorphs of the past/nonpast tense affixes -i/∅ by Holmberg et al; in negated past tense sentences, the past/nonpast distinction is realized as a participle on an auxiliary stem and the agreement appears on the element of negation:

36) a. Minä men-i-n   kauppa-an eilen.
    I(nom) go-past-1s shop-to yesterday
    'I went to the shop yesterday'

    b. Minä e-n   men-nyt   kauppa-an eilen.
    I(nom) neg-1s go-pcp/past shop-to yesterday
    'I didn't go the shop yesterday'

37) Aili   korja-a   ikkuna-a.
    Aili(nom) repair-3s window-part
    'Aili is repairing the window'

In a later section it is proposed that the participle -NUT can also project as Perfect (PERF).

Conditional and Potential Moods

Two nonindicative mood markers, conditional *-isi* and the increasingly infrequent potential form *-ne/-nne*, appear in the same position affixed to the verb:

38) a. Sinä tunte-ne-t   Aili-n   jo   hyvin.
       you know-pot-2s Aili-acc already well
       'You may/probably already know Aili well'

    b. Mi-hin   matkusta-isi-t, jos sinu-lla ol-isi   paljon raha-a?
       where-ill travel-cond-2s if you-adess be-cond a lot money-part
       'Where would you travel, if you had a lot of money?'

Mood markers cannot co-occur with the past tense affix *-i*:

39) a. *tunte-ne-i-t   *tunte-i-ne-t
       know-pot-past-2s   know-past-pot-2s

    b. *matkusta-isi-i-t   *matkusta-i-isi-t
       travel-cond-past-2s   travel-past-cond-2s

Furthermore, Mitchell (1991a) notes that conditional and potential mood morphology cannot co-occur with lexical elements signalling tense without an auxiliary (in a separate projection) to support a perfect participle, indicating that Tense and Mood share a projection:

40) a. *Syö-isi-n   keitto-a   eilen
       eat-cond-1s soup-part yesterday

   b. Ol-isi-n   syö-nyt   keitto-a   eilen.
       be-cond-1s eat-pcp   soup-part yesterday
       'I would have eaten soup yesterday'

The fact that (40b) is possible rules out a hypothesis that the Mood-Tense co-occurrence restriction is semantic.

Imperatives

The imperative mood in Finnish is expressed by a 'bare' weak-grade verbal stem in the second person singular; the historical imperative marker *-k is overtly realized in a paradigm of 'agreement' suffixes which signal the person and number of the imperative referent in four of the six possible paradigm slots:

41)   From *ottaa*, 'to take'

       1s: (no form)
       2s: Ota (sinä) se!   'Take (sg. addressee) it!'
       3s: Otta-koon (hän) sen!   'Let him/her take it!'
       1p: Otta-kaamme (me) se!   'Let us take it!'
       2p: Otta-kaa (te) se!   'Take (pl. addressee) it!'
       3p: Otta-koot (he) sen!   'Let them take it!'

In the second person singular form of the imperative, no 'agreement' affix appears. Holmberg et al. (1993:185) assume that imperative might be classified as a mood, but do not go into greater detail on the subject. Mitchell (1991b) suggests that the imperative mood marker projects as head of an Obligation (OBL) phrase. Her arguments for this derive from data from negated imperatives, discussed below.

Tense/Mood and Negation

The hypothesized structural relation between Tense/Mood and Negation, that Negation dominates T/M, is supported by the fact that when a sentence marked for nonindicative mood is negated, the negation element hosts an agreement affix, the mood element remains affixed to the main verb, and pluperfect or perfect tense is hosted by an auxiliary:

42) a. He   e-ivät   tietä-ne,   että Maija on   koto-na
       they neg-3p   know-pot   that Maija be/3s home-at
       'They probably don't know that Maija is at home'

   b. He e-ivät lie-ne[9] tietä-neet,   että Maija ol-i   koto-na
      they neg-3p be-pot know-pcp/pl   that Maija be-past/3s home-at
      'They probably didn't know that Maija was at home'

If Negation were below T/M, the mood element rather than the negation element would be expected to host agreement.

Imperative Mood and Negation

Mitchell (1991b) specifically does not analyse the imperative as a mood, but as an instantiation of the functional head [OBL] (Obligation) along with the modal verbs *täytyy* and *pitää*. She posits this functional projection as occurring between AGR and NEG, on the basis of evidence from negated imperatives:

43)   Äl-k-ää   otta-ko   si-tä!
      neg-*k*-2p   take-imp   it-part
      'Don't (pl. referent) take it!'

In Mitchell's model, the imperative affix paradigm given in (41) above projects as AGR (in this case surfacing as -*ää*), dominating OBLP (headed by the imperative morph -*k*-), which dominates NEG (headed by *äl*-), which in turn takes T/MP as a complement:

Introduction

44)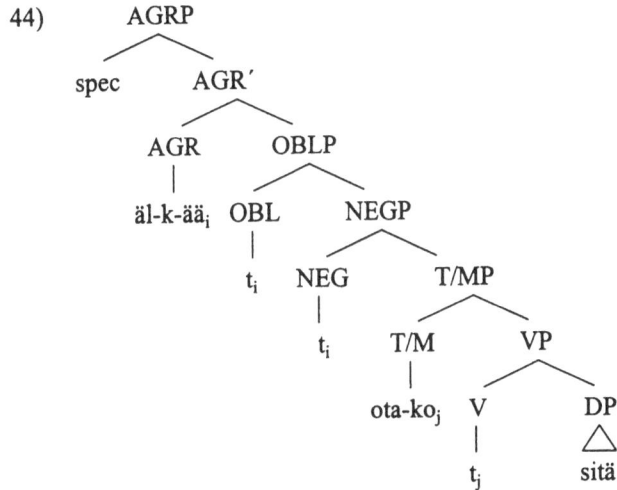

However, the subdivision of imperative 'agreement' markers such as -*kää* into two components -*k*- and -*ää* is not justified on the grounds of morphological productivity: they do not occur with any other morphs in modern Finnish. Similarly, the modal verbs of Obligation which she suggests raise to the OBL node are not morphologically marked as distinct from other verbs; their properties of obligation are clearly lexical rather than inflectional as Mitchell suggests.

Holmberg and Nikanne (1993:5) interpret elements such as -*kää* as representing a conflation of imperative and agreement morphemes, presumably projecting as a single element in the syntax. In the same analysis, the -*ko* element is interpreted as an imperative marker. Holmberg and Nikanne's interpretation of imperative agreement elements as single morphological units is adopted here, as is their analysis of -*ko* as an imperative marker. However, if their analysis of the morphology is merged with Holmberg et al's proposed structure of IP for Finnish, a problem emerges in that two discontinuous imperative mood markers (and by extension Tense/Mood) project in the syntax, one conflated with AGR as -*kää* and one affixed to the auxiliary as -*ko*. One possible solution to this problem is to analyse elements such as -*kää* as nonheads, which cliticize onto the host NEG. The imperative 'agreement' paradigm occurs in conjunction with the imperative mood but these morphemes do not carry imperative mood features. Instead, the imperative mood in negated imperative sentences projects as -*ko*, an allomorph of the other imperative markers. Additional evidence in support of the hypothesis that -*ko* projects as T/M is presented in the next section.

1.2.2.4 Auxiliaries

In sentences with pluperfect tense, auxiliary verbal stems *ole-* and *lie-*, 'to be,' host Tense/Mood, while the verb appears in a participial form:

45) Hanna   ol-i   rakenta-nut   talo-a.
    Hanna(nom) be-past/3s build-pcp/past house-part
    'Hanna had built a house'

In negative perfect imperatives, the imperative marker -*ko* is hosted by an allomorph of the stem of the auxiliary verb 'to be,' *ol-*:

46) Äl-kää   ol-ko   otta-neet   si-tä![10]
    neg-2p be-*ko* take-pcp past/pl it-part
    'Don't have taken it!'

(The participle -*neet* which appears affixed to the verbal stem in the example above is analysed as a projection of Perfect in the next section). The hypothesis presented above that -*ko* projects as T/M is supported by the fact that inflection for negative pluperfect is ungrammatical, indicating that -*ko* cannot share a node with Tense:

47) *Äl-kää   ol-i-ko   otta-neet   se!
    neg-2p be-past-*ko* take-pcp past/pl it(nom)
    'Don't had taken it!'

Mitchell does not posit a separate node for AUX but allows auxiliary stems to be base-generated in T/MP with the Tense/Mood affix. Holmberg et al. posit a node below T/MP in which auxiliaries (AUX) are base-generated to provide adequate structure to form compound past tenses. In their phrase-structure template for Finnish, AUX projects between T/MP and V, since in sentences like (45) the auxiliary rather than the verb hosts the past tense marker. In support of their argument that auxiliary *ole-* and *lie-* project as heads separate from the main copular verb *olla*, 'to be,' they note that auxiliary *ole-* cannot occur in some of the same non-finite clauses which permit main verb *olla*. Holmberg et al. suggest that the matrix verbs in such non-finite clauses subcategorize for Tense/Aspect complements (posited in the next section as the functional projection below AUX), a category which includes infinitival verb forms such as *olla*; however, *ole-* projects as a different functional category, AUX, and so cannot select the subcategorization frame of the matrix verb.

1.2.2.5 Perfect tense

Both Holmberg et al. (1993) and Mitchell (1991a) posit a projection for the perfect and pluperfect participles which appear attached to the verb when supported by an auxiliary, as in (45) and (46). The former name the projection Tense, but distinguish it from Tense/Mood; in the latter analysis the projection is named Aspect. Because this position hosts perfect and pluperfect tense participles over and above those distinguishing past from nonpast tense, this projection is termed Perfect (PERF) in the current work.

Negative Pluperfect

The participial morpheme -NUT (plus variants involving the assimilation of an initial consonant) supported by auxiliaries was analysed as Tense/Mood in a previous section. It is possible for a Finnish sentence to contain two participial verb forms, one base-generated in Tense and one in Perfect. Evidence that two projections are required for two separate participles is given by Holmberg et al. and derives from negated pluperfect sentences:

48) Hanna e-i ol-lut vielä rakenta-nut talo-a.
    Hanna neg-3s be-pcp yet build-pcp house-part
    'Hanna hadn't yet built a house'

In a negated pluperfect sentence, the negation element hosts agreement, the auxiliary hosts (participial) tense, and the verb appears in a participial form, so nodes are required for Agreement (*-i*),

Negation (*e*-), Tense/Mood (-*lut*), Auxiliary (*ol*-), Perfect (-*nut*), and Verb (*raken*-).

Negative perfect imperatives

Negative imperatives can also occur with perfect tense (data given as 46 above):

  49) Äl-kää ol-ko otta-neet   si-tä!
       neg-2p be-*ko* take-pcp/pl it-part
       'Don't have taken it!'

The negative pluperfect imperative sentence in (49) above shares properties of indicative negative pluperfect sentences as in (45): the negative stem *äl-* is quasi-verbal, and appears with an 'agreement' marker -*kää* to signal the person and number of the addressee.

1.2.2.6 Passive and Voice

Finnish has an impersonal passive formed by affixation of the verbal stem with the morpheme -TA+AN. Both previous analyses posit a node below Perfect tense in which Passive elements are base-generated; Mitchell (1991a) terms this node Voice while Holmberg et al. posit a PASS node. Holmberg et al's term PASS is used here.

    The passive markers in Finnish comprise a finite, impersonal passive morpheme -TAAN (composed of two subparts TA+AN; as discussed in a previous section this is evident in negated passives, where the second element fails to appear in the morphology) plus a participial form -TTU. -TAAN occurs without a copula and can reflect past and nonpast Tense with a suffixed -*i*. The passive participle appears as either a lexicalized adjective or as an adjectival predicate with copula, and can reflect past and nonpast tense (which is interpreted as expressing obligation). The surface forms of both morphemes are conditioned by consonant gradation and vowel harmony:

50) Koulu-ssa opiskel-tiin ranska-a
 school-in study-pass/past French-part
 'In school they studied French'

51) Suome-ssa syö-dään viili-ä
 Finland-in eat-pass viili-part
 'In Finland they eat *viili*'

52) Maala-ttu pöytä on myy-tävä-nä.
 paint-pcp pass/past table(nom) be/3s sell-pcp pass/np-ess
 'The painted table is for sale'

53) Pöytä on maala-ttava.
 table(nom) be/3s paint-pcp pass/np
 'The table should be painted'

In (50) and (51) the past/nonpast Tense distinction is realized by the infixes -*ii*-/-*ää*- within the passive morpheme. In (52) and (53) above the passive participles -TTU and -TTAVA reflect a distinction involving the completedness of the painting and selling events. Adopting the tree structure proposed so far, the structural differences between (50) and (51) on the one hand and the predicates in (52) and (53) on the other is proposed as follows: in (50) and (51) the passive morpheme -TAAN is base-generated in PASS and raises to Tense; no auxiliaries project in this structure. There are two possible analyses for the morphology of (52) and (53). One possibility is that the passive morpheme in these cases is actually comprised of -TTA-, conditioned by consonant gradation in (53) to -*ta*-, plus a tense element -AVA (alternating with -U in examples like *maala-ttu* in (52)). The passive element then raises from PASS to PERF to collect the tense marker, yielding the resulting participial verb in PERF, while further up the tree the auxiliary *ole*- raises to Tense and Agreement. The other structural option for these examples, and the one apparently favoured by Holmberg et al, is that the morphemes -TTAVA and -TTU are base-generated in Voice but conflate Perfect and Passive features, so that the elements are required to raise to Perfect. The productivity of the morpheme -VA independent of the passive -TTA supports the former analysis, also adopted by Holmberg and Nikanne (1993:2).

1.2.3 Summary

Adopting the proposed maximal phrase structure representations from Holmberg et al. (1993) and Mitchell (1991a and 1991b) with some relatively minor alterations, the functional categories that make up INFL in Finnish finite clauses can be summarized thus far, in order of dominance from the top of the structure downwards:

1. AGR- verbal agreement affixes
2. NEG- verbal negation elements *e-* and *älä-* (imperatives only)
3. T/M-
    Tense (indicative Mood):
       Finite past/nonpast, *-i/Ø*,
       Participial -NUT and -VA (with negation only)
    Mood:
       Conditional *-isi-*
       Potential *-ne-*
4. AUX- auxiliary verb stems *ole-* and *lie-*
5. PERF- participles -NUT, -VA, -(TT)U, -(TT)AVA
6. PASS-
    Voice:
       Impersonal passive -TA+AN
       Passive participial stem -TT

The present analysis, then, assumes that finite clauses are headed by subject agreement (AGR), governing the functional heads Negation, Tense/Mood, Auxiliary, Perfect, and finally, Voice. The maximal expansion of IP in any one finite Finnish sentence, a negated passive pluperfect, would have the following syntactic structure (specifiers omitted):

54)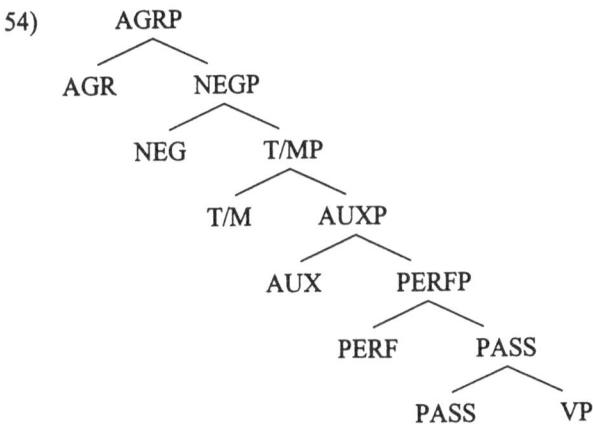

Having posited the structure of the maximal Finnish IP as (54) above, the question remains as to whether all of these heads project in all sentences, as assumed in Mitchell (1991b), or whether elements not overt in the morphology of a given sentence are also missing from the underlying syntactic representation, as assumed by Holmberg et al. (1993) This issue is addressed in chapter 4.

1.2.4 Other functional categories

1.2.4.1 CP and Topic

COMP in Finnish is licensed by complementizers such as *että* (55):

55) Minä toivo-n, että aurinko paista-a huomenna.
    I   hope-1s that sun   shine-3s tomorrow
   'I hope that it will be sunny tomorrow'

Wh-movement in Finnish is assumed to involve movement to spec(CP) in the usual way:

56) Miksi sinä   itke-t?
    why   you(nom) cry-2s
    'Why are you crying?'

Moreover, CP has been identified (Vainikka 1989c) as the position which hosts stressed elements; Vilkuna (1989) posits a discourse-linked position K for contrastive elements, question particles, and relative pronouns, which roughly corresponds to C and spec(CP). Movement of elements to a sentence-initial position is often referred to as 'topicalization,' but this term may be misleading since stressed elements in this position in Finnish may receive a contrastive focus interpretation rather than an interpretation as a topic. Vilkuna and Vainikka also posit a position to the right of K or spec(CP) (T and spec(IP), respectively) which generally must be licensed with phonologically realized material. This position may arguably be associated with Topics.

1.2.4.2 DET

Following Abney (1987), determiners are assumed to project as the functional head of NP. Written Finnish lacks articles, but evidence for a projection of DET is available from demonstrative pronouns:

57) a. Tuo siili   b. Nuo   siili-t
       that hedgehog   those hedgehog-pl
       'that hedgehog'   'those hedgehogs'

    c. Nä-i-n   tuo-n   siili-n.
       see-past-1s   that-acc hedgehog-acc
       'I saw that hedgehog'

Demonstrative pronouns in the examples above show concord with the head noun.

1.2.4.3 Infinitives

In addition to the inflectional elements described above, Finnish has two productive infinitive markers, -MA and -TA, the forms of which are conditioned by consonant gradation, vowel harmony and phonemics of the verb stem:

58) a. E-n   minä halua vasta-ta   kysymykse-en.
        neg-1s I(nom) want answer-TA question-ill
        'I don't want to answer the question.'

    b. Miehe-n tarvitse-e myy-dä tietokonee-nsa.
        man-gen need-3s sell-TA computer-Px3
        'The man must sell his computer'

59) a. Auli men-i   Turku-un osta-ma-an uude-n lompako-n.
        Auli go-past/3s Turku-to buy-MA-ill new-acc wallet-acc
        'Auli went to Turku to buy a new wallet'

    b. Velje-ni   tul-i   etsi-mä-stä   ystävä-ä-nsä.
        brother-Px1s come-past/3s look for-MA-ela friend-part-Px3
        'My brother came from looking for his friend'

Infinitive forms are selected as complements by a wide variety of verbs, particularly modals and raising verbs. Holmberg et al. (1993:188) argue that the infinitival morpheme -TA projects in Tense (Perfect). Vainikka (1989c) proposes that the two elements head their own functional projections; her analysis is adopted in the current work.

In the next chapter, data are presented illustrating some of the case-marking phenomena to be examined in Chapters 3 and 4. In Chapter 5, the properties of nominal AGR (Possessive affixes) are contrasted with those of verbal AGR, and in Chapter 6 an account of complex predicates and nominalized constructions is outlined.

Notes

1. *se-* is the stem form of the derivational suffix *-nen*, which derives nouns and adjectives, and translates roughly as 'having the qualities of.'

2. *-n*, *-t*, and zero and listed as the three forms of the accusative in most traditional grammars. However, in recent syntactic analyses of Finnish (including the current work), the identity of the *abstract* case represented by these three forms has been the subject of debate. Various proposals from the literature are summarised in Chapter 2. In Chapter 4, *-t* and zero alternating in the same environments are argued to signal the assignment of both nominative and accusative case to an argument.

3. Nikanne (1989, 1991, and 1993) has proposed an analysis of the semantic cases in Finnish in which case affixes are assigned by a phonologically empty head P. However, Nikanne's analysis presents a violation of the PFLP, a theoretical constraint on representation and acquistion assumed in the current work (discussed in Chapter 4) which bars nonovert heads; in this dissertation the agreeing of heads and modifiers for case will be assumed to be an instantiation of generalised agreement within a phrase via feature percolation.

4. In section 4.4.2 it is argued that verbs may not theta-mark complements until D-structure.

5. The stem vowel of the verb *laulaa*, 'to sing' is *laula-* in nonpast tense but is conditioned by the affixation of the past tense morph *-i* to trigger a change in the stem vowel to *-o*. This phonological rule applies to an entire class of stems.

6. Past participles such as *-neet* do reflect plural vs singular number; however, this is not interpreted in the literature as full subject agreement, since agreement for person is not signalled.

Introduction

7. In word-final position (i.e. when first and second person agreement affixes are not present) the present indicative tense marker is signalled by a glottal stop word-finally or by a lengthening of the following consonant. (35b) above is thus realized as /söikkalaa/.

8. The diphthong -*yö* in the verb stem undergoes a phonological stem change to -*ö* conditioned by the affixation of the past tense morph.

9. *lie-* is a suppletive form of the auxiliary *ole-* (derived from the stem of the verb 'to be') which is restricted in distribution to the potential mood only.

10. In this example, the imperative verb might express a wish for a certain state of affairs rather than have an imperative reading.

CHAPTER 2
Grammatical Case Assignment in Finnish

2.1 INTRODUCTION

Patterns of objective case in Finnish, or, more precisely, case marking on internal arguments and quasi-arguments, are problematic for Case Theory for a number of reasons and so have attracted scrutiny in the previous literature on Finnish. In simple transitives, subjects appear in nominative case and objects in accusative (identical in form to singular genitive case in full DPs) or partitive case. However, despite predictions made by Case Theory and Burzio's Generalization, full DP 'nominative objects' (here referred to as 'zero accusatives') surface in certain well-defined syntactic contexts, but alternate with accusative-marked animate pronouns in the same environments. Moreover, the distribution of both of these accusative forms alternates freely with partitive case. A separate form for plurals also exists, which is identical for nominative and accusative cases.

Data is presented first illustrating nominative and objective case marking in transitive sentences. Next, the partitive/accusative alternation is examined. Finally, data illustrating the theoretically problematic zero-accusative case form is discussed, followed by a review of the previous literature on the topic.

2.2 SUBJECT AND OBJECT CASE

Canonical subjects appear in nominative, morphologically unmarked, case and agree with the verb. Plural nominative case is signalled by a suffix, -*t*:[1]

1) a. Nainen   laulo-i.
   woman(nom) sing-past/3s
   'The woman sang'

   b. Naise-t   laulo-i-vat
   woman-nom/pl sing-past-3p
   'The women sang'

Nominative pronouns occur within the following paradigm:

2) minä 1s, 'I'   me 1p, 'we'
   sinä   2s, 'you' (sing)   te   2p, 'you' (pl)
   hän   3s, 'he/she'   he   3p, 'they'
   se   3s, 'it'   ne   3p, 'they' [-ANIMATE]

Objective case in simple transitive sentences may be marked with one of three suffix forms, accusative -*n* and -*t*, and partitive -TA. The distribution of the -*n* case morph as a marker of accusativity is limited to singular full DPs and inanimate pronouns:

3) a. Henna   ott-i   avaime-n.
   Henna(nom) took-past/3s key-acc
   'Henna took the key'

   b. Henna   ott-i   se-n.
   Henna(nom) took-past/3s it-acc
   'Henna took it'

The singular accusative -*n* affix is identical in form to the singular genitive case affix for both full DPs and pronouns[2]:

4) se-n   takana
   it-gen behind
   'behind it' (cf ex. 3b above)

The accusative -*t* affix appears with plural DPs, homophonous with the nominative plural marker:

5) Naise-t   näk-i-vät   naise-t.
   woman-nom/pl see-past-3p woman- acc/pl
   'The women saw the women'

Plural DPs which are marked for other cases, however, e.g. locatives, appear with a different plural marker, -*i*, which precedes the case affix:

6) talo-i-ssa
   house-pl-iness
   'in the houses'

The -*t* morph is thus not simply a plural marker; it is part of a case paradigm, and triggered by the assignment of nominative or accusative case.

The accusative -*t* also appears within the animate pronominal paradigm (cf. 2 above):

7) minu-t   1s, 'me'   meidä-t   1p, 'us'
   sinu-t   2s, 'you' (sing)   teidä-t   2p, 'you' (pl)
   häne-t   3s, 'him/her'   heidä-t   3p, 'them'

The fact that accusative pronouns are clearly distinguishable from nominative pronouns becomes particularly relevant in section 2.2.2 below.

The third objective case form, the partitive, is signalled by the morpheme -TA, which is conditioned by consonant gradation, vowel harmony, and the morphophonemics of the stem to yield surface forms /-tä/, /-tta/, /-ttä/, /-a/, and /ä/:

8) Henna   ott-i   si-tä.
   Henna(nom) take-past/3s it-part
   'Henna was taking it/took part of it'

Pronouns also appear in a partitive case paradigm:

9) minu-a   1s, 'of me'   mei-tä   1p, 'of us'
    sinu-a   2s, 'of you' (sing) tei-tä   2p, 'of you' (pl)
    hän-tä   3s, 'of him/her'   hei-tä   3p, 'of them'
    si-tä   3s, 'of it'   nii-tä   3p, 'of them'

In sum, the following grammatical case morphemes appear in transitive sentences:

10)

Argument type	Nom.	Acc.	Part.	Gen.
singular DPs	zero	-*n*	-TA	-*n*
animate pron.	zero	-*t*	-TA	-*n*
plural DPs	-*t*	-*t*	-i-TA	-iTEN
plural inan. pron	zero	zero	/niitä/	/niitten/

Syncretization of form has occurred among plural nominatives and accusatives, and among singular DP accusatives and genitives.

2.2.1 The partitive / accusative alternation

We have seen that in transitive sentences, the distribution of the accusative forms -*n* and -*t* is dependent on the lexical properties of the argument; animate pronouns and plural DPs receive the accusative -*t* while singular DPs receive -*n*. In this section the complex semantic factors that condition the distribution of these accusative forms versus the partitive case is discussed.

As an objective case, the partitive has arguably a wider distribution than the accusative (Yli-Vakkuri 1987). Linked with the event structure of a given verb, partitive objective case signals a variety of aspectual states including irresultativity, unboundedness, and atelicity, some of which may be determined purely by inherent properties of the verb (*Aktionsart*). The partitive also induces a partially affected or indefinite reading, and is assigned by numerals and negation. Finally, the partitive is linked with presupposition. Aspectual distinctions signalled via partitive case marking are also independent of perfect and pluperfect tense, which are marked via participial verb endings. Because the partitive/accusative alternation tends to express aspectual oppositions, there is some debate in the literature as to which, if either, is structurally assigned and which is inherent, or which is marked and which is unmarked (Heinämäki 1984, Belletti 1988, Vainikka and Maling 1996, Rigler 1992). This issue is explored more fully in Chapter 4.

One of the main roles of the partitive case in Finnish is to induce an interpretation of the event structure of the predicate as [-BOUND]. If the verb is lexically unspecified for boundedness (e.g. *lukea*, 'to read'), the partitive/accusative case alternation on the object signals that the event is completed or ongoing:

11) a. Ulla   luk-i   lehte-ä.
       Ulla(nom) read-past/3s magazine-part
       'Ulla was reading the magazine'

   b. Ulla   luk-i   lehde-n.
       Ulla(nom) read-past/3s magazine-acc
       'Ulla read the magazine'

Broadly speaking, if the verb is inherently [+BOUND] (e.g. *nähdä*, 'to see'), or requires a telic interpretation of the object, partitive objects are ruled out for an irresultative or atelic reading:

12) a. Ulla näk-i   valaa-n.
       Ulla see-past/3s whale-acc
       'Ulla saw the whale'

   b. *Ulla näk-i   valas-ta
       Ulla see-past/3s whale-part
       'Ulla was seeing the whale'

If a verb is inherently [-BOUND] (e.g. *rakastaa*, 'to love'), accusative objects are ruled out (13b):

13) a. Rakasta-n sinu-a.
    love-1s you-part
    'I love you'

b. *Rakasta-n sinu-t.
    love-1s you-acc

Adverbs of duration also signal boundedness; certain adverbial modifiers are inflected with objective case in the same way as full DPs:

14) Laulo-i-n minuuti-n.
    sing-past-1s minute-acc
    'I sang for a minute'

Where a transitive verb takes a partitive object, the reading may be irresultative but [+BOUND] if an adverbial modifier delimits the duration of the event:

15) Te-i-n pulla-a tunni-n.
    make-past-1s pulla-part hour-acc
    'I made *pulla* for an hour' (but did not necessarily finish it)

Heinämäki (1984) proposes that the function of the accusative case in such pairs as (11) is to signal that there is a bounding element present, either to be inferred by the hearer based on contextual information, or explicitly specified via e.g. an adverbial modifier. Thus bounding phrases such as adverbs of duration do not act as independent bounds, but are interpreted as such as a result of accusative case being assigned to some element in the sentence. Rigler (1992) also argues that the boundedness value for an entire sentence cannot be signalled by a single constituent.

One fact seems to indicate that the partitive may be assigned syntactically rather than semantically, and has been used as evidence that the partitive/accusative alternation is not entirely semantic (Heinämäki 1984). Under negation, accusative rather than partitive objects are ungrammatical (16b):[3]

16) a. Soili   e-i   luke-nut   kuvakirja-a.
       Soili(nom) neg-3s   read-pcp   magazine-part
       'Soili didn't read the magazine'

    b. *Soili   e-i   luke-nut   kuvakirja-n.
       Soili(nom) neg-3s   read-pcp   magazine-acc

However, to a certain extent this 'syntactic' assignment of partitive case may be accounted for as a reflex of the semantics of negation; Vainikka (1989c) argues that negation is semantically incompatible with the verbal feature [+COMPLETED], which assigns accusative case in her model.

The other main function of the partitive/accusative alternation in Finnish is to signal definiteness and the relative affectedness or partiality of the object, if the verb denotes a process (17); the interpretation of the argument as definite or affected is also dependent on whether it is a mass or count noun (17 and 18). In this sense the partitive patterns with De Hoop's (1992) Weak Structural case and the accusative with Strong Structural case:

17) a. Mikko   sö-i   kakku-a.
       Mikko(nom) eat/past 3s cake-part
       'Mikko ate some of the cake'

    b. Mikko   sö-i   kaku-n.
       Mikko(nom) eat/past 3s cake-acc
       'Mikko ate the entire cake'

18) a. Pekka   ampu-i   kyyhkys-tä.
       Pekka(nom) shoot-past/3s pigeon-part
       'Pekka shot a pigeon'

    b. Pekka   ampu-i   kyyhkyse-n.
       Pekka(nom) shoot-past/3s pigeon-acc
       'Pekka shot the pigeon'

Definiteness is assumed to be sensitive to discourse-based distinctions such as given versus new information. Perhaps not surprisingly, then, the partitive/accusative alternation can express distinctions involving the assumption of background knowledge about a state or event. This use of the partitive is most clearly illustrated in yes-no questions and can reflect levels of politeness (Heinämäki 1984:172; data from same source) and emotional overtones (Yli-Vakkuri 1987):

19) a. Ot-i-t-ko   telta-n?
       take-past-2s-qu tent-acc
       'Did you take the tent?'

   b. Ot-i-t-ko   teltta-a?
      take-past-2s-qu tent-part
      'Did you take a tent?'

In (19a), there is an implicit reminder to the hearer that s/he was supposed to have taken a tent. In (19b), no such assumption is made, and the form is politer.

Partitive case in Finnish is also assigned by numerals larger than one:

20) a. Yhdeksän   omena-a   puto-si   maa-han.
       nine(nom) apple-part fall-past/3s earth-to
       'Nine apples fell to the earth'

   b. *Yhdeksän omena
        nine   apple(nom)

In such cases the numeral is assumed to head a DP, assigning partitive case to the noun it governs. Numerals themselves may be case-marked as arguments; see Vainikka (1989a) for an interesting discussion of related phenomena.

As will become particularly relevant in the next section, the distribution of partitive versus accusative case is conditioned by semantic factors. The semantic oppositions signalled by the partitive/accusative alternation are, broady speaking, related to (a) the boundedness of the event structure in a given sentence and (b) to the interpretation of the object as definite/indefinite or partial/total. The syntactic phenomena that condition the distribution of the various accusative forms, on the other hand, never have a bearing on the accusative/partitive contrast.

2.2.2 Zero-accusative environments

In certain syntactic environments, singular full DP internal arguments do not receive the *-n* accusative case morph. Instead, singular full DPs in these sentence types receive what appears to be nominative case inflection; they appear in their lexical, uninflected form. 'Nominative objects' (or 'zero-accusatives') alternate with accusative human pronouns and are restricted in their distribution to a limited number of sentence types, which share defective agreement morphology and may fail to license an external argument. In some cases these properties are the result of morphosyntactic processes (imperative and passive inflectional morphology) while in other cases these properties appear to originate in the lexicon. The problem with analyses of these phenomena which rely on verbs losing their ability to assign case is that zero-accusative singular full DPs contrast with accusative pronouns in the same environments. Data is given below to illustrate the alternation.

2.2.2.1 Impersonal Passives

Formal models of abstract Case as it relates to grammatical function and argument structure often focus on data from passives and unaccusatives because of apparently Case-related effects which appear in these contexts, such as NP-movement to subject position in English and case marking in Italian unaccusatives. Because grammatical case marking in Finnish is overt in the morphology, a fair amount of attention has been paid in the literature to impersonal passive sentences (van Nes-Felius 1983, Taraldsen 1986, Belletti 1988, Vainikka and Maling 1996) in order to test predictions made by Case Theory and the Unaccusative Hypothesis (Perlmutter 1978 and Burzio 1986) in particular.

The facts about Finnish impersonal passives are interesting for several reasons: firstly, there is no requirement for passivized DPs to move out of complement position; secondly, nearly all verbs can undergo passivization, including copulae and unergatives, but excluding unaccusatives; and perhaps most relevantly, internal arguments of passivized verbs show an alternation between nominative and accusative case depending on the relative animacy of the DP. Impersonal passives also show interesting morphology.

Impersonal passive morphology consists of a verbal stem, generally 'weak' depending on the verb class, plus an impersonal morpheme -TAAN, which varies in surface form depending on consonant gradation and vowel harmony:

21) Kalakukko syö-dään.
 fish pie   eat-pass
 'The fish pie is being eaten'

Impersonal passive main clauses are tensed. The impersonal passive marker -TAAN has a nonpast form and a past tense form:

22) a. Ovi   ava-taan.
    door(nom) open-pass/np
    'The door is being / will be opened'

 b. Ovi   ava-ttiin.
    door(nom) open-pass/past
    'The door was opened'

Impersonal passives can be marked for mood, e.g. conditional:

23) Saa-ta-isiin   raha-a
 get-pass-cond   money-part
 'They would get money / Money would be got'

There is both synchronic and diachronic evidence to suggest that the impersonal passive morpheme -TAAN is actually composed of two smaller morphological units. When the verb is negated, the second portion of the morpheme (the -Vn affix composed of a lengthening of the preceding vowel plus -n) fails to appear on the impersonal passive element, while the negation element stem e- is inflected for third person singular agreement:

Grammatical Case Assignment in Finnish

24) a. Kalakukko syö-dä-än
     fish pie   eat-pass-Vn
     'The fish pie is being eaten'

b. Kalakukko-a e-i   syö-dä
   fish pie-part neg-3s eat-pass
   'The fish pie is not eaten'

This pattern of negation and agreement is mirrored in finite clauses, where finite AGR is absent from the finite verb stem in negated sentences but appears instead on the quasi-verbal negation stem. These data are discussed in section 1.2.2 of the previous chapter.

Diachronically, the suffix -Vn appears to be derived from a third person pronominal possessive affix (Hakulinen 1964:157 and in subsequent literature). The third person possessive affix (Px3) may be signalled by a lengthening of the preceding vowel plus -n. Pxes host pronominal agreement in various non-finite constructions, such as temporal clauses formed with the affix /-ttua/:

25) Tul-tua-an   koti-in   Minna   men-i   nukku-ma-an.
    come-tua-Px3 home-to Minna(nom) go-past/3s sleep-MA-ill
    'After coming home Minna went to sleep'

In (25) above, the third person possessive affix -*an* in the non-finite adverbial clause agrees with the main clause subject *Minna*. The homophonous -Vn morpheme in the impersonal passive is not coindexed with an overt argument, but according to some analyses of passivization (e.g. Baker 1988) this element may itself have the status of an argument and receive an external theta-role. However, even if the -Vn element realizes AGR, it is unproductive, restricted to third person agreement only. In this respect the 'agreement' marker in impersonal passives resembles similar markers in other zero-accusative contexts (discussed below), where agreement, if present, is depleted of person and/or number features or associated with a defective paradigm.

Impersonal passives have been interpreted as being similar to English-type passives in the literature (Vainikka 1989c and van Nes-Felius 1983), but there are several important syntactic differences. As (23) above demonstrates, passivized 'subjects' are not required to raise to a preverbal subject position (though as Vainikka 1989c notes, the syntactic subject position in passives is required to be licensed by lexical material of some sort). As is the case in several Indo-European languages (e.g. Russian and Spanish) they may remain *in situ* in object position.

Impersonal passive morphology in Finnish is extremely productive, more so than English passive morphology (26b and 27b). Unlike in English, unergative verbs and copulae can be passivized; in fact, any verb that can be conceived of as having a human subject/agent can be passivized (Laitinen and Vilkuna 1993:38, fn 11):

26) a. Uiskennel-tiin.
    swim around-pass/past
    'They swam around'

   b. *It was swum around
      *It was blushed

27) a. Eilen   ol-tiin   sauna-ssa.
       yesterday be-pass/past sauna-in
       'Yesterday (they) were in the sauna'

   b. *It was being/been in the sauna

Verbs which cannot be conceived of as having a human agent, such as verbs of motion or change-of-state, cannot take impersonal passive morphology (28b):

28) a. Asema-lle tul-i   juna.
       station-to come-past/3s   train(nom)
       'A train came to the station'

   b. *Asema-lle tul-tiin   juna
        station-to come-pass/past train(nom)

Weather verbs cannot be passivized either (29b):

29) a. Sata-a.
    rain-pres/3s
    'It's raining'

b. *Sade-taan
   rain-pass

The most problematic feature of impersonal passives for theoretical analyses is the case alternation between singular full DPs and animate pronouns. Passivized full DPs appear in nominative case (30a), but animate pronouns in the same environment receive the accusative -*t* form (30b):

30) a. Asema-lta tuo-tiin   laukku.
       station-from bring-pass/past bag(nom)
       'The bag was brought from the station'

b. Heidä-t tuo-tiin   asema-lta.
   they-acc bring-pass/past   station-from
   'They were brought from the station'

The case facts related to impersonal passives show a pattern visible throughout the grammar of Finnish: accusative human pronouns alternate with nominative full DPs in a range of sentence types discussed throughout this chapter.

There has been some debate in the literature as to whether or not Finnish has a passive at all, and there is evidence to support both arguments. Shore (1988) argues at length against the analysis of the Finnish impersonal as a passive. She asserts that the impersonal passive verb (or 'indefinite') assigns an implicit plural agent theta-role, despite the fact that an overt, oblique subject (as in English passives) is ungrammatical.[4] Shore notes that the impersonal passive verb may not describe an act of nature, or one performed by an animal or God; the reading must be for a plural and specifically human agent:

31) Kaupunki   tuho-ttiin.
    town(nom)   destroyed-pass/past
    'The town was destroyed (by a crowd)'
    *'The town was destroyed (by a hurricane)'

Largely on the basis of evidence relating to case assignment, and following from his assertion that the Case Filter is inactive in Finnish, Milsark (1985:323) also argues against the impersonal construction as a passive, and interprets it as an active sentence with PRO as its subject.

Previous analyses of Finnish impersonal passives are unanimous in acknowledging that productive verbal agreement is not present in this construction. The most contentious issue that emerges from this observation is to what extent verbal agreement morphology reflects argument structure, and what effect argument structure has on the ability of the verb to assign accusative case. Differences of opinion on this point are reflected in the literature on Finnish. Contra Shore (1988), van Nes-Felius (1983) interprets this construction as having a suppressed external theta-role as in an English passive. She argues that the 'passive' morphology absorbs the nominative case of the subject but fails to assign accusative to its object. Mitchell (1991a) and Holmberg et al. (1993) both argue that Finnish has passives, but that passivized DPs do not undergo movement to subject position as in English passives.

Vainikka (1989c) assumes that Finnish has passives, but also rejects the validity of the Case Filter for Finnish because, among other reasons, accusative pronouns violate Burzio's Generalization. Burzio's Generalization predicts case-assignment and theta-marking properties for verbs which lack external arguments (Burzio 1986:178-9):

32) i. A verb which lacks an external argument fails to assign accusative case.

ii. A verb which fails to assign accusative case fails to theta-mark an external argument.

The appearance of an accusative internal argument of a passive as in (30b), then, contradicts this generalization. There are a number of languages in which passive verbs retain their ability to assign accusative case (Jaeggli 1986), but the Finnish data constitute a particularly serious counterexample to both halves of Burzio's Generalization, since (32i) is violated by impersonal passives and copular constructions, while (32ii) is violated by imperatives (discussed later in this section).

An important issue in analysing Finnish impersonal passives, then, lies in the status of their external arguments: do they truly get absorbed by the passive morphology, i.e. does the process of passivization fundamentally alter argument structure (Chomsky 1981, Marantz 1984), or are external arguments of impersonal 'passive' verbs still active in the syntax although not phonetically overt (Baker 1988)? The choice of analyses has important consequences for Burzio's Generalization, discussed in greater detail in section 3.2, which links the failure of certain verbs to assign accusative case with a failure to license an external argument. In Chapter 4 it is argued that the presence of an overt external argument indirectly determines the case-assigning properties of the verb.

2.2.2.2 Unaccusatives

According to the Unaccusative Hypothesis (Perlmutter 1978), subjects of certain intransitive verbs originate as underlying objects (unaccusatives), while subjects of other intransitives originate as subjects (unergatives). The proposed distinction between unaccusatives and unergatives is essentially a semantic one. Although the single argument of an unaccusative verb may originate as an object, Perlmutter also formalizes the following rule (Perlmutter 1978:161):

33) The Final 1 Law:

Every clause with an unaccusative substratum involves an advancement to 1.

This rule of Relational Grammar entails that unaccusative verbs always promote their underlying objects (2) to the status of subjects (1). The rule is designed to capture effects related to 'promotion to subject' for both unaccusatives, which are argued to lack subjects at the lexical/semantic level, and impersonal passives, the whose subjects have been absorbed by passive morphology (i.e. at the syntactic level, according to most transformational accounts of passivization).

Lexical unaccusatives, according to Perlmutter, typically involve motion, state or change-of-state, and their subjects are less agentive/volitional than unergative subjects. Unaccusatives share various distinctive syntactic properties cross-linguistically which suggest that Perlmutter's hypothesis is valid. In Romance languages, a different auxiliary is used with unaccusative verbs as opposed to unergatives and transitives. In Italian, unaccusative subjects occur postverbally in unmarked word order, and they accept clitics of negation as if they were objects. Moreover, unaccusatives fail to assign accusative case in Italian, leading Burzio (1986) to posit his generalization that verbs lacking external arguments also fail to assign accusative case.

Despite the evidence from Italian and English, not all linguists are convinced that the Unaccusative Hypothesis holds true as a linguistic universal. Mithun (1991) calls into question the basic lexical distinction between unergative and unaccusative verbs, noting that in many languages effects related to unaccusativity are linked to the relative animacy of arguments and aspect rather than to lexical properties of the verb. Also, unaccusative subjects in many languages may appear either in subject or object position, with various semantic effects (e.g. relative animacy or volition) depending on the position of the argument. The question remains as to whether the Unaccusative Hypothesis is universally true for all verbs in all languages, or if unaccusative subjects may in fact be base-generated *either* external or internal to VP, depending on semantic factors such as animacy and aspect.

Like Italian, Finnish is characterized as an SVO language with relatively free word order that allows pro-drop (in some paradigm slots). Traditional Finnish grammars describe an 'existential' and several related inverted constructions that broadly encompass Perlmutter's unaccusative verb class. Verbs in these constructions show default third person agreement morphology regardless of whether the argument is singular or plural, and the internal argument may receive either nominative or partitive case (34 and 35):

34) Siellä hävis-i nainen.
    there vanish-past/3s woman(nom)
    'There vanished a woman'

35) a. Koulu-ssa on uude-t opettaja-t.
    school-in be/3s new-nom/pl teacher-nom/pl
    'The school has new teachers'

   b. *Koulu-ssa ovat uude-t opettaja-t
    school-in is/3p new-nom/pl teacher-nom/pl

Under negation, postverbal 'subjects' in these sentences occur in the partitive case (36), unlike nominative preverbal subjects (37):

36) a. Perhee-seen synty-i kaunii-t tyttö-t.
    family-to born-past/3s beautiful-nom/pl girl-nom/pl
    'To the family were born beautiful daughters'

   b. Perhee-seen e-i synty-nyt kauni-i-ta tyttö-j-ä.
    family-to neg-3s born-pcp beautiful-pl-part girl-pl-part
    'To the family weren't born beautiful daughters'

   c. *Perhee-seen e-i synty-nyt kaunii-t tyttö-t
    family-to neg-3s born-pcp beautiful-nom/pl girl-nom/pl

37) a. Kaunii-t tytö-t synty-i-vät perhee-seen.
    beautiful-nom/pl girl-nom/pl born-past-3p family-to
    'The beautiful daughters were born to the family'

   b. Kaunii-t tytö-t e-ivät synny-neet perhee-seen.
    beautiful-nom/pl girl-nom/pl neg-3p born-pcp/pl family-to
    'The beautiful daughters weren't born to the family'

   c.*Kaunii-ta tyttö-jä e-ivät synny-neet perhee-seen
    beautiful-part/pl girl-part/pl neg-3p born-pcp/pl family-to

Despite the fact that nominative and partitive case may both be assigned in this construction, the case alternations involving accusative pronouns described in section 2.2.2.1 above fail to show up in unaccusative sentences because unstressed pronominal 'subjects' in the same environment are ungrammatical (38):[5]

38) *Perhee-seen synty-i sinu-t
    family-to born-past/3s you-acc
    'To the family you were born'

Vilkuna (1989:155-64) discusses these sentences and notes various other object-like properties of the existential 'subject,' including similarities with impersonal passive 'subjects' with respect to reflexive binding. However, she also notes several subject-like properties of the same DPs: verbs which can occur in these constructions can all take nominative subjects; in certain cases, existential subjects can 'escape' the scope of negation and occur in nominative case; and finally, unlike genuine objects and passivized DPs, single count nouns cannot occur in the partitive, which suggests that existential sentences in Finnish have distinct aspectual properties. Vilkuna concludes that although subjects of these sentences are syntactically ambiguous, within a structural, configurationally-based account of Finnish they would be best analysed as originating within VP. Thus despite Vilkuna's rejection of the term 'unaccusative' for existential sentences in Finnish, the term will be retained in the current work.

2.2.2.3 Possessive copular constructions

In possessive copular constructions, the third person copular verb assigns nominative, partitive, or accusative case to the predicate DP:

39) a. Häne-llä   on   hevonen.
       s/he-adess be/3s horse(nom)
       'S/he has a horse'

    b. Häne-llä   on   hevos-i-a.
       s/he-adess be/3s horse-pl-part
       'S/he has horses'

    c. Häne-llä   on   sinu-t.
       s/he-adess be/3s you-acc
       'S/he has you'

These data illustrate the same case-related patterns discussed in the previous section on impersonal passives: human pronouns (39c) appear in accusative case and alternate with nominative (39a) and partitive (39b) full DPs. A plural predicate of the copular verb fails to trigger agreement morphology (39b), providing evidence that verbs in this construction are also depleted of agreement features.

2.2.2.4 Imperatives

Perhaps because typically they involve only one overt argument, imperatives show idiosyncratic case marking cross-linguistically (Sadock and Zwicky 1985:174-5). Case in Finnish imperatives patterns like that in other zero-accusative syntactic environments. In first and second person Finnish imperative sentences, accusative full DP and inanimate pronominal complements appear zero-marked:

40) a. Tuo   sateenvarjo!
       bring(imp) umbrella(nom)
       'Bring the umbrella!'

    b. Tuo   se!
       bring(imp) it(nom)
       'Bring it!'

Animate pronouns in the same distribution occur in accusative -*t* case:

41) Tuo   häne-t   koti-in!
    bring(imp) him/her-acc home-to
    'Bring him/her home!'

When the referent is second person singular, imperative mood appears in written Finnish as the bare, uninflected stem of the verb.

Generally speaking, the referent signalled by the imperative is implicit, and assumed to be equivalent to the hearer or hearers. An overt nominative subject referring to the hearer is possible, but only in postverbal position (42):

42) a. Ota   sinä   laukku!
       take(imp) you(nom) bag(nom)
       'You take the bag!'

   b. *Sinä   ota   laukku!
       you(nom) take(imp) bag(nom)

It is also possible to specify a pronominal referent with an imperative agreement element; these markers signify optative mood in the third person (Sulkala and Karjalainen 1992:316):

43) From *ottaa*, 'to take':

   1s: (no form)
   2s: Ota (sinä) se!   'Take (sg. addressee) it!'
   3s: Otta-koon (hän) sen!   'Let him/her take it!'
   1p: Otta-kaamme (me) se!   'Let us take it!'
   2p: Otta-kaa (te) se!   'Take (pl. addressee) it!
   3p: Otta-koot (he) sen!   'Let them take it!'

Overt referents are felicitous in all of the above paradigm slots.[6]

Negative imperatives include a special negative auxiliary stem *äl-* to which the morphs listed above are attached, plus an additional marker *ko-* on the verbal stem in all but second person singular forms:

44) From *liikuttaa*, 'to move':

   1s: (no form)
   2s: älä liiku, liikutta   'Don't move!' (sg. addressee)
   3s: äl-köön (hän) liikutta-ko   'Let him/her not move'
   1p: äl-käämme liikutta-ko   'Let us not move'
   2p: äl-kää liikutta-ko   'Don't move!' (pl. addressee)
   3p: äl-kööt (he) liikutta-ko   'Let them not move!'

In affirmative imperative sentences[7] with first and second person referents, singular full DP objects appear zero-marked for objective case, but in third person imperatives, objects are marked for *-n* accusative case (45):

45) a. Herätä   Matti!
       wake up(imp/2s) Matti(nom)
       'Wake up Matti!'

   b. Herättä-köön   Matti-n!
      wake up-imp/3s Matti-acc
      'Let him/her wake up Matti!'

On the basis of this paradigm of 'agreement' markers, Mitchell (1991:220) has proposed that imperatives in Finnish show syntactic agreement with subjects. However, the status of these affixes as full verbal agreement remains ambiguous; in phonological terms these morphs share features with clitics, distinct from inflectional affixes and possessive affixes. This is indicated by the fact that overt imperative agreement markers fail to trigger consonant gradation in the preceding syllable (45b). The argument structure of imperatives is discussed in greater detail in section 3.4.

2.2.2.5 Complex predicates

Case marking in complex predicates is unusual in that singular DP complements of the infinitival[8] lower clause are case-marked -*n* or zero-accusative depending on the agreement morphology and/or argument structure of the *matrix* verb:

46) Minä   halua-n   osta-a   olue-n.
    I(nom)   want-1s   buy-MA   beer-acc
    'I want to buy a beer'

47) Minu-n   tarvitse-e osta-a   olut.
    I-gen   want-3s   buy-MA   beer(nom)
    'I need to buy a beer'

In (46) the matrix verb agrees with its subject, and accusative case is assigned to the complement of the lower VP. In (47) the matrix verb shows defective agreement marking, and the full DP complement of the lower VP is assigned nominative case. This pattern of case marking may extend to the subjects of infinitival complements (48):

48) a. Hän   pakott-i   lapse-n   avaa-ma-an   ove-n.
       s/he(nom) force-past/3s child-acc open-MA-ill door-acc
       'S/he forced the child to open the door'

   b. Pakota   lapsi   avaa-ma-an   ovi!
      force(imp) child(nom) open-MA-ill door(nom)!
      'Force the child to open the door!'

One set of constructions in which zero-accusative case gets assigned includes a class of verbs which takes infinitival complements and assigns genitive case to their subjects.[9] Genitive subject verbs often share semantic features associated with deontic modality, hence the traditional term 'necessive' for this type of verb. The matrix verb in this construction is marked for a default third person agreement; if the matrix subject appears in the plural, agreement morphology on the verb does not change (49b):

49) a. Häne-n   täyty-y   teh-dä   se.
       s/he-gen   must-3s   do-TA   it(nom)
       'He/she must do it'

   b. Heidä-n   täyty-y   teh-dä   se.
      they-gen   must-3s   do-TA   it(nom)
      'They must do it'

Consistent with the general pattern for verbs lacking syntactic subject agreement, the complement of the lower VP appears in nominative case if it is an inanimate pronoun (or singular full DP) (50a) and accusative case if it is an animate pronoun (50b):

50) a. Häne-n   täyty-y   teh-dä   se.
       s/he-gen   must-3s   do-TA   it(nom)
       'He/she must do it'

   b. Sinu-n   pitäisi   tuo-da   heidä-t   koti-in.
      you-gen   should/3s bring-TA they-acc   home-to
      'You should bring them home'

Matrix verbs in this construction can be marked for both tense and mood. The tense and mood morphs appear with no overt agreement, signalling default third person singular marking:

51) a. Sinu-n   pitä-isi   men-nä   koti-in.
      you-gen   must-cond/3s   go-TA   home-to
      'You should go home'

    b. Aili-n   on   täyty-nyt   men-nä   koti-in.
       Aili-gen   be/3s   must-pcp   go-TA   home-to
       'Aili had to go home'

Another set of verbs selecting infinitival complements show assignment of zero-accusative case to singular full DPs alternating with accusative pronouns. These verbs have surface Experiencer subjects in the partitive case:

52) a. Minu-a   pelotta-a   ava-ta   ovi.
       I-part   scare-3s   open-TA   door(nom)
       'I'm afraid to open the door'

    b. Minu-a   pelotta-a   näh-dä   heidä-t.
        I-part   scare-3s   see-TA   they-acc
        'I'm afraid to see them'

The morphology of these verbs includes a causative suffix, -*tt*. The structure of the partitive subject construction mirrors that of the genitive subject construction; the verbs select infinitive clauses as complements, where the object DP of the *lower* clause is marked for zero-accusative case or accusative -*t* if pronominal. Partitive subject verbs also fail to agree with their surface subjects. They are, however, tensed:

53) Hän-tä   harmitt-i   keskeyttä-ä   työ.
      s/he-part   annoy-past/3s   interrupt-TA   work(nom)
      'It annoyed him/her to interrupt work'

Whereas necessive verbs involve obligation, partitive subjects are linked with a non-agential EXPERIENCER role. Subjects in this Finnish construction resemble 'quirky' subjects in Icelandic (Andrews 1985:102):

54) Mér líkar vel við henni
    me/dat likes/3s well with her/dat
    'I like her'

In Chapter 6 this construction is analysed as having a similar underlying structure to the genitive subject construction.

2.2.2.6 Summary

From the data it is evident that there is a link in Finnish between the form of the subject and the form of the object; accusative objects pattern with nominative subjects, and nominative objects with oblique or omitted subjects. More specifically, this correlation is related to the presence or absence of productive agreement morphology on the verb. Assuming that verbal agreement morphology is a reflex of the person and number features of the subject, this pattern suggests a syntactic dependency in Finnish between two discontinuous elements, inside and outside the maximal projection of the verb. In order to provide an account of this dependency, the relationships between case (both abstract and morphological), agreement and argument structure must be investigated more thoroughly.

2.3 OBJECT CASE ASSIGNMENT AND AGREEMENT IN FINNISH: PREVIOUS ACCOUNTS

Several questions emerge from the data outlined in the previous section. Firstly and most importantly is that of the nature of the zero-accusative case: is the zero inflection an allomorph of the genitive/accusative case -*n*, is it nominative case, or does it represent the lack of any case inflection? If the zero object form is a case, what is assigning it? If it is nominative case, what distinguishes it from structural accusative case, and why do animate pronouns get accusative case in the same environments? Although there is no clear consensus in the existing literature on the topic, previous analyses tend to focus on either the lack of a lexical subject in zero-accusative constructions or the presence or absence of inflection or agreement on the governing verb.

The second issue that arises from the Finnish data relates to the accusative/partitive case alternation. Which, if either, is the more marked objective case? Because the distribution of the two cases often reflects aspectual and other types of semantic dichotomies, it is difficult to determine whether one or the other case is a structural default. Vainikka's (1989c, 1993) and Vainikka and Maling's (1996) hypothesis that the partitive is a structural default case for complements of categories V and P provides one mechanism for accounting for the distribution of the two cases. In Chapter 4 another approach is outlined in which both cases are assigned structurally via theta-marking of aspectual roles by the verb. Before an analysis of the data is presented, however, existing literature on the topic is examined in this chapter.

The data presented in the sections above has been mentioned in several traditional grammars, e.g. Setälä (1891/1952:18-19), who mentions the dependency between the valency of the matrix verb and the form of the lower clause object in complex predicates; Eliot (1890:182), who mentions the lack of agreement morphology in the context of nominatively-marked objects; and Hakulinen (1946/1964).

Timberlake (1975) disputes a traditional contention that zero-object constructions are those in which the logical subject has been deleted, noting that imperatives may take a postverbal subject for emphasis, and yet the object NP remains zero-marked (Timberlake 1975):

55) Ota   sinä   kahvi   kaapi-sta!
    take(imp) you(nom) coffee(nom) cupboard-from
    '*You* take the coffee from the cupboard!'

Timberlake's own account takes a functional approach. Following Jakobson (1936), he correlates the accusative case with 'personal' verbs (i.e. verbs which allow a grammatical subject). In such sentences, the presence of multiple (possible) GFs allows for ambiguity of interpretation, hence the function of the accusative is to signal a possible conflict of interpretation and thus avoid ambiguity. The nominative case, on the other hand, surfaces as an "elsewhere" case, and may appear on objects where the verb is "nonpersonal". Nonpersonal verbs, he argues, are morphologically simpler than personal verbs and do not allow the possibility of a grammatical subject. Since there is no possible conflict of GF interpretation, the accusative fails to appear and the nominative is used as a default. Multiple nominative-marked nouns in imperatives and impersonal passives are possible because the verbs are impersonal and lack grammatical subjects. Hakulinen and Karlsson (1979:187) adopt Timberlake's account and assume that the nominative object is a form of the accusative.

Later analyses within the Principles and Parameters framework have focused on the existence of syntactic/semantic features (e.g. +COMPLETED in Vainikka 1989c) and major category features (Reime 1989, 1993) which might trigger a surface case form. To illustrate this pattern of features and cases, the following general schema for case assignment (56) has been adopted in various forms by van Nes-Felius (1983), Renault (1984), Reime (1989, 1993), and Vainikka (1989c):

56)

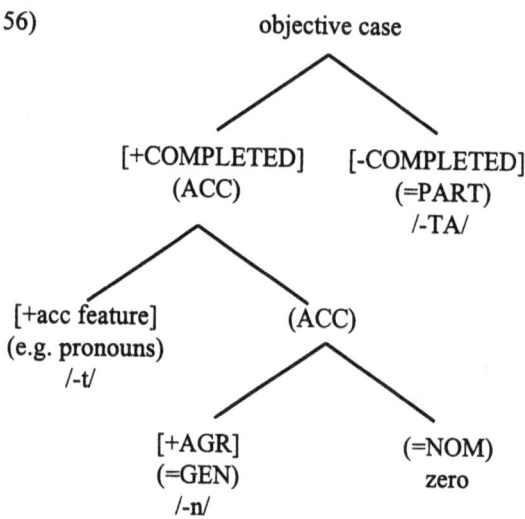

The first binary branching node in this representation of case involves the aspectual feature [+COMPLETED]. If the verb lacks this feature, partitive case is assigned to the NP complement. If the verb does have this feature, a choice exists between three forms of the accusative case.

According to this schema, if the NP in question has a pre-determined accusative form in its paradigm, i.e. is a human pronoun or plural, the accusative case form will be -*t*. At the next branching point in the tree, if the verb has the feature [+AGREEMENT], case is realized as 'genitive-accusative,' or -*n*; if not, it is realized as 'nominative-accusative,' or zero. This analysis assumes a fact which in the past has been a matter of some debate, namely, that the zero morph marking NPs in certain constructions is a form of accusative case rather than nominative case. It also assumes that such relatively complex systems as aspect and verbal agreement can be accounted for as a single binary feature in the syntax. Some consensus in the literature thus exists that the partitive/accusative alternation is essentially semantic; that the -*t* accusative feature is lexically derived; and that the -*n*/zero accusative alternation among singular full DPs is syntactic. Over and above these generalizations, however, the main focus of debate has been as to whether the distribution of cases can be accounted for within Case Theory or not.

Milsark (1985) is the first to propose that the Case Filter is actually encoded as a parameter of UG (rather than a linguistic universal) that is inoperative in Finnish. Leaving aside the issue of case assignment to pronouns, Milsark notes that the traditional grammarians' account of the Finnish data, in which objects appear in nominative case when no overt subject is present, is problematic for several reasons. Firstly, in spoken colloquial Finnish two nominative elements are possible in a single imperative or impersonal passive sentence; and secondly, he argues that to posit a case-assigning metric sensitive to information external to the governing domain of the verb would be to compromise the integrity of the configurational VP. He also notes that the morphological case alternation between -*n* and zero cannot be the result of differing spellouts of the same abstract case, because word-formation processes are meant to be insensitive to syntactic environment. To account for the data, he argues that nominative case is not a case, i.e. 'lexical,' uninflected NPs are Caseless at all levels. Accusative case is only assigned under government by inflected verbs with no intransitivizing morphology such as passive or imperative. Milsark's perceptive discussion of the motivations for, and validity of, the Case Filter cross-linguistically highlights many of the themes to be discussed at length in later chapters of this thesis, including the link between agreement morphology and nominative case assignment, the difficulties in accounting for the realization of abstract case via morphological spellout rules, and the relationship between argument structure and case assignment. Milsark's analysis unfortunately fails to account for all of the relevant data: since he rules out -*n* and zero as allomorphs of abstract accusative Case conditioned by syntactic environment, there is no way his model can account for the presence of the -*t* affix on accusative animate pronouns alternating with 'caseless' NPs. If a verb is unable to assign accusative case to full DPs because of its argument structure or inflectional morphology, then there is no way to account for accusative morphology on animate pronouns in such environments without positing -*t* as an allomorph of zero.

Taraldsen (1986) rejects the standard notion that AGR is essential for the assignment of nominative case, instead arguing that nominative is not a case and that its distribution can be accounted for in purely structural terms. He argues that Finnish is non-configurational, lacking VPs, and that nominative is linked with the coindexation of the feature [+EA] (External Argument) to a chain. His arguments are partly based on data from Finnish unaccusatives, where despite a lack of subject case agreement, nominative case gets assigned to the complement (Taraldsen 1986:139):

57) Tul-i   vaikea-t   aja-t.
    came-past3s hard-nom/pl   time-nom/pl
    'There came hard times'

Taraldsen does not, however, consider the data from accusative animate pronouns, and so his analysis fails to achieve descriptive adequacy.

Vainikka (1989c) is to date the most comprehensive syntactic analysis of Finnish within the Principles and Parameters framework. Her thesis provides an account for phenomena as diverse as word order, anaphoric binding and case assignment and posits several innovative theoretical features to account for the data, including an additional level of representation in the syntax ('M'-structure), a reworking of trace theory ('pointer theory') and a model of licensing for elements in spec(IP).

Most relevant for the current study is Vainikka's analysis of case assignment. With Milsark (1985) and to a certain extent Taraldsen

(1986) she accepts the traditional view (Jakobson 1936)[10] that nominative case is not a case. She rejects Case Theory

> ... because it does not account for morphological cases in Finnish; Finnish has no 'ECM'; in Passive and Raising in English, where NPs move to get case, the comparable Finnish NP clearly has case or Case, yet its movement pattern is quite similar to the case-seeking NP in English; that is, a theory of Passive and Raising is required for Finnish that is not based on any notion of case/Case. (Vainikka 1989c:16)

Vainikka also posits a system of structural default case assignment to account for the patterning of most surface case forms. She argues that genitive is the structural default case for all specifiers (and by extension, subjects), as long as the element is lexical. No structural default case is proposed for complements in general, but partitive is taken to be the structural default case for complements of V and P and elative the default for complements of N and A. For oblique case she adopts Nikanne's (1989) model in which oblique cases head their own projections and oblique case features percolate to other elements in the phrase.

In Vainikka's model, abstract accusative case appears only as a result of the aspectual feature [+COMPLETED] on the verb, which prevents partitive case from appearing. Pronouns appear with -*t* because that morph is available within the pronominal paradigm. Following from her assumption that the Case Filter is inactive, she suggests that the accusative -*n* case form is not assigned by the verb, but is actually the same case feature as the genitive subject case, which has percolated across from the spec(VP) position. The default case for the position spec(VP) in her model is genitive. When subjects agree with the verb (either via theta-role assignment or lexically) agreement features are base-generated in INFL. The subject raises to (spec)IP to become coindexed with these features, 'stranding' its genitive features behind in spec(VP). Later in the derivation, the genitive features percolate to complement position to mark accusative case. If there is no agreeing subject in spec(IP), the genitive feature remains in spec(VP), and the complement NP appears 'caseless.' This is internally consistent with her analysis, since she argues that nominative case is the lack of any case inflection, and it accounts for the distribution of genitive subjects in certain zero-accusative constructions. Vainikka's hypothesis is referred back to throughout this thesis.

Two analyses provide a structural account of the Finnish data without rejecting the basic tenets of Case Theory. Reime (1989, 1993) proposes a theory of case assignment which involves the interaction of major category features and agreement features. He suggests that verbs in Finnish contain the category features [+V, (-N)], and that the feature [-N] is dependent on the presence of the inflectional element AGR. V, he argues, assigns objective case to its complement, but stipulates that verbs which lack the feature [-N] (i.e. which occur in clauses not headed by AGR) require the accusative suffix -*n* in order for their complements to be visible to the Case Filter at PF. Verbs which have the [-N] feature can assign objective case, under a head-government relation, which is interpreted at PF without the -*n* affix. Like Vainikka, he assumes that plurals and animate pronouns have the -*t* affix available to them (presumably lexically) and so do not require an additional affix for visibility to the Case Filter. Several of Reime's proposals, for instance the notion that nominal (Px) AGR is related in the syntax to verbal AGR, are adopted in the current work.

Mitchell (1991b) is the first work to apply Pollock's (1989) Split-INFL Hypothesis to case assignment in Finnish. She interprets subjects as being base-generated outside VP, in a functional projection called PredP, where nominative case is also assigned. To account for case in passives and related constructions, she proposes that nominative case comprises two distinct forms, nominative(nom)inative and nominative-accusative; the surface case form of the single argument depends on the presence of agreement features in the verbal inflection.

Another theoretical approach to have been applied to the issue of case assignment in Finnish is the Case-Tier (Yip, Maling and Jackendoff 1987; Nikanne 1991), a syntactic model based on autosegmental phonology. In this model of grammar, case is assigned to encode grammatical function according to a hierarchy which is mapped from left to right onto the NPs of a given clause:

58) GF Tier: SUBJ   >   OBJ>   ADV
                  | |
    Case Tier: NOM   ACC

Where an NP (or adverbial) is unavailable for mapping onto a Case-Tier, a 'shift' occurs so that the appropriate case gets assigned to the next available NP. The Case-Tier is applied to Finnish in Maling

(1993), who attempts to account for the familiar grammatical case data as well as the complex case patterns that appear when a verb is modified by several adverbials (data from Maling 1993:59):

59) a. Luot-i-n Kekkose-en yhde-n vuode-n kolmanne-n kerra-n.
    trust-past-1s K.-ill one-acc year-acc third-acc time-acc
    'I trusted Kekkonen for a year for the third time'

   b. Kekkose-en luote-tiin yksi vuosi kolmanne-n kerra-n.
      K.-ill trust-pass one(nom) year(nom) third-acc time-acc
      'Kekkonen was trusted for a year for the third time'

   c. Kekkose-en luote-tiin kolmanne-n kerra-n yksi vuosi.
      K.-ill trust-pass third-acc time-acc one(nom) year(nom)
      'Kekkonen was trusted for a year for the first time'

In (59a) above, where agreement morphology is present on the verb, both adverbial modifier phrases are assigned accusative case. In (59b), the impersonal passive verb assigns zero-accusative case to one of the adverbial modifiers, the duration phrase, while the frequency phrase gets accusative case, regardless of the linear order of the constituents.

To account for this ranked assignment of zero-accusative (nominative) case, she proposes the following version of the Case-Tier which incorporates a hierarchy of case assignment that extends beyond the core functions usually signalled by grammatical case (Maling 1993:60):

60) a.) NOM is assigned before ACC.
    b.) Only one XP can get assigned NOM, any remaining NPs get ACC.
    c.) Which XP gets NOM reflects the hierarchy of GFs, where SUBJ > OBJ > MEASURE > DUR > FREQ

In this system, the zero-accusative case form is taken to be an instance of nominative, rather than accusative case, assigned to the highest GF in a given sentence. Although Maling's hierarchy successfully predicts the assignment of multiple accusatives in a single sentence (which is ruled out by Vainikka's 1989c analysis), she is forced to make minor stipulations to account for instances of multiple nominative elements in a sentence.

Another recent model of case assignment in Finnish, Case Position Theory, is proposed by Toivanen (1993). In this theory, each sentence in Finnish of capable of supporting up to 6 positions in a flat, rather than configurational, structure. Position 2 is occupied by the verb and 1,3,4 for the complements, with 5 and 6 remaining for local and instumental functions (Toivanen 1993:112):

61) 1.   2.   3.   4.   5.   6.
    NOM V   ACC/   PAR/   LOCAL   INSTR
              NOM   NOM

NPs occur in the various positions according to three basic principles: that cases are associated primarily with certain positions; that cases can perform more than one function; but that the same case cannot be use for the same function at the same syntactic level. Like Maling's Case-Tier approach, nominative case in this model is preferred in what is effectively a case hierarchy.

2.4 CONCLUSION

Several themes recur in the analyses summarized above. Firstly, given the existence of 'nominative objects' which alternate with accusative animate pronouns in certain syntactic contexts, the nature of nominative case itself is an extremely contentious issue. For some linguists (Milsark 1985, Taraldsen 1986, Vainikka 1989c), nominative case is not a case at all, and elements which occur in their zero-marked, lexical forms are caseless. In other work which invokes the notion of case hierarchies (Maling 1993 and Toivanen 1993), nominative case is the highest-ranked grammatical case, assigned before all others. In other analyses (Reime 1989, 1993; Mitchell 1991) nominative case when it appears on complements is essentially a variant of accusative case, triggered by the absence of agreement features on the verb. These various interpretations of the Finnish data attempt to resolve the fundamental, and not recent, conundrum of the nature of morphological case: given an inflectionally rich language like Finnish, to what extent does surface case form reflect grammatical

Grammatical Case Assignment in Finnish

function? And to what extent can the data be captured within a theory of abstract case assignment?

In the following chapters, an attempt is made to resolve at least some of these questions. The distribution of 'zero-accusative' case is found to correlate with the failure of the verb to license an external theta-role coindexed with AGR. Finnish is argued to show split-S ergativity (an 'active' pattern) in these sentences, as the result of double case assignment of two case features simultaneously to a single argument. An individual case, then, may reflect the assignment of more than one feature, but feature type turns out to be relevant as well. While accusative and partitive case are closely related to verbal semantics and theta-role assignment, nominative case is argued to be associated with the case-assigning requirement of a particular functional category.

Notes

1. The issue of whether or not the -*t* affix is encoded as a single [+PLURAL]/[+PRONOMINAL] feature in the syntax will be addressed in Chapter 4, where morphological spellout rules will be posited for various argument types that yield surface forms that are sensitive to syntactic environment.

2. Vainikka (1989c) suggests that the -*n* accusative case form is actually the same case feature as the genitive case, which has percolated across from the spec(VP) position. However, the two need not be analysed as being the same 'feature.' Diachronically, the two are not identical. In proto-Uralic the accusative marker was *-*m*, which during a phonological shift developed into -*n*; the genitive -*n*, on the other hand, is ancient (Comrie 1976:11, Hakulinen 1964:67). Also, the case forms have conflated only in the singular; the accusative plural form is -*t*, while the genitive plural form is /-iten/. See Reime (1993:106) for additional arguments on this point.

3. But see Almqvist (1989), who provides evidence that accusative objects *can* appear under the scope of negation, and that the alternation is systematic; however, the accusative appears in only 1 - 3% of negated sentences.

4. In most dialects of spoken Finnish, the impersonal passive form has replaced the first person plural verbal agreement affix -*mme* and may occur with an overt, nominative subject pronoun:

    i. Me   oste-ttiin   auto
       we(nom) buy-pass/past car(nom)
       'We bought a car'

The verb remains unmarked for agreement despite the presence of a nominative subject, and the object DP appears in nominative case. This construction is extremely problematic for many theories of case-assignment. However, it is (at present, at least) confined to spoken rather than written Finnish only, and it is well-attested that the syntactic properties of spoken

Finnish differ markedly from those of the standard written language (Vainikka 1989c); therefore no analysis of this construction is attempted in the current work.

5. A similar restriction on postverbal pronouns in unaccusatives appears in other languages that allow VS-word order for this type of verb, for example English. Although this topic will be left for further research, it is tentatively suggested here that this restriction is the result of a complex interaction of factors related to the relationship between syntax, verbal semantics and pragmatics.

6. First person plural *me* is stylistically marked as pompous, according to one informant.

7. In negated sentences partitive case is assigned to the complement DP.

8. Infinitives may be formed with either of two affixal morphemes, -MA and -TA, the realisation of which are conditioned by consonant gradation, vowel harmony and stem class. Both types may have overt subjects, depending on the governing verb. Only the -TA type given in these examples has subjects which are case-marked structurally; -TA infinitives assign lexical genitive case to their subjects.

9. Laitinen and Vilkuna (1993) observe that in certain dialects of Finnish genitive subjects alternate with nominative subjects, and that the alternation is systematic and is associated with agreement.

10. Based on data from Russian, Jakobson argues that nominative is not a case because although it appears on elements designated as 'subjects,' it actually serves a heterogeneous function, signalling topics, naming referents, or appearing as an unmarked opposition to marked accusative case in passives and copular constructions. Jakobson reaches an insightful conclusion about the different functions of nominative and accusative case: while the appearance of accusative case entails the existence of a hierarchy of meanings, and signals that the element occupies a low point on that hierarchy, nominative case refers to a single function and does not entail the existence of a hierarchy.

CHAPTER 3
Patterns of Case Assignment

3.1 INTRODUCTION

The Finnish case system, in which all arguments appear overtly marked for one of 15 productive morphological cases, provides data which exemplify classic debates in the field of linguistics over the relationship between form and function. On the one hand, the system seems relatively straightforward: accepting the "zero", unmarked lexical form as nominative case, every noun phrase in Finnish does receive overt morphological case. This fact should lend support to, or at least pose no problems for, the Case Filter in the Principles and Parameters framework, which requires all arguments to receive abstract Case. However, Case Theory does not provide a straightforward mechanism to account for the systematic alternation between the -*t*, -*n*, and zero accusative forms. In this light the data from Finnish are so problematic that they have been used as evidence by several theoretical syntacticians (Vainikka 1989c, Milsark 1985, and Taraldsen 1986) to dispute the very existence of the Case Filter.

It is the distribution of the four grammatical cases, nominative, accusative, genitive, and partitive, which has generated such intense debate in the literature on Finnish. The data presented in the previous chapter illustrate the following patterns of case assignment. In general, syntactic subjects appear in nominative case in finite clauses and in genitive case in non-finite clauses. The form of object DPs varies depending on a set of syntactic and semantic criteria. Firstly, an alternation between accusative and partitive case is determined by a complex set of semantic factors. If a DP does not receive partitive case, it may appear in any one of three 'accusative' forms. One form, *-t,* is distinct from the other two and appears with plurals and animate pronominals only, thus must be in some sense lexically determined. The other two realizations of accusative case, *-n* and zero (nominative case), are conditioned by syntactic environment. In this chapter, this syntactic environment is characterized more precisely.

Data was given in Chapter 2 to illustrate patterns of case assignment in transitives, impersonal passives, unaccusatives, imperatives, and complex predicates. In the previous literature on the topic, an interesting correlation has been noted: in sentences where nominative objects surface, the verb lacks full subject agreement morphology and/or a nominative subject. If agreement marking is taken to be the morphological reflex of a coindexed subject, this apparent correlation between elements internal and external to VP may present a theoretical problem in frameworks that assume a hierarchical, configurational structure. Milsark makes this point in response to earlier suggestions that nominative objects appear when subjects are absent (1985:324-5):

> A somewhat more interesting difficulty faced by the traditional analysis is that it implies a rather bizarre and powerful principle of case assignment. If indeed Finnish has a standard phrase structure containing a phrasal projection of V, as I am assuming, any principle which determines object case as a direct consequence of the presence or absence of an overt subject, however the notion of overt subject is to be construed, will be structurally global to a degree that is unprecedented and undesirable. If one takes the distinction between overt nominative and overt accusative case-marking in objects to be a reflex of the assignment of different abstract Case in NO [Nominative Object] and AO [Accusative Object] structures, the object Case assignment metric would be sensitive to structural information represented outside the government domain of V.

Burzio's Generalization (Burzio 1986) was formulated to capture this type of nonlocal dependency between constituents in terms of the verb's ability to theta-mark an external argument and assign case. This generalization is tested for Finnish in the current chapter.[1] In section 3.2 the relationship between a verb's compositional semantics, encoded in the syntax via theta-role assignment, and its ability to assign objective case is explored. Following a review of the structural definitions of internal versus external argumenthood, the predictions

Patterns of Case Assignment

made by Burzio's Generalization are tested for a variety of case-related phenomena in Finnish. Next, the relationship between verbal agreement morphology and case is discussed, including previous accounts which postulate a direct link between the presence of a verbal agreement feature and the case-assigning properties of the verb. External arguments are argued to be base-generated in spec(AGRP), coindexed with agreement morphemes. Finally, it is proposed that Finnish grammatical case patterns as an active or split-S ergative system.

3.2 CASE AND EXTERNAL ARGUMENTS

3.2.1 Argument structure and the Theta Criterion: Theoretical assumptions

How exactly does a verb theta-mark its arguments? Following proposals by Williams (summarized in Williams 1995), the theta-marking of arguments by a verb is assumed to encode a relation between V and an NP (or DP) which must be realized at all levels of representation according to the Projection Principle (Chomsky 1981:29). The argument structure of the verb encodes the (minimum) number of constituents required for interpretation.[2] There is a structural distinction between *internal* arguments (canonically objects), for which V subcategorizes as complements, and *external* arguments (canonically subjects), which are theta-marked by the VP predicate composed of the verb plus its internal argument(s) (if any); the verbal predicate VP is therefore a one-place predicate whose head binds the external argument like an operator (Williams 1995:106). Given the phrase structure generated by X-bar theory, relations between a transitive verb and its internal argument(s) are local, i.e. the head V and its complement are sisters, while the relations between V and its external argument are non-local, since the external argument is located external to VP:

1) $\text{NP}_\alpha \Leftarrow \theta \ [_{VPi} \ V(\alpha_i, \beta) \ \theta \Rightarrow \text{NP}_\beta]$
       external   internal

In the diagram above, the verb requires two arguments, α and β; it theta-marks its complement β as an internal argument. The external argument α is coindexed as an operator with the predicate VP, which in turn theta-marks the external argument outside the VP. In order to allow theta-relations to be maximally local, Williams (1995:106) restricts the position of the external argument to that of sister of the maximal projection of the verb. The position of base-generation of subjects in Finnish is discussed in greater depth later in the chapter.

In its most basic conception, argument structure simply specifies the number of participants required for interpretation; transitivity or intransitivity of verbal predicates is accounted for in terms of the number of arguments licensed by V. Among predicates which license a single argument, a distinction is drawn between unergatives such as *blush* and *sneeze*, which do not require an internal argument, and unaccusatives such as *vanish* and *arrive*, which fail to theta-mark an external argument. Although the syntactic status of external versus internal arguments is clearly defined, the precise mechanism underlying their interpretation is less so. Theta Theory does not offer a particularly detailed account of *why* external arguments tend to be assigned 'subject' roles such as AGENT or INSTRUMENT, and whether or not their syntactic position has any bearing on their eventual interpretation.

3.2.2 Finnish and Burzio's Generalization

In Chapter 2, previous literature was reviewed on the topic of case in Finnish. Particularly relevant for the current work is Burzio's Generalization (Burzio 1986), discussed in the context of Finnish by Milsark (1985) and Vainikka (1989c), which makes predications about the link between case and argument structure. Specifically, the generalization captures a distributional correlation cross-linguistically between verbs which license external arguments and verbs which can assign accusative case.

The theoretical cornerstone of Vainikka's (1989c) account of case assignment is that the Case Filter does not operate in Finnish, a position also held by Taraldsen (1986) and Milsark (1985). One of the main reasons for Vainikka's rejection of the Case Filter is the apparent violation of Burzio's Generalization by pronouns in Finnish passives.

Patterns of Case Assignment

Burzio's Generalization states that if a verb fails to license an external theta-role, it is unable to assign accusative case, and conversely, if a verb fails to assign accusative case, then it also fails to theta-mark an external argument. As a corollary, the generalization predicts that verbs that assign accusative case license an external theta-role, and vice-versa (Burzio 1986: 178-9):

2) $\quad -\Theta_S \rightarrow -A$
$\quad\;\; -A \;\rightarrow -\Theta_S$

$\quad\;\; A \leftrightarrow \Theta_S$

The generalization makes predictions across a wide range of data cross-linguistic data from a variety of sentence types, including unaccusatives, raising verbs and copular constructions. In particular, the attested data from passives in languages like English are predicted.

Within the Principles & Parameters framework, two main analyses of passivization have emerged. Marantz (1984) argues that passivization is essentially a lexical property of the passive morpheme. According to this proposal, the morpheme itself has the property [-log sub] (i.e. it lacks a logical subject), disallowing the licensing of an external theta-role. Affixation of the passive transfers these syntactic properties to the verb. Baker (1988) and Jaeggli (1986) argue that the passive morpheme itself receives the verb's external theta-role; in Baker's analysis, the passive element has the status of an argument and receives the objective Case feature assigned by the verb, thus preventing the verb's internal argument from receiving Case. Although the two analyses differ with respect to the specific mechanism of passivization, they both provide explanations for the range of attested data captured by Burzio's Generalization.

Whichever approach is adopted for Finnish,[3] the data is problematic. As Vainikka (1989c) notes, the generalization is violated because pronominal arguments in Finnish passives appear in accusative case:

3) Häne-t   valokuva-ttiin   lentoasema-lla.
   s/he-acc photograph-pass/past airport-at
   'He/she was photographed at the airport'

Full DP arguments, however, conform to the generalization, appearing in nonaccusative (nominative) case as predicted:

4) Opettaja valokuva-ttiin lentoasema-lla.
   teacher(nom) photograph-pass/past airport-at
   'The teacher was photographed at the airport'

The questions to be addressed here are to what extent can Burzio's Generalization capture the data from Finnish to account for the distribution of zero-accusative ('nominative object') case among full DP arguments, and do animate pronouns consistently violate the generalization? In other words, given that the generalization is designed to predict the distribution of *nonaccusative* case in passives and unaccusatives, can it predict the occurrence of nominative internal arguments elsewhere? And does the appearance of zero-accusative objects in Finnish correlate with the verb's failure to theta-mark an external argument?

Recall that the generalization (2 above) is formulated as a two-way implication: if a verb fails to theta-mark an external argument then it fails to assign accusative case, and if a verb fails to assign accusative case then it fails to theta-mark an external argument. The first half of the hypothesis is tested first.

3.2.3 Testing Burzio's Generalization I

As mentioned above, passive verbs either fail to theta-mark an external argument or the argument is absorbed by passive morphology and so is unavailable for case-marking.[4] Other types of verbs argued to lack an external argument include 'ergative' or unaccusative verbs, copular constructions and raising verbs (Chomsky 1981, Burzio 1986, Belletti 1988, etc.).

Certain verbs in Finnish show properties of raising. Standard Principles and Parameters accounts of raising motivate movement on Case-theoretic grounds: since raising verbs are unaccusative (i.e. fail to license an external argument), they cannot assign case to the lower clause subject, which forces it to raise to the higher subject position to get Case. As we have seen in the case of Finnish passives, and as noted by Vainikka (1989c), Finnish DPs in general do not appear to undergo

Case-seeking movement. Instead, Finnish has relatively free word order and movement appears to be motivated by a more general licensing condition that requires spec(IP) (Vainikka 1989c) or T (Vilkuna 1989) to be filled by lexical material. However, unusual case-related effects do surface on the *object* of the lower VP in certain raising-type constructions.

Finnish has several verbs which have been given a straightforward raising analysis by Finnish grammarians (e.g. Hakulinen and Karlsson 1979:162-163 and Vainikka 1989c:55-58), such as *näyttää*, 'to appear,' 'to seem'; *kuulua*, 'to sound'; and *vaikuttaa*, 'to seem.' (Other verbs which also may show properties of raising are discussed in section 3.2.4 below.) These verbs take two types of clausal complement, participial and finite, headed by the complementizer *että*. When the lower clause is finite, both singular full DPs and animate pronouns in subject position of the lower clause appear in nominative case (5):

5) a. Näyttä-ä si-ltä, että Mauno on väsynyt.
   appear-3s it-abl that Mauno(nom) be/3s tired
   'It appears that Mauno is tired'

   b. Näyttä-ä si-ltä, että hän on väsynyt.
   appear-3s it-abl that s/he(nom) be/3s tired
   'It appears that he/she is tired'

In contrast to the data from impersonal passives, both pronouns (7 and 8) and full DPs (6) raised to subject position appear in nominative case and trigger agreement on the raising verb (8):

6) a. Mauno näyttä-ä ole-van väsynyt.
   Mauno(nom) appear-3s be-pcp/np tired
   'Mauno appears to be tired'

   b. *Mauno-n näyttä-ä ole-van väsynyt.
   Mauno-acc appear-3s be-pcp/np tired

7) a. Hän   näyttä-ä   ole-van   väsynyt.
      s/he(nom) appear-3s   be-pcp/np   tired
      'S/he appears to be tired'

   b. *Hane-t   näyttä-ä   ole-van   väsynyt.
      S/he-acc   appear-3s   be-pcp/np   tired

8) Sinä   näytä-t   ole-van   väsynyt.
   you(nom)   appear-2s   be-pcp/np   tired
   'You appear to be tired'

However, pronouns raised from a passivised lower clause may appear in accusative case (9b) (Hakulinen and Karlsson 1979:162):

9) a. Sinä   näy-t   asete-tun   ensimmäise-lle   ehdokassija-lle.
      you(nom) seem-2s   run for-pcp/pass first-all   candidate-all

   b. Sinu-t   näky-y   asete-tun   ensimmäise-lle   ehdokassija-lle.
      you-acc   seem-3s   run for-pcp/pass first-all   candidate-all
      'You seem to been been chosen as the first candidate'

This pattern of case assignment suggests that the zero-accusative alternation with accusative pronouns surfaces when the DP in question originates as a theta-marked internal argument, but not when it has undergone subject-to-subject raising. We will return to this issue in Chapter 6.

Along with raising verbs and passives, unaccusatives and copular verbs are also described as failing to license an external argument (Burzio 1986, Belletti 1988 and Lasnik 1992). In traditional Finnish grammars, the term 'existential' is used for a range of sentence types that broadly encompass unaccusatives and most copular constructions. These constructions are described in sections 2.2.2.2 and 2.2.2.3 of the previous chapter. Finnish unaccusative verbs, like their Italian counterparts, may allow inversion; in this construction, internal DP arguments appear in nominative case:

Patterns of Case Assignment

10) a. Perhee-seen   synty-i   tyttö.
       family-to   born-past/3s   girl(nom)
       'To the family was born a girl'

    b. *Perhee-seen   synty-i   tytö-n
        family-to   born-past/3s   girl-acc

As mentioned previously, animate pronouns in postverbal position are ungrammatical:

11) a. *Perhee-seen   synty-i   minu-t
        family-to   born-past/3s   I-acc

    b. *Perhee-seen   synty-i   minä
        family-to   born-past/3s   I(nom)

Animate pronouns in subject position of the same class of verb are, in contrast, felicitious, and trigger agreement morphology on the verb:

12) Minä   synnyi-n   perhee-seen
    I(nom)   born-1s   family-to
    'I was born to the family'

Leaving aside for the moment the question as to why pronouns are ungrammatical in complement position, examples like (12) raise interesting issues about the Unaccusative Hypothesis in general. If unaccusativity is indeed a lexical phenomenon, than the subject in (12) must be base-generated as an internal argument and raise to subject position, triggering agreement morphology in the process. If this is the case, however, then unaccusatives pattern radically different from all other similar sentence types in Finnish, in particular impersonal passives, where derived subjects fail to trigger agreement. Data from various native American languages (Mithun 1991) illustrate that the unergative/unaccusative distinction is not a cross-linguistic inherent *lexical* property but may be a *syntactic* expression of differing values for aspect, agency and/or affectedness; Laitinen and Vilkuna (1993) have argued among similar lines for Finnish. On the basis of these arguments, it is suggested here that unaccusativity, whether lexically or syntactically-driven, allows single arguments to be base-generated either internal or external to VP. The surface subject in (12), therefore, is taken to be a subject (external argument) at all levels of the derivation, which accounts for the presence of agreement morphology.

Similar effects surface in Finnish existential copular constructions with respect to both word order and agreement facts, and the possibility of pronouns occurring postverbally. Full DPs may occur postverbally in nominative case or as subjects:

13) a. Koulu-ssa on   uude-t   opettaja-t
       school-in be/3s   new(nom)/pl   teacher(nom)/pl
       'The school has new teachers'

   b. Uude-t   opettaja-t   ovat   koulu-ssa
      new(nom)/pl   teacher-pl/nom   is/3p school-in
      'The new teachers are at the school'

Animate pronouns in this construction are restricted to preverbal subject position (14):

14) a. Me   ole-mme   koulu-ssa.
       we(nom)   be-1p   school-in
       'We are at the school'

   b. *Koulu-ssa   on   me / meidät
       school-in   be/3s   we(nom) / we-acc

However, there is a similar construction,[5] the possessive, in which animate pronouns may occur in complement position, and in accusative case (15):

15) a. Minu-lla   on   kynä.
       I-adess   be/3s   pen(nom)
       'I have a pen'

   b. Minu-lla   on   sinu-t.
      I-adess   be/3s   you-acc
      'I have you'

   c. *Minu-lla on   sinä.
      I-adess   be/3s   you(nom)

The evidence from possessive copular constructions suggests that copular verbs may assign accusative case despite failing to assign an external theta-role, but only to animate pronouns. Again, assuming that copular verbs are unaccusative, Burzio's Generalization holds for full DPs but not for pronouns.

3.2.4 Testing Burzio's Generalization II

The second half of Burzio's Generalization states that where verbs fail to assign accusative case, they also fail to theta-mark an external argument. The remaining zero-accusative sentence types are examined in this section to test this half of the generalization.

One environment in which zero-accusatives occur is in the clausal complements of modal-like necessive verbs such as *täytyä*, 'must'; *pitää*, 'must/should,' and *tarvita*, 'need.' The surface subject of the necessive verb in these constructions occurs in genitive case (in contrast to accusative pronominal subjects in passives). This holds true for both full DPs (16) and pronouns (17):

16) a. Nais-ten[6]   pitäisi   matkusta-a   Ranska-an.
       woman-gen/pl   should/3s   travel-TA   France-to
       'The women should travel to France'

    b. *Naise-t   pitäisi   matkusta-a   Ranska-an.
       woman-acc/pl   should/3s   travel-TA   France-to

17) a. Sinu-n   pitäisi   matkusta-a   Ranska-an.
       you-gen   should/3s travel-TA   France-to
       'You should travel to France'

   b. *Sinu-t   pitäisi   matkusta-a   Ranska-an.
       you-acc should/3s travel-TA   France-to

Laitinen and Vilkuna (1993) argue that these verbs are monadic predicates taking an infinitival complement.[7] Their analysis entails that the genitive 'subject' is actually an argument of the lower infinitival clause. If their analysis is adopted, then Burzio's Generalization predicts nonaccusative case for both pronominal and full DP surface subjects.

However, the situation is complicated by patterns of case assignment in the lower VP. Although the subjects of necessive constructions appear in genitive case, the object of the *lower* clause in this construction shows the familiar nominative-accusative case effects (18 and 19):

18) a. Nais-ten   pitäisi   tava-ta   presidentti.
       woman-gen/pl   should/3s   meet-TA   president(nom)
       'The women should meet the president'

   b. *Nais-ten   pitäisi   tava-ta   presidenti-n.
       woman-gen/pl   should/3s   meet-TA   president-acc

19) a. Nais-ten   pitäisi   tava-ta   heidä-t.
       woman-gen/pl   should/3s   meet-TA   they-acc
       'The women should meet them'

   b. *Nais-ten   pitäisi   tava-ta   he.
       woman-gen/pl   should/3s   meet-TA   they(nom)

These data suggest that like impersonal passives and unaccusatives, necessive verbs fail to license an external argument, but moreover, that infinitive verbs in Finnish are non-case-assigning. Assuming that the necessive verb governs the lower clause object, Burzio's Generalization again predicts the data for full DPs but not for animate pronouns in this construction.

A slightly more problematic construction for Burzio's Generalization is the data from Experiencer verbs with partitive subjects. Case marking in the lower clause in this construction mirrors that in clauses headed by necessive verbs:

20) a. Minu-a pelotta-a ava-ta   ovi.
       I-part scare-3s   open-TA door(nom)
       'I'm afraid to open the door'

   b. Minu-a pelotta-a näh-dä   häne-t.
      I-part scare-3s   see-TA   s/he-acc
      'I'm afraid to see him/her'

If the Experiencer subject of these sentences is base-generated as an external argument, then the generalization appears to be violated. The -*tt* suffix in these verbs is diachronically a causative; however, the subject is interpreted as affected, not agentive. The agent 'causer' appears to have been absorbed by the morphology. Furthermore, no agreement morphology is present on the verb, further evidence that no external argument is base-generated.

Burzio's Generalization has so far predicted the Finnish data. However, there is one sentence type in Finnish which is *not* predicted by the second part of Burzio's Generalization. In first- and second-person imperative sentences, the internal argument of the verb cannot be assigned accusative case if it is a full DP or inanimate pronoun (21):

21) a. Osta   kartta!
       buy(imp)   map(nom)
       'Buy a map!'

    b. *Osta   karta-n!
        buy(imp) map-acc

Although the argument structure of imperatives has been little discussed in the generative literature, it seems unlikely the imperatives actually fail to assign an external theta-role. Failure to assign an external theta-role is generally attributed to either lexical properties of the verb, as is the case of raising and unaccusative verbs, or as the result of valency-changing morphosyntactic processes as in the case of passivization. Since imperative morphology is extremely productive, the latter hypothesis seems the more likely of the two; however, the 'missing' external arguments of imperatives and passives have fundamentally different properties. Firstly, the subject of passives is interpreted in various ways, depending on the language in question; in English, the subject of an agentless passive verb is interpreted as non-specific, although semantic properties of the verb might restrict interpretation, as in *The branch was chewed* or *Songs were sung*. In Finnish, the subject of impersonal passives receive an interpretation as [+HUMAN] and [+PLURAL], but the referent is still non-specific. The referent in first and second person imperatives, however, is specific. The second difference between the subjects of passives and imperatives lies in the fact that overt subject referents in impersonal passive sentences are ungrammatical, while overt referents in imperatives are grammatical (though restricted to postverbal position):

22) a. Sinä sö-i-t banaani-n.
   you(nom) eat-past-2s banana-acc
   'You ate the banana'

   b. Syö sinä banaani!
   eat-imp/2s you(nom) banana(nom)
   '*You* eat the banana!'

   c. *Sinä syö banaani!

23) a. Soita isoäidi-lle!
   call(imp) grandmother-all
   'Call grandmother!'

   b. Soita sinä isoäidi-lle!
   call(imp) you(nom) grandmother-all
   '*You* call grandmother!'

   c. *Sinä soita isoäidi-lle!
   you(nom) call(imp) grandmother-all

These facts suggest that imperatives may theta-mark an overt external argument, and thus differ from the other sentence types where

Patterns of Case Assignment

accusative case fails to be assigned to internal arguments. However, subjects licensed by imperatives do not behave like standard transitive subjects in a number of important ways, discussed in section 3.5.

With the exception of imperatives, then, Burzio's Generalization consistently predicts the distribution of zero-accusative case among full DP arguments, and consistently fails to predict the appearance of accusative animate pronouns in the same environments. In the next section, a possible relationship between a verb's case-assigning ability and the presence of agreement morphology is explored.

3.3 AGREEMENT MORPHOLOGY AND CASE

In Chapter 1 a functional head AGR was posited that hosts verbal subject agreement features. Previous accounts of case marking phenomena in Finnish (Eliot 1890:182; Reime 1989, 1993; Vainikka 1989c; Mitchell 1991b) have focussed on verbal agreement as the pivotal syntactic feature which determines the case-marking of the complement DP. This section will examine the hypothesis that an agreement feature (or functional head) is involved in accusative case assignment, as has been claimed in previous analyses.

In environments where zero-accusative case is assigned, subject agreement is underspecified. In these contexts, which include impersonal passive, unaccusative, necessive, causative, and some imperative constructions, verbs appear with third person singular agreement morphology as a default (with the exception of imperatives). The relevant data is presented in section 2.2.2 in the previous chapter. In contrast, in transitive sentences where the verbal complex contains productive subject agreement, full DP internal arguments receive accusative case. There appears to be a correspondence, then, between morphologically overt subject agreement and the assignment of accusative case to full DPs.

Both Vainikka (1989c) and Reime (1989,1993) propose analyses in which a verbal agreement feature is required for the assignment of accusative case. In Vainikka's model, the accusative case ending originates in spec(VP) as the structural genitive case, the default for subjects. Subjects are generated VP-internally, and get genitive case by structural default. If agreement features in IP require the subject to raise, the genitive *-n* affix is "stranded" in VP and percolates to the object, surfacing as accusative case. The subject NP, having left its genitive case features behind in VP, raises to IP as a caseless argument. Verbs whose subjects are not required to raise to IP due to a lack of agreement features there remain in VP, keeping the genitive case feature in spec(VP). Vainikka's analysis essentially relies on the notion that agreement features in INFL are always present but can be strong or weak, the former forcing the subject to raise out of spec(VP), the latter allowing the subject to remain *in situ*.

Reime's analysis involves the major category features [+V, (-N)]. He formalizes the dependency between subject agreement and accusative case by in terms of visibility under the Case Filter; verbs which are [-AGR] (and therefore (-N)) can assign 'visible' zero-objective case, while [+AGR] verbs fail to assign 'visible' case, so a *-n* affix is required for the object NP to pass the Case Filter. The main drawback to Reime's proposal is that he does not offer any motivation for his initial stipulation that verbs require an AGR feature to be able to assign visible case.

Both of these models attempt to reconcile an observed dependency between verbal agreement, which encodes a relation between a verb and its external argument, and accusative case, which encodes a syntactic relation internal to VP. Vainikka achieves this by equating genitive subject case features with accusative case features, while Reime postulates a link between AGR and the verb's ability to assign visible case.

The complex relationship between agreement morphology and case is highlighted in data from impersonal passives and generics (see Hakulinen and Karttunen 1973 for a more detailed characterization of 'missing person' sentences in Finnish). Singular generic referents in Finnish are signalled by third person singular verbal morphology with no overt pronominal element (cf. French *on*). Timberlake (1975) notes that Finnish generics lack an overt subject yet assign accusative case to full DP and inanimate pronoun objects:

24) Se-n arva-a.
    it-acc guess-3s
    'One guesses it'

Under a hypothesis linking agreement with accusative case, the verb in (24) is predicted to be inflected with verbal agreement in order for

Patterns of Case Assignment

accusative case to be assigned. Unfortunately the morphology in such examples is uninformative; third person singular is the default person and number marking in sentences which lack subject agreement. However, the singular generic reading of the subject cannot be made plural by changing the verbal agreement morphology to third person plural:

25) *Se-n   arvaa-vat
    it-acc guess-3p
    'They (nonspecific) guess it'

Third person plural nonspecific referents in Finnish are instead signalled by impersonal passive morphology, which also shows default agreement:

26) Se   arva-taan.
    it(nom) guess-pass
    'They (nonspecific) guess it'

The data in (25) and (26) suggest that the third person agreement morph in generic sentences is not productive, and may encode a default weak agreement feature. However, there is also evidence to suggest that strong agreement features are present in generics: impersonal passives cannot bind third person possessive affixes, but singular generics can (Hakulinen and Karlsson 1979:254):

27) a. Täällä pidäte-tään   hengitys-tä.
        here   hold-pass   breath-part
        'They're holding (their) breath here'

    b. *Täällä pidäte-tään   hengitys-tä-än
        here   hold-pass   breath-part-Px3

28) Jos [pro] pidättä-ä   hengitys-tä-än, ...
    if   pro   hold-3s   breath-part-Px3
    'If one holds one's breath ... '

In (27b) above, no antecedent is available to bind the possessive affix. This can be accounted for as the result of passivization, since the impersonal passive morphology has absorbed the external argument. In (28), the only third person argument available to bind the anaphoric possessive affix is the nonovert pronoun pro[8], which, if present, must be coindexed with the third person agreement morph. Vainikka (1989c:232-236) notes that spec(IP) is required to be filled in this construction, and that this position may be licensed by nonarguments. She posits a nonovert pronominal subject for this construction that remains *in situ* in spec(VP), allowing spec(IP) to be available as a landing site for other elements. Despite the apparent lack of productivity in generic agreement morphology, Vainikka's proposal finds support in case-related data. DP objects within clausal complements of generic verbs get assigned accusative case as if the matrix verb licenses an external argument, in contrast to similar constructions headed by impersonal passive verbs:

29) a. Täällä voi luke-a se-n.
    here may/3s read-TA it-acc
    'Here one may read it'

   b. Täällä voi-daan luke-a se.
    here may-pass read-TA it(nom)
    'Here people may read it'

The examples above show that the verb's ability to license an external argument (in the case of generics, this argument may be nonovert pro[9]) is as relevant for case assignment as the presence of overt agreement morphology per se. This hypothesis predicts that matrix verbs that are unaccusative (or [-log sub] in Marantz' (1984) terminology) can take generic third person singular morphology but will fail to assign accusative case. The examples in (30) bear out this generalization:

30) a. Baari-ssa voi osta-a olu-en.
    bar-in can/3s buy-TA beer-acc
    'In the bar one can buy a beer'

   b. Baari-ssa täyty-y osta-a olut.
    bar-in must-3s buy-TA beer(nom)
    'In the bar one must buy a beer'

In (30), both matrix verbs show third person agreement morphology and the subjects of both receive a generic interpretation. However, the lower clause DP complement in (30a) gets assigned accusative case, whereas the complement in (30b) is assigned nominative case. Clearly in these cases agreement morphology has no bearing on the ability of the verb to assign case. The relevant fact about *voida* 'may/can' and *täytyä* 'must' is that *voida* licenses an external argument which gets assigned nominative case and agrees with the verb when it selects a clausal complement, while *täytyä* fails to license a nominative coindexed external argument:

31) a. Minä   voi-n   osta-a   olue-n.
       I(nom) can-1s   buy-TA   beer-acc
       'I can buy a beer'

   b. Minu-n   täyty-y   osta-a   olut.
      I-gen   must-3s   buy-TA   beer(nom)
      'I must buy a beer'

In Chapter 6 examples such as (31b) are given a raising analysis, wherein the matrix subject originates as an argument of the lower clause. This movement would be ruled out if pro was licensed as the implicit subject of the modal verb, since the subject position would be unavailable as a landing site for the lower clause subject.

The proposed focus on argument structure rather than agreement morphology as the more important condition for predicting the appearance of nominative-marked objects reinforces the correlations stated in Burzio's Generalization. Imperatives, however, remain the most problematic data for the generalization. The argument structure of imperatives is discussed later in this chapter.

3.4 WEAK AND STRONG AGR

Throughout the literature related to inflectional categories, the terms 'weak' and 'strong' have been used to describe agreement features in two different senses, language-specific and construction-specific. Languages with impoverished agreement morphology have been described as having weak agreement; in Chomsky (1993), weak AGR features in English mean that elements do not raise to AGR to check features until after Spell-Out. In contrast, the phenomenon of pro-drop has traditionally been ascribed to the relative strength of agreement features in certain languages. Given that Finnish inflectional morphology is rich, and pro-drop is possible in first and second person, Finnish presumably falls into the same loosely-defined category as Spanish and Italian in the 'strength' of its agreement.

Within a given language, however, agreement features have also been described as weak or strong within a particular construction. Vainikka (1989c) accounts for the appearance of genitive subjects in necessive constructions in terms of the strength of agreement features in INFL: because agreement features are weak in this construction, the subject of the modal verb fails to raise to become coindexed with agreement in INFL, instead remaining in spec(VP) in genitive case.

The notion that AGR may vary in strength depending on construction type is a particularly relevant one for Finnish. In an entire range of sentence types, described in detail in Chapter 2, agreement morphology is set as a default third person, not coindexed with any argument. What then licenses a functional head containing defective/default agreement? If the head is devoid of φ-features, can it still head a projection?

Consider the following sentences with 'default' agreement:

32) Koulu-sta tule-e laps-i-a.
school-from come-3s child-pl-part
'Some children are coming from school'

33) Laulu-t laule-ttiin.
song-nom/pl sing-pass/past
'The songs were sung'

34) Huomenna kuulu-u matkusta-a Helskinki-in.
tomorrow must-3s travel-TA Helsinki-to
'Tomorrow one has to travel to Helsinki'

In all three examples, the default third person agreement morpheme fails to be coindexed with an external argument, yet it surfaces anyway. However, if agreement morphology were absent altogether, the resulting verb forms would be unacceptable.[10] This suggests that 'weak' AGR in Finnish is licensed by morphophonological rules rather than the syntax; verb stems in Finnish require affixes to be phonologically acceptable. Although devoid of syntactic and semantic content, agreement affixes are nevertheless required by verbal stems. Phonological material itself is sufficient to license a projection of AGR under the PF-Licensing Principle, a constraint on representation discussed in greater detail in the next chapter. Therefore, it is proposed that 'weak' AGR is still licensed as a syntactic projection even when in does not encode φ-features (-φ).

3.5 THE ARGUMENT STRUCTURE OF IMPERATIVES

Imperatives are one of the sentence types in which zero-accusative objects appear. Cross-linguistically, Finnish is unusual in having nominative objects of imperatives (Sadock and Zwicky 1985:174-5), which, according to the various generalizations described above, indicates that first and second person imperatives seem to behave as monadic predicates for the purposes of case assignment. However, as is evident from the discussion above on argument structure, the first and second person imperative data are not predicted by Burzio's Generalization, since imperatives do appear to assign an external theta-role. Before an account of case assignment is given in the next chapter, the status of the external argument of imperative verbs needs to be clarified.

In the context of Finnish syntax and morphology imperatives show several interesting features. Firstly, the morpheme that signals the imperative mood fails to show consistent morphophonological properties throughout the paradigm: there is no single imperative morph for all paradigm slots and all sentence types. In the second person singular, the imperative is marked by a zero morph that triggers consonant gradation in the verbal stem (35):

35) Anna kirje äidi-lle! (from *antaa*, 'to give')
 give(imp/2s) letter(nom) mother-to
 'Give the letter to mother!'

In the rest of the paradigm, the imperative mood is associated with a set of agreement morphs, all beginning with the consonant *k-* but which fail to trigger consonant gradation in the preceding syllable (36a and 36b):

36) a. Anta-kaamme kirje äidi -lle!
    give-imp/1p letter(nom) mother-to
    'Let us give the letter to mother!'

   b. Anta-kaa kirje äidi -lle!
      give-imp/2p letter(nom) mother-to
      'Give (pl. addressee) the letter to mother!'

Although the addressee referent can be overt (surfacing in nominative case), it can only occur in postverbal position, in contrast to most finite clauses where word order is generally free (previously given as (22) above):

37) a. Sinä sö-i-t banaani-n.
       you(nom) eat-past-2s banana-acc
       'You ate the banana'

   b. Syö sinä banaani!
      eat(imp/2s) you(nom) banana(nom)
      '*You* eat the banana!'

   c. *Sinä syö banaani!

Sentences like (37b) have been interpreted as evidence that the presence or absence of an overt subject is not an important diagnostic for predicting the distribution of nominative objects in Finnish (Timberlake 1975). Such sentences also pose difficulties for models of case assignment in which nominative case is uniquely assigned to a single argument (e.g. Maling 1993).

Imperatives, which occur in nearly all if not all languages, show various unusual properties. Sadock and Zwicky (1985:170-8) note that verbs in these constructions are typically morphologically reduced, tending to disallow tense and agreement affixes. Subject pronouns are usually omitted, and where present fail to trigger verbal agreement. The data from Finnish is consistent with these cross-linguistic tendencies.[11]

Patterns of Case Assignment

Another feature attributed to the subjects of imperatives is that of obligation. Mitchell (1991b) argues that, with subjects of necessive verbs and a related copular construction expressing obligation, subjects of imperatives are base-generated in a functional projection of the feature [+OBLIGATION] along with genitive subjects of necessives and deontic copular constructions. Schmerling (1982) takes issue with accounts wherein subjects of imperatives are interpreted as agential, and the putative correlation between imperatives and obligation imposed on the addressee, noting that speakers frequently use imperatives when the addressee has no (human) agentive control over the state of affairs whatsoever. Thus *Get well* might be said to someone ill, *Stay!* to a dog, or *Start, dammit!* to a car refusing to start. Furthermore, she discusses various types of exhortations such as *Save 10c* (where the imperative verb relates to a state which results from the act of purchasing), *Please don't rain*, and *Be big and strong*, and concludes that "the uttering of a (categorical) imperative is an attempt thereby to bring about a state of affairs in which the proposition expressed by the imperatives is true" (Schmerling 1982:212). Schmerling's observations as well as the data from various exhortatives to nonagentive addressees illustrate the link between 'agentivity' and the imperative mood to be a tenuous one.

Thus at least three facts suggest that imperative subjects do not share important syntactic properties with indicative transitive subjects. Firstly, as Schmerling has argued, the semantics of imperative 'subjects' are not necessarily agentive, and may be interpreted as having roles closer to THEME than AGENT. In this sense imperative verbs resemble unaccusatives semantically. Secondly, overt subject referents in Finnish imperatives must occur postverbally, unlike transitive subjects. Finally, imperative 'agreement' is signalled by a distinct morphological paradigm that fails to behave like full verbal agreement with respect to consonant gradation and productivity. These unusual features of imperative subjects suggest that the first and second person imperative mood marker in Finnish, like the impersonal passive morpheme, renders the external argument syntactically inactive.

3.6 SPLIT-S ERGATIVITY

In the previous sections, the link between external arguments, agreement and accusative case was explored. Finnish pronouns were found to consistently violate Burzio's Generalization, while for full DPs, the assignment of accusative case turned out to correlate with a relation of coindexation between AGR and an external argument. In this section, the patterns of grammatical case assignment in Finnish are described in the context of cross-linguistic studies of ergativity. Finnish is argued to conform to a split-S ergative (Dixon 1979; 1995) or active system, with the two grammatical functions S_A and S_O corresponding to external and internal arguments, respectively.

3.6.1 Case coding for Grammatical Function

Across languages, the coding of the grammatical functions of arguments in a given clause is described as being organized into two main systems, Nominative-Accusative and Ergative-Absolutive. The following conventional notation appears in the typological literature in discussions of grammatical function:[12]

> A= agent in transitive sentences
> S= subject in intransitive sentences
> O= patient in transitive sentences

Nominative-Accusative systems fail to overtly mark a distinction between A and S, but mark O as distinct from the other two roles. In ergative systems the marking for S and O converges, but A is marked distinct from the other two argument types. Languages may show syntactic or morphological ergativity. Cross-linguistic studies of ergativity and ergative splits tend to equate nominative case with ergative case and accusative case with absolutive, following Dixon (1979).[13]

38) a. Nominative-Accusative languages

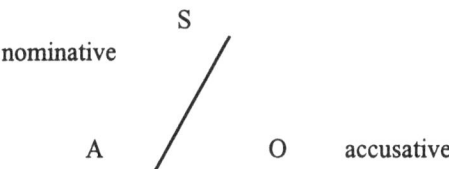

b. Ergative-Absolutive languages

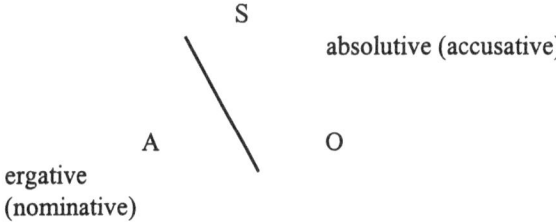

The distinction between the two systems becomes most apparent in intransitive (unaccusative/unergative) sentences. In a Nominative system, the single argument appears in nominative case, so subjects of unergatives in English and the internal argument in passives and unaccusatives pattern as subjects of transitive sentences. In a (morphologically) ergative system, the single argument in both unaccusatives and unergatives appears in accusative or absolutive case, i.e. marked for the same grammatical function as an object in a transitive sentence.

These two types of coding systems for grammatical function have been argued (Marantz 1984, Chomsky 1993) to be the result of parametric variation across languages, resulting in either an Ergative or Nominative case-marking system in any given language. However, the Nominative/Ergative distinction, as is the case with many phenomena ascribed to parametrization, is rarely canonical, with languages often incorporating both systems. Dixon (1995), for example, notes that no language is completely ergative. Instead, most languages show features of both case marking systems. These ergative 'splits' occur cross-linguistically in various syntactic contexts: for instance, in Hindi, Sumerian, and a number of Mayan languages ergativity is associated with perfective aspect (Dixon 1994:100), and in many Native American languages, splits are linked with person and number hierarchies (Jelinek 1993).

3.6.2 Accounts of ergativity in Finnish

Patterns of case assignment in Finnish have been described as ergative or ergative-like in previous work. The first analysis of Finnish involving ergativity describes the NOM DP / ACC pronoun alternation and is presented in Comrie (1975). In his analysis, animate pronouns in Finnish pattern as Nominative-Accusative, while full DPs show 'antiergativity' (as given in Comrie 1975:114-15):

39) a. Case-assignment in a Nominative-Accusative language:

    S (nom)   V
    S (nom)   V   O (acc)
                V   O (acc)[14]

b. Case-assignment in an Ergative language:

    S (abs)   V
    S (erg)   V   O (abs)
                V   O (abs)

c. Case-assignment in an 'Antiergative' language:

    S (abs)   V
    S (abs)   V   O (antierg)
                V   O (abs)

Finnish animate pronouns, he proposes, pattern as (39a), while singular full DPs pattern as (39c), with the *-n* affix marking "antiergative" case.

This proposal is criticized in Dixon (1994:62) because it fails to differentiate between transitive and intransitive sentence types.

Moravcsik (1978) suggests that the Finnish partitive-accusative objective case alternation under negation is best described as ergative, because the domain of the case split includes objects and some intransitive subjects (in existential constructions with copular predicates) but not transitive subjects. Vilkuna (1989:156) adopts Moravcsik's analysis but uses the term 'absolutive' rather than 'ergative.'

Itkonen (1979) also characterizes the Finnish objective-nominative alternation as showing ergativity. He detects an ergative-type split between 'existential' and 'non-existential' sentences: subjects of existential sentences occur either in nominative or partitive case, while subjects of other sentence types occur in nominative case. Itkonen's examples of 'existential' predicates, including *tulla*, 'to come,' *syntyä*, 'to be born,' and *tarttua*, 'to get stuck' fall into the general semantic class of unaccusatives (Itkonen 1979:82):

40) a. Kissa-lle synty-i   pentu/   pennu-t/   pentu-ja
       cat-all born-past/3s kitten(nom)/kitten-nom/pl/kitten-pl-part
       'The cat had a kitten/kittens/some kittens' (lit. 'to the cat was born kitten(s)')

    b. Verkko-on tul-i   kala   / kala-a
       net-ill   come-past/3s fish(nom)/   fish-part
       'A fish/some fish got caught in the net'

In section 2.2.2.1 the object-like properties of unaccusative 'subjects' are discussed, in particular the lack of verbal agreement and the fact that partitive case is assigned to these DPs under scope of negation.

The nominative:accusative/partitive case alternation, Itkonen argues, patterns with the ergative:absolutive case distinction, and correlates with agentivity. However, because nominative in Finnish is unmarked and ergative case is typically marked, he describes the system as 'inverted ergative.' Furthermore, he links patterns of ergativity with agentivity in genitive subject constructions and permission clauses and classifies Finnish as having an 'ideal' ergative subsystem, which distinguishes agentive from non-agentive subjects.

Itkonen (1979:87) captures his generalizations in the following diagram:

41)

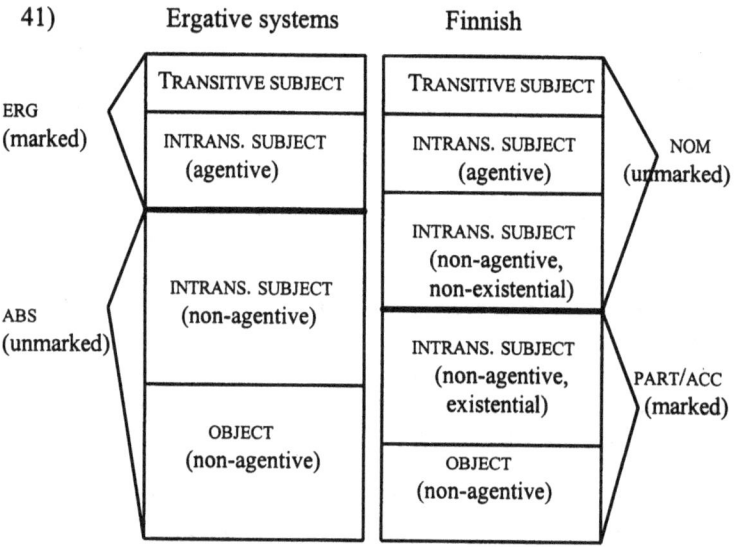

3.6.3 Split-S systems

Itkonen's and Moravcsik's characterization of the accusative-partitive case alternation in Finnish relates to a typological classification of certain languages as 'active,' 'split intransitive' or 'split S,' all notions associated with the unaccusative/unergative distinction proposed by Perlmutter (1978).[15] In this type of system, intransitive verbs are subdivided into two semantic classes which may be based on the relative level of agency, animacy or volition of the argument; aspectual properties of the predicate; or 'lexical aspect' (*Aktionsart*) which distinguishes event from stative predicates. Case in these languages marks some intransitive 'subjects' as objects, and some as agents (42):

Patterns of Case Assignment

42) Split-S

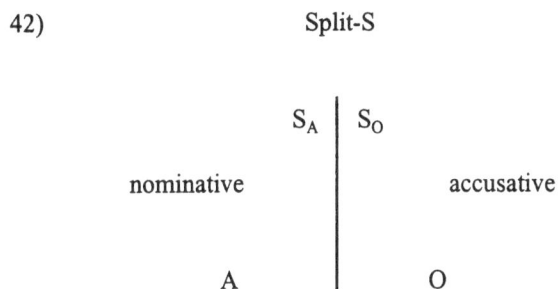

Although split-S systems broadly divide intransitive verbs into the two types described by Perlmutter (1978), the patterns of case marking they employ are *not* predicted by the Unaccusative Hypothesis, and by extension, Burzio's Generalization. Unaccusative predicates in these languages do not show effects related to raising to subject, but appear marked in objective case. Languages which are argued to show this pattern include Lakhota, Icelandic, Italian, and Eastern Pomo, data from which is given below (Andrews 1986:147-8):

43) a. mí-p' káluhuya
 he (A) went-home
 'He went home'

b. mí-pal xá-ba-kú-ma
 he(O) in-the-water fell
 'He fell into the water (accidentally)'

c. mí-p' mí-pal šá-k'a
 he(A) him(O) killed
 'He killed him'

In Eastern Pomo, the relative volition of the unergative/unaccusative subject is associated with the case-marking of the argument. The S_O non-volitional noun in (43b) receives the same object case-marking as an object in a transitive clause, while the volitional S_A noun in (43a) receives the same case-marking as the agent of a transitive verb.

Earlier in this chapter, it was argued that 'zero-accusative' environments were those in which no external argument is licensed, or in which the external argument has been rendered syntactically inactive by inflectional morphology (impersonal passives and imperatives). Although certain unaccusative sentence types disallow animate pronouns postverbally, the fact that partitive DPs may occur in the same position suggests that these are nonetheless unaccusative predicates. To account for the Finnish data, a split-S analysis of case is adopted: those intransitive environments where no internal argument is coindexed with AGR are taken to be S_O; unergative predicates with coindexed nominative subjects are S_A.

Case in Finnish is significantly less straightforward than that of a language like Eastern Pomo because there are two distinct objective cases available, the choice of which is conditioned by semantic factors. A multiple split is in fact evident: the distribution of the partitive versus the other two core grammatical cases shows a split-S type pattern conditioned by aspect. But accusative, rather than partitive, objective case marking produces another split conditioned by animacy, between [+HUMAN] pronouns and all other DPs.

Firstly, Itkonen's (1979) analysis is adopted to characterize the split between nominative case and the two objective cases, but the distribution of accusative case he describes only actually applies to [+HUMAN] pronouns:

44) Split-S in Finnish

(unergatives)	S_A	S_O	(unaccusatives)
nominative			partitive/accusative pronouns
	A	O	

The split conditioned by animacy produces a different case-marking schema for full DPs, which pattern as a strongly Nominative-Accusative language (45):

Patterns of Case Assignment

45)   Case marking in full DPs

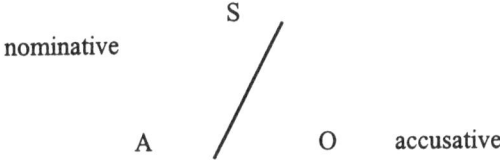

Case marking of full DP arguments is actually predicted by Burzio's Generalization, with the exception of imperatives, which are discussed in a later section. However, Laka (1993:169) observes that Burzio's Generalization accounts for case patterns in Nominative-Accusative languages, but it cannot predict case marking in ergative languages, where the single argument in an intransitive sentence typically may fail to receive an external theta-role and still be assigned accusative/absolutive case. As argued in this section, pronominal arguments in Finnish are assigned case within an ergative-type subsystem, and so fall outside the generalization.

3.7 CONCLUSION

In this chapter, dependencies between argument structure and case assignment were examined. Finnish full DPs, including zero-accusative elements, were found to conform to the predictions made by Burzio's Generalization. The generalization establishes a link between the licensing of an external argument by a verb and its ability to assign accusative case. However, it fails to account for zero-accusative objects in imperative constructions, and animate pronouns in Finnish appear to consistently violate the generalization. The properties of subject agreement were then discussed; it was proposed that AGR always projects, but may or may not be coindexed with an external argument. In the case where no external argument is licensed, the projection is licensed phonologically but not syntactically, i.e. is devoid of ϕ-features. The structural distinction between internal and external arguments and case was then found to correspond to typological definitions of ergative splits in intransitives. The violation of Burzio's Generalization is accounted for as the result of split-S ergativity in animate pronouns. In the next chapter, a syntactic account for split-ergativity is proposed in which the case-assigning properties of the functional head Tense/Mood and the argument structure of subjectless predicates results in the internal argument being assigned two case features simultaneously.

Notes

1. To a certain extent, the difficulties described by Milsark in suggesting a dependency between structurally nonlocal arguments of the verb has been resolved since Chomsky (1993), where a lower projection of AGR ($AGR_O P$) is postulated external to V' in which accusative case may be assigned to an object. Within this framework, both arguments are external to VP by LF, eliminating the basic structural asymmetry inherent in previous approaches. However, this model has spawned new problems; for example Koopman and Sportiche (1991) argue that AGR_O is external to V but internal to the maximal projection of V. Even if a lower objective case-assigning node is assumed to project external to V, the reconciliation of an apparent dependency between the case assigned by AGR_O and information encoded in AGR_S would still have wide-ranging theoretical ramifications.

2. These relations may be formalised in various ways, e.g. by the use of brackets as in TOAST(A, B), where A and B repesent the arguments necessary for the interpretation of the verb *toast*, namely an agent (the person who is toasting) and a patient (the thing being toasted, e.g. a slice of bread).

3. The facts that the passive morpheme contains an agreement-like element (-V*n*) diachronically derived from a third person possessive affix, and that the agent of an impersonal passive in Finnish is interpreted as being third person, human and plural suggest that Baker's (1988) analysis is the correct one for Finnish. Adoption of Baker's proposal entails that the Finnish passive morpheme is theta-marked as the external argument of the passive verb. However, Baker's suggestion that the same element is also assigned accusative case by V runs into familiar problems with the data from accusative Finnish pronouns.

4. In fact, as described in section 2.2.2 of the previous chapter, only Finnish verbs which can be conceived of as having a human agent can take impersonal passive morphology, a requirement that excludes unaccusative verbs. Moreover, Shore (1988) notes that the implicit subject of a passive must be interpreted as human and plural; the builder(s) of the island in the

example below could not be interpreted as being animals, for example beavers, or as God:

    i. Rakenne-taan   pieni   saari.
       build-pass   small(nom) island(nom)
       'A small island will be built'

The underlying plurality of the absorbed external argument of impersonal passive verbs surfaces as plural agreement on predicate adjectives:

    ii. Venee-ssä   ol-laan   varovais-i-a
        boat-in   be-pass   careful-pl-part
        'In a boat people are careful'

    iii. *Venee-ssä   ol-laan   varovais-ta
         boat-in   be-pass   careful-part

5. Freeze (1992) provides extensive cross-linguistic evidence that existentials and possessive copular constructions share identical structures. His analysis will be discussed in greater detail in Chapter 4.

6. Because the surface case forms of the singular genitive and the singular accusative are homophonous, plural DPs have been used in these examples to make the distinction between accusative and genitive case visible.

7. Based on a large corpus of Finnish dialect data, Laitinen and Vilkuna distinguish between necessive verbs which have genitive surface subjects from those which have nominative subjects. They analyse genitive subjects as arguments of the clausal complement and nominative subjects as arguments of the necessive matrix. They also note interesting correlations between the relative animacy of the surface subject of the necessive predicate and the choice of case among speakers. Because genitive subjects occur with greater frequency in standard Finnish and are nearly always judged to be felicitous in all dialects, only the genitive necessive construction is discussed in the current work.

8. To posit pro as the nonovert subject of generics is admittedly an oversimplification; Hakulinen and Karttunen (1973) note that the semantics of Finnish generics are actually quite complex. Only a subset of verbs may appear with third person singular generic agreement, and not all adverbial modifiers may appear in generic sentences. The generic referent may actually be the speaker, or a generic pronoun corresponding to English *one*, or the quantifier *whoever*, depending on the context.

9. It is suggested here that generics license pro, but since a VP-external subject hypothesis is adopted, the question remains as to how nonarguments may move into spec(AGRP) in generic constructions if pro is coindexed with AGR in spec(AGRP). Vainikka's adoption of VP-internal subjects allows movement into this position; in the current analysis, it may be that nonarguments must be located in spec(T/M) rather than spec(AGR) in generics.

10. In negated impersonal passives, the 'agreement' morpheme is absent, and a participial affix appears on the passivised verb:

    i. Laulu-j-a   e-i   laule-ttu.
       song-pl-part neg-3s sing-pass/pcp
       'The songs were not sung'

Although a phonological rule allows the passive stem to surface without agreement, the default agreement morpheme resurfaces on the negation marker bound stem *e-* instead.

11. Sadock and Zwicky (1985:171) note that an interesting fact about imperatives emerges from ergative languages. In Ergative-Absolutive languages, agents of transitive verbs are marked with ergative case, while patients of transitive verbs and subjects of intransitives appear in absolutive case. Within this system, one might predict that the subject of transitive imperative verbs would be interpreted as absolutive, i.e. as non-agentive, while subjects of intransitive imperatives would be interpreted as ergative, i.e. agentive. In other words, in an ergative language, the imperative of a verb such as 'go' should be interpreted as 'you go,' and the imperative of a verb such as 'convince' should be interpreted as 'you be convinced.' However, in Sadock and Zwicky's sample of strongly ergative languages

such as Eskimo and Dyirbal, the predicted interpretation does not surface. Instead, subjects of all imperatives in ergative languages are interpreted as agents. The authors attribute this to an inherent property of the semantics of imperatives: addressees must be agentive subjects with direct control over the state of affairs being evinced. Their hypothesis is supported by the fact that in most languages, verbs whose subjects are not agents tend not to occur in imperatives (e.g. *Weigh 120 lbs!)

12. These terms first appeared in Dixon (1968) and have been employed throughout Dixon's subsequent work and much of the typological literature.

13. The justification for this is grounded in the functions of the various cases in transitive clauses, where ergative and nominative cases signal the role of agent/subject and accusative and absolutive cases signal an object function. However, the cases differ in morphological markedness: nominative and absolutive cases tend to be unmarked while ergative and accusative cases tend to be marked. This does not pose a particular problem for the current analysis, given that Finnish patterns largely as a Nominative-Accusative language with an ergative *subsystem*.

14. Comrie's 'VO' sentence type refers to imperatives and impersonal constructions rather than passives and unaccusatives; in a Nominative-Accusative language like English the internal argument in such sentences appears in accusative case.

15. There is a difference of opinion as to whether split-S systems are actually ergative. Mithun (1991) argues for a separate classification between what she terms 'active/agentive' case marking and ergative case marking, but Dixon (1994) does classify split-S patterns as ergative. Dixon's terminology is adopted here.

CHAPTER 4
Mechanisms of Case Assignment

4.1 INTRODUCTION

In the previous chapter Finnish was argued to show split-S ergativity. The predictions made by Burzio's Generalization were also examined for Finnish, and the distribution of 'zero-accusative' case among full DP objects was found to correlate with the verb's failure to license an external theta-role and with the absence of agreement morphology. In this chapter, a structural account of patterns of grammatical case in Finnish is outlined in which syntactic properties encoded as lexical features within a single functional head (Tense/Mood) produce a split in the case marking of intransitive clauses and some complex predicates. Before an account of split-S ergativity is attempted, the structure of the finite clause is reviewed. A review of Case Theory follows in section 4.3, and mechanisms of case assignment are discussed. Tense/Mood is argued to assign Case both under government and spec-head agreement. Verbs (V) are proposed as objective case assigners under government, following evidence that objective case cannot be assigned under spec-head agreement in Finnish. The partitive-accusative case alternation is examined, and accusative case linked with a particular type of aspectual theta-role assigned by the verb. Finally, case in subjectless predicates is discussed. An ergative split is shown to surface when two structural cases get assigned to a single internal argument.

4.2 FINITE CLAUSE STRUCTURE

Before an analysis is presented detailing the mechanisms of case assignment which produce the patterns described in the last three chapters, the structure of finite clauses is reviewed.

4.2.1 Heads and structure

In Chapter 1 the following structure was posited as a maximal (possible) expansion of IP in Finnish (e.g. a negative pluperfect passive):

1)
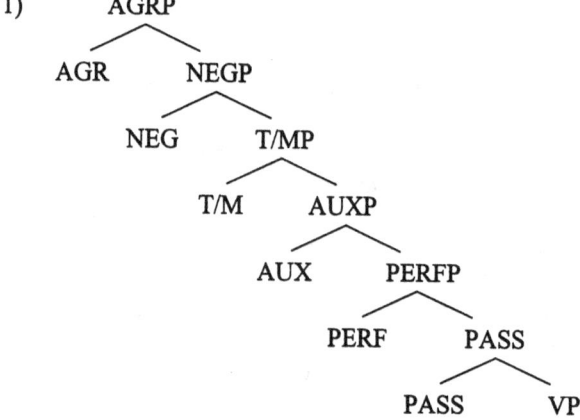

In assuming the independent projection of functional heads in the syntax, a further principle is assumed: The PF Licensing Principle (Cann and Tait (1989), Tait and Cann (1990), Tait (1991), and Cann (1993)) formulates a constraint on representation and acquisition which restricts the set of possible projections in a given language to those whose heads contain or are coindexed with phonetically realized material.[1]

2) *PF Licensing Principle* (Cann and Tait 1989:9)

α is PF-licensed iff.

a. the head of α contains phonologically realized material or
b. the head of α is bound by a PF-licensed position or
c. α binds a PF-licensed trace

In the framework detailed by Cann and Tait, all X^0 elements have lexical entries in which syntactic and semantic properties are encoded. Syntactic structure is determined by properties specified in the lexical entries of functional heads, which then combine with other functional heads and contentive heads according to the principles of X-bar Theory to yield derivations. Principles of UG in this model are thus reduced to lexically-specified selectional criteria and X-bar Theory itself. Because a language learner can only acquire those elements which are overt at PF, the contents of the functional (f-) lexicon in a given language are necessarily language-specific. No cross-linguistic template can be posited containing functional heads which are morphologically overt in some languages but not in others. Language variation emerges as the result of the lexical properties of the particular functional elements available as input to an acquirer of a language.[2]

Given the evidence presented in Chapter 1 for the maximal expansion of IP for a finite clause, the question remains as to whether all possible functional heads project in every clause, the 'Maximal IP'[3] hypothesis assumed in Mitchell (1991) following Chomsky (1986a), or whether the underlying structure of a given representation must be licensed by phonetically realized morphological material, the 'Minimal IP' hypothesis suggested by Holmberg et al. (1993). Maximal IP assumes that there is a language-specific (or universal) template for all possible sentences, the individual nodes of which may or may not be licensed by phonetically realized material; however, all nodes of the entire extended IP are available as landing sites for movement, and perhaps for case assignment, in all derivations. In such a model, all possible functional heads which comprise IP are always part of the extended projection of V, the structure of which can be accounted for in terms of c-selection of functional categories for their complements. Furthermore, functional heads are assumed to have syntactic and semantic feature values which are relevant in all sentences. For example, the functional head Negation actually encodes a binary value for assertion or negation; the projection of the Passive morpheme encodes a binary value for active or passive voice; and Perfect encodes a binary value for +/- PERFECT. The only functional head posited which does not encode such a syntactic or semantic feature is AUX, which projects only to serve as a host for T/M affixes. Not surprisingly, Mitchell does not posit a projection for auxiliary verbs, presumably for this very reason. The main advantage of this approach is that the structure-building mechanism for deriving trees can be reduced more or less entirely to that of categorial selection, either 'top-down' or 'bottom up': AGR, the head of a clause, c-selects a projection of AST (Assertion) as a complement, which in turn c-selects T/M, and so on until a finite clause is generated which satsifies all of the relevant selectional requirements. The main drawback to this approach is that many structures generated would contain functional projections devoid of semantic and phonetic content, the specifier positions of all of which would theoretically be available as landing sites for relatively unconstrained movement of elements within the structure.

The second hypothesis (Minimal IP), that functional heads only project when overt in the phonology, encounters problems involving selection. If the principles of X-bar theory are assumed to underlie the generation of trees, then the head-complement relation of functional heads to each other in a binary branching tree must be one of selection, be it lexical, categorial or otherwise. The assumption made by Holmberg et al, that elements only project when they are overt in the morphology, entails that functional heads can select complements of varying category, e.g. that a projection of Tense/Mood can c-select AUX, PERF, passive Voice *or* V as complements, depending on what morphemes are overt in the morphology in a given sentence. The strength of hypothesis over Maximal IP is that representations are minimal in scale, with projections such as Negation licensed only by both sentential semantics and phonology. If heads can select complements of varying category, however, then the ordering of the morphemes in IP becomes inherently unpredictable. In such a model of structure building, the correct linear order of elements in the template might be ensured by appealing to a mechanism of 'transitive selection,' such that if X selects Y and Y selects Z, then X also selects Z. However, this also proves too unconstrained, as it fails to rule out

Mechanisms of Case Assignment

strings such as V+PASS+PERF and V+PERF+T/M+AGR, given as (3a) and (3b) below:

3) a. *kirjoite-taan-nut
   write-pass-perf

b. *ui-neet-isi-mme
   swim-perf-cond-1p

In the derivations given above, the heads occur in the correct linear order, and do not violate any obvious phonological rules. If the Minimal IP hypothesis with transitive selection is adopted, these structures might be ruled out on other grounds: PASS and PERF might be specified in the f-lexicon as word-final suffixes so any further affixation to these morphemes produces an ill-formed string.[4]

The relative universality of functional projections cross-linguistically or within a given language is an issue still under debate within syntactic frameworks assuming the projection of functional heads.[5] Problems involving selection that emerge if heads such as Negation are assumed not to project in all cases (see e.g. Zanuttini 1991:74 fn. 13 for a discussion) also remain unresolved. In the framework assumed in the current work, syntactic structure is built according to selectional properties of X^0 elements encoded in the lexicon, so the issue of selection arising from the adoption of Minimal IP is a crucial one; concurrently, the PF-Licensing Principle requires the projection of functional elements to be licensed at PF, posing problems for the Maximal IP hypothesis.

Part of the solution to this problem concerns the heterogeneous nature of the various functional categories. In the previous chapter, the syntax and semantics of AGR were discussed, and it was argued that AGR projects in all clauses but may or may not have syntactic or semantic content. In cases where AGR is devoid of ϕ-features, it is licensed by the phonology of verbs in Finnish; these may not occur as bare stems, so a default agreement morph is required to prevent a phonological violation. On the other hand, a putative projection of Negation in affirmative finite clauses would be devoid of phonological, semantic *and* syntactic content. When NEG does project in Finnish, it functions as a semantic operator and also as a semi-verbal stem hosting agreement affixes. Auxiliaries (AUX) serve a similar morphological function as stem hosts for tense and aspect markers, but are completely devoid of semantic content. PERF must be licensed by perfective or progressive participles, and is therefore associated with verbal semantics. PASS is licensed by the passive morpheme, which alters argument structure and therefore has wide-ranging syntactic and semantic effects.

Given the observation that projections of functional heads are associated with phonological, semantic or syntactic content, the Minimal IP hypothesis is adopted in the current work, i.e. elements not licensed are also assumed to be missing from syntactic representations. IP in Finnish is assumed to be generated in the following way: AGRP dominates the structure, and may c-select either NEG or T/M as a complement. NEG selects T/M as a complement. T/M is a transitive selector, and may c-select either AUX, PERF, or PASS, which in turn also c-select complements based on transitive selection. However, the resulting structure generated must be sensitive to morpheme-specific properties of affixation, namely, whether a given element is a stem (NEG, AUX, and V) or an affix, and which elements must occur word-finally (PERF, PASS, AGR). At PF, the PFLP operates to rule out derivations containing heads unlicensed by phonological material. This hypothesis predicts that given these constraints, unfelicitous structures are ruled out while still retaining the minimal number of elements licensed in a derivation.

4.2.2 Base-generation of arguments

The Projection Principle requires that all arguments theta-marked by verbs must be present at every level of representation. This entails that all arguments, internal and external, must be base-generated at D-structure in a position where they can be theta-marked. Leaving aside the issue of the structure of ditransitives, there is a general consensus that internal arguments of transitive verbs are base-generated inside V' as complements of V, where they are theta-marked directly by the verb and from where they may move to satisfy the Case Filter if necessary.

The base-generation of external arguments, on the other hand, is a more contentious issue. Chomsky (1981:52) proposes that subjects are base-generated in spec(IP), within the maximal projection of the sentential head. INFL in this analysis may be marked for +/- Tense, and governs the subject only if it contains AGR. Thus subjects of infinitives are base-generated in INFL[-TENSE], and in languages where AGR is present in infinitives (e.g. Portuguese) may agree with the verb. Following Pollock (1989) and subsequent work in which the inflectional features in INFL are analysed as heading separate projections, the question of where subjects are base-generated becomes more complex. If subjects are assumed to originate in INFL, then TNS, AGR, NEG, PERF and various other proposed functional heads become possible sites for the base-generation of external arguments. Mitchell (1991b), for example, suggests that subjects in Finnish may be base-generated in the specifier positions of either of two functional categories located between CP and VP, Predication and Obligation. Ramchand (1995) allows subjects in Scottish Gaelic to be base-generated in either spec(IP) or spec(PERFP), depending on whether the predicate is stage-level or individual-level.[6]

An alternate view has been proposed by, among others, Koopman and Sportiche (1991). In this analysis, all subjects are base-generated and theta-marked in spec(VP),[7] that is, internal to VP. Positing VP as the site of base-generation of subjects captures the locality of the relation signalled by theta-role assignment between verbs and their external arguments more elegantly than does the spec(IP) subject hypothesis. The analysis also entails that INFL is a 'raising category' along with modals and raising verbs, i.e. that it induces raising of subjects to IP. Vainikka (1989c) adopts this proposal for Finnish, arguing that subjects receive structural default genitive case in spec(VP) when they are base-generated, then raise to spec(IP) to become coindexed with agreement features (if any). The subject leaves behind its genitive case feature and appears caseless (i.e. in nominative case) in spec(IP). The 'unrealized' genitive case feature in spec(VP) percolates to within VP and case-marks the object NP. Chomsky (1993) also assumes that subjects originate in spec(VP), raising to spec(AGR_S) to check φ-features and nominative case features.

In the syntactic framework adopted here, however, feature-checking mechanisms are not assumed to motivate movement of arguments to specifier positions as in Chomsky (1993). This creates problems for the VP-internal subject hypothesis: why exactly do subjects raise to spec(IP)? One motivation for movement may be case-related: to be assigned nominative case by tense and/or AGR in INFL, external arguments must raise from spec(VP) to surface subject position in spec(IP). This model encounters problems when faced with postverbal nominative objects, and in languages where subjects may receive nominative case *in situ* in VP. These cases are discussed in section 4.4.2.

Vainikka (1989c) offers another explanation for the raising of subjects out of spec(VP): subjects raise when agreement features in IP are 'strong,' then become coindexed (presumably under spec-head agreement). However, this hypothesis brings up further problems involving discontinuous dependencies. If subject and agreement are not coindexed until after movement, how does the strength of features external to VP induce movement from inside VP? In other words, how is the subject sensitive to the strength of features elsewhere in the structure? If subjects are base-generated in IP (T/MP or AGRP), however, they are already coindexed with the relevant inflectional features at D-structure[8] and need not be sensitive to feature values elsewhere in the structure. On these grounds, external arguments are assumed to be base-generated in spec(AGRP) in Finnish, rather than VP-internally.

4.3 MECHANISMS OF CASE ASSIGNMENT

Case Theory as formulated in Chomsky (1981) has several functions as a theoretical construct. Firstly, it accounts for the distribution of morphological case in a variety of Indo-European languages: for example, by associating nominative (i.e. unmarked) case with a structural, abstract nominative Case assigned by INFL, the distribution of nominative case morphology in English finite clauses can be captured. Secondly, positing the Case Filter as a condition that all phonetically overt NPs receive Case provides an explanation for various syntactic phenomena, including movement between D-structure and S-structure in passive constructions in English and other Indo-European languages. Finally, the assignment of abstract case functions as a visibility condition for theta-role assignment (Chomsky 1981); V cannot theta-mark[9] unless a given argument has been made 'visible' via the assignment of abstract Case. Case Theory, then, seeks to explain a variety of disparate phenomena, including word order, case morphology, and the interpretation of arguments.

All three of these explanatory tasks, however, are challenged by cross-linguistic data. Languages such as Chinese employ no overt case (or agreement) morphology whatsoever and have relatively free word order, yet speakers are able to interpret the thematic roles of arguments. Passive morphology in many languages does not always induce movement, and/or the internal argument may appear in accusative or objective case (Jaeggli 1986). Finally, postulating structural abstract case as a condition required for theta-role assignment must necessarily dissociate specific theta-roles from specific abstract cases, as the well-known English data from ECM constructions and passives illustrates. However, this last provision of the theory as it is formulated in earlier work within Principles & Parameters requires refinement, since certain morphological cases do appear to correlate with specific theta-roles.

One question that arises from earlier formulations of Case Theory is whether Case is assigned to arguments, or to structural positions. The first hypothesis entails a strong correlation between thematic roles and case morphology, and associates abstract Case assignment with deep levels of representation closely linked with verbal semantics. The latter hypothesis removes such a correlation between meaning and form, or form and function, and elevates Case licensing to a more abstract level. Chomsky (1986a) differentiates between these two types of Case, and posits diagnostic features for both: inherent (lexical) case is linked with a particular theta-role and is assigned to arguments at D-structure (i.e. to NP-trace at S-structure if movement has occured) under lexical government; structural case is assigned at S-structure (i.e. not to NP-trace at S-structure) and is not associated with a particular theta-role. The formulation of the Minimalist Program (Chomsky 1993) has also involved some radical refinements to Case Theory. These are addressed in later sections.

The least well-defined notions integral to Case Theory are a) the precise definition of 'case assignment under government' and b) the level of representation at which Case is assigned. The theoretical inconsistencies resulting from (a) have been noted extensively in the literature: if head-government entails a governing relation between head and complement *and* head and specifier, why does the head V assign case to its complement but the head INFL only to its specifier? Koopman and Sportiche (1991) note that in some languages (e.g. Arabic and Welsh) subjects base-generated internal to VP remain *in situ*, but still receive nominative case. To account for this cross-linguistic variation, they redefine government for the purposes of case assignment as *i-command*, restricting government by heads to complements and specifiers of daughters, but not their own specifiers (Koopman and Sportiche 1991:229):

4) I-Command:

A i-commands (immediate command) B if the first constituent (distinct from A) containing A contains B.

Assuming that no complements are barriers to government, they argue that INFL may assign nominative case under i-command to subjects in spec(VP) or to subjects in specifier positions of ASPP, the projection proposed to intervene between IP and VP. However, they note that nominative case can also be assigned to spec(IP) through spec-head agreement, which triggers verbal agreement morphology with the subject. Languages in their model are parametrized as to whether INFL assigns case under government, under spec-head agreement, or via both. If INFL in a given language can assign only under government, subjects may remain *in situ* with no resulting violation of the Case Filter; if INFL assigns case via spec-head agreement only, the external argument must raise out of VP to get case. By proposing this parameter Koopman and Sportiche account for both SVO and VSO word orders from an underlying SVO order. This approach retains a distinction between two mechanisms of case assignment (spec-head agreement and head-government) for two abstract Cases, although it assumes that languages may vary as to which mechanisms are employed.

Formulations of Case Theory also tend to be ambiguous with respect to the level of representation at which case is assigned. Given that the Case Filter is held to operate at S-structure, if V-to-I raising (Chomsky 1986a) is assumed rather than the lowering of INFL to V, how can V assign case to its complement if V has moved out of VP by S-structure? This difficulty is addressed by Koopman (1987), who proposes a parameter +/- Case Chain (CC), which in some languages allows the tail of a chain (i.e. a coindexed trace at S-structure) to license case, while others (e.g. Bambara) require that case can only be assigned by the head of a chain. Chomsky (1991) suggests that the

+/-CC parameter can be reduced to lexical properties of heads; English and French allow all heads (X^0) to enter into a case relation, whereas other languages allow only lexical X^0 to license case. In any event, if V raising to INFL is assumed, some mechanism for case assignment must be operational if the complement of V is to be assigned case at S-structure.

Another proposed property of moved heads becomes relevant to this discussion. Baker's (1988) Government Transparency Corollary states that heads inherit the governing domain of an incorporated element:

5) Government Transparency Corollary:

A lexical category which has an item incorporated into it governs everything which the incorporated item governed in its original structural position.

This principle also provides a mechanism for V to assign accusative case after moving out of VP, since it ensures that the verbal complex formed when V moves to INFL still governs the verbal complement. However, if INFL incorporates V, it then governs the complement formerly governed by V. If Koopman and Sportiche's (1991) proposal that INFL can assign case under government is adopted, then INFL can also case-mark the verbal complement with nominative case at S-structure. Since both V and INFL govern the complement of V, the adoption of both Baker's corollary and Koopman and Sportiche's case-assigning parameter entails that the object may be assigned both nominative and accusative case features simultaneously at S-structure, a situation clearly not consistent with the explanatory goals of Case Theory. However, since it will emerge that both of the principles mentioned appear to hold for Finnish, the case-assigning properties of both INFL and V need to be more explicitly defined before an analysis can be attempted.

4.4 NOMINATIVE CASE ASSIGNMENT

4.4.1 Is nominative case a case?

As discussed in Chapter 2, some previous analyses of the distribution of case in Finnish (Milsark 1985, Taraldsen 1986, and Vainikka 1989c and 1993) have suggested that nominative case is not a case, signalling instead the absence of abstract case features. The evidence from Finnish would support this hypothesis much more strongly if zero-accusative objects alternated with nominative animate pronouns. However, the fact that pronouns clearly appear in accusative case in the same environments is problematic: by what mechanism can accusative case *not* be assigned singular full DPs but still be assigned to pronouns in exactly the same structural position? Taraldsen (1986) accounts for data from Finnish unaccusatives as well as other zero-accusative sentence types and argues that nominative case is not a case, but is a form associated with the theta-marking of an external theta-role.

Vainikka (1989c) also argues that nominative is not a case. In her model, accusative case is assigned as a result of the feature [+COMPLETED] being present on the verb, while partitive case is assigned as a structural default (i.e. if the feature [+COMPLETED] is lacking). In a simple transitive sentence, a complement which receives abstract accusative case appears with -*t* if it is an animate pronoun because pronouns are paradigmatically specified for the -*t* accusative. Singular full DP accusatives in her model receive the affix -*n* via a feature percolation process from spec(VP), from where the external argument raises to INFL if coindexed with AGR. Subjects are base-generated inspec(VP) and receive the genitive case feature by structural default; when they raise to INFL, they 'strand' their genitive case feature in spec(VP), and appear in spec(IP) as 'caseless' nominative arguments. In zero-accusative environments, no external argument is coindexed with AGR in INFL, so the DP appears without any case feature, in nominative case. In Vainikka's model, then, nominative case may realize abstract accusative case features, but is not actually assigned to subjects; in both subjects and objects, nominative case surfaces when no genitive case affix is available.

Mechanisms of Case Assignment

Vainikka's analysis therefore equates structural case for subjects (genitive) with accusative case for objects as the same case feature.

4.4.2 Mechanisms of nominative case assignment

Given the distribution of nominative case described in Chapter 2, and assuming that nominative case *is* a case, how can the structural mechanism(s) for nominative case assignment be defined? Discussions of nominative case assignment in the literature tend to focus on Tense/Agreement features in INFL as the mechanism for nominative case assigment, but immediately encounter problems when faced with data such as unaccusatives in Italian and postverbal subjects in Arabic, where it appears that nominative case may be assigned to elements lower in the structure than canonical subject position. To account for the Finnish data, it is necessary to posit more than one possible structural position in which nominative case can be assigned.

Analyses which assume the existence of the Case Filter usually posit the locus of nominative case assignment to be in IP. Chomsky (1981) argues that subjects are assigned nominative case in spec(IP) at S-structure if INFL is [+AGR]. INFL according to this analysis may be specified for [+/- TENSE], so that subjects of infinitives may be base-generated under INFL and still show subject agreement, as is the case in Portuguese. Nominative case assignment in Chomsky (1986a) is assigned under spec-head agreement by the functional head INFL to the argument in its specifier position. In Pollock (1989) and in subsequent work, INFL is further articulated into feature-specific units of verbal inflection, projecting as the functional heads Tense, Agreement, Negation, etc. Despite the fact that INFL in this analysis is decomposed into several functional heads, the general assumption remains that both Tense and Agreement are involved in the assignment of nominative case;[10] for example, Ouhalla (1991) specifies a parameter that associates AGR with case-marking properties. Chomsky (1993) associates nominative case (in Nominative-Accusative languages) with the movement of Tense into the head AGR; subjects check case and agreement features in spec(AGR$_S$), where they are assigned nominative case. In Ergative-Absolutive languages, where subjects of intransitives appear in absolutive (=accusative) case, the lower projection of AGR is assumed to be active and case-assigning, resulting in external arguments with absolutive case marking.

Two distinct ideas emerge from these proposals: first, that nominative case is assigned to the left by INFL, and is therefore associated with a structural subject position; and second, that nominative case is linked with agreement features (or a functional head AGR). One interesting test of these hypotheses is data from Italian inverted sentences and unaccusatives ('ergatives') (Burzio 1986:96):

6) a. Arriva Giovanni.
arrives Giovanni
'Giovanni arrives'

b. Telephona Giovanni.
telephones Giovanni
'Giovanni telephones'

In each of these sentences, nominative case is assigned to a DP post-verbally; in (6a), the verb is unaccusative, and in (6b), the sentence is an inverted unergative. Based on what is effectively a rule for lowering INFL to V, whereby agreement affixes attach to a verbal stem in VP forcing the insertion of subject PRO, Chomsky (1981:256-265) develops a rule for nominative case assignment to account for such data, suggesting that nominative is assigned under the following rule:

7) At S-structure, assign nominative case to NP co-superscripted with and governed by AGR.

He then suggests that PRO is coindexed with AGR and the post-verbal NP. By the case-assignment rule posited above, the internal argument of the unaccusative verb in (6a) and the inverted subject in (6b) get assigned nominative case. Since this rule depends on AGR lowering to V rather than V raising to AGR, as is being assumed in the current analysis, there is no mechanism by which the internal argument of an accusative might be coindexed with AGR.

Burzio (1986:96-98) accounts for (6b) above as an instance of lowering, where the subject NP has left a coindexed trace in spec(IP) which is then assigned nominative case. Explaining nominative case assignment in (6a) is more problematic. Adopting the Unaccusative

Hypothesis (Perlmutter 1978), he assumes that *Giovanni* is base-generated as an internal argument but is coindexed with a nonovert, non-argument expletive pronoun in subject position, corresponding to an overt pronominal expletive in English raising constructions as in (8) below:

8) It was expected [that Caroline would sing.]

Burzio's analysis allows for the nonovert expletive element by assuming that in pro-drop languages INFL can have the status of a pronoun. This analysis differs slightly from Chomsky's, in that no PRO-insertion rule is required. Burzio's proposed coindexation relation provides a mechanism for nominative case assignment *in situ* while retaining the leftward directionality of case assignment by INFL. The main problem with this analysis concerns the status of AGR in unaccusatives. Featureless ('weak') AGR lacks semantic content and coindexation with an external argument. Since pronouns are the lexical realization of bundles of ϕ-features, it seems unlikely that AGR could have the syntactic status of a pronoun in such constructions. Analyses of this type assume a mechanism of 'case transmission' whereby a pleonastic element coindexed with a lexical noun can transmit case because the two elements form a syntactic chain to which case is assigned. Lasnik (1992) argues against the possibility of case transmission in any language, proposing instead that all case is assigned directly under government; from this follows the hypothesis that, contrary to Burzio (1986), unaccusatives do assign Case.

An alternate mechanism for nominative case assignment to arguments postverbally arises out of the VP-Internal Subject Hypothesis (VISH). Koopman and Sportiche (1991) examine data from English and French (SVO), Irish and Welsh (VSO), and Arabic (SVO and VSO). In explaining why subjects may have to raise out of VP once subjects have been base-generated there, they argue that case-assigning properties of INFL parametrized in three possible ways. Nominative case may be assigned by INFL under spec-head agreement, in which case subjects must raise to INFL in order to avoid a violation of the Case Filter (SVO); by head-government, in which case subjects must remain in spec(VP) to get nominative case (VSO); or by both mechanisms, as in Arabic. This model accounts for the fact that certain languages appear to allow the option for movement of the subject out of VP. Interestingly, the data from Arabic suggests an association between derived subjects in spec(IP) and subject agreement: nominative case-marked subjects *in situ* in spec(VP) do not appear to trigger agreement morphology on the verb. However, the model fails to capture inversion of subject and verb in Italian unaccusatives, where *internal* arguments get assigned nominative case postverbally.

Koopman and Sportiche's proposal that INFL in some languages may assign case either under spec-head agreement or under government is adopted in the current analysis, but must be modified to account for nominative case assignment to internal arguments. In addition, a disassociation of nominative case and subject agreement is required to allow an account of pre- and postverbal case assignment in sentences such as (9) and (10) below:

9) Ovi   ava-ttiin
   door(nom) open-pass/past
   'The door was opened/They opened the door'

10) Minu-a   pelotta-a   ava-ta   ovi
    me-part   fear-3s   open-TA door(nom)
    'I'm afraid to open the door'

In (9) above, the impersonal passive verb is unmarked for subject agreement. In (10), the finite causative verb is marked for third person singular default agreement, and the infinitive is also umarked for agreement. However, nominative case is still assigned to an argument in the clause.

Given that AGR is assumed to project even when devoid of pronominal features, however, this does not rule out the possibility that AGR still assigns nominative case in such sentences. Data from nominalizations provides more evidence that agreement and nominative case are not necessarily linked. Like many other languages, Finnish has a set of nominal agreement markers or Possessive Affixes (Pxes) which encode pronominal subject agreement features in non-finite verbs, such as those formed with the affix /-ttua/ (11):

11) Lue-ttua-ni kirjee-n lähd-i-n pois.
read-ttua-Px1s letter-acc leave-past-1s away
'After reading the letter I went away'

Arguments have been made (Ouhalla 1991, Reime 1993) that possessive affixes such as Finnish Pxes encode syntactic AGR, and related proposals are made in Chapter 5 of the current work. However, in sentences with Px agreement, both nominative subjects and nominative objects are ungrammatical (12):

12) a. *Minä lue-ttua-ni kirjee-n lähd-i-n pois.
I(nom) read-ttua-Px1s letter-acc leave-past-1s away
'After reading the letter I went away'

b. *Lue-ttua-ni kirje lähd-i-n pois.
read-ttua-Px1s letter(nom) leave-past-1s away
'After reading the letter I went away'

Data such as these indicate that in Finnish, finite tense is required in INFL for nominative case to be assigned. It is therefore proposed that the functional head responsible for nominative case assignment is Tense/Mood. The lexical entries for category Tense/Mood elements contain the relevant case-assigning feature as follows:

13) T/M^0: Assign nominative case under government.

Because the Tense/Mood element in Finnish undergoes head movement to AGR in non-negated sentences, nominative case can be assigned under spec-head agreement to a DP in spec(AGRP) at S-structure.

14)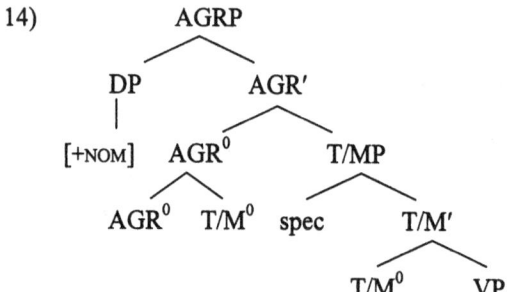

Subjects base-generated in spec(AGRP) are coindexed with verbal AGR, and are assigned nominative case in spec(AGR) by the functional head T/M, which is in AGR at S-structure.

Following Koopman and Sportiche (1991), nominative case can also be assigned rightward to positions governed (i-commanded) by T/M, including spec(VP):

15)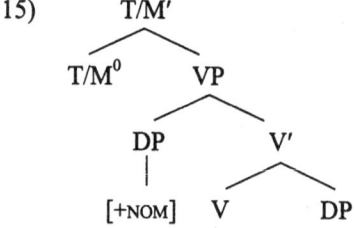

Following Tait (1991), the head Tense/Mood is argued to have the following property:

16) Tense/Mood is a bi-unique case-assigner.

If a head is a bi-unique assigner of nominative case, then there is a single case feature available to assign, and the assigner must assign that feature to some element within its governing domain. Tait (1991:276) breaks down the notion of 'bi-uniqueness' into two component properties, UNIQUE and NECESSARY. From a case-theoretic perspective, bi-uniqueness entails that lexical elements need to satisfy a condition of case licensing imposed on them by a non-lexical X^0 *in addition to* satisfying the requirements of the Case Filter, which requires all elements to be assigned abstract case by S-structure. The property of bi-uniqueness in a case-assigning node therefore creates a situation which runs counter the technical device Greed in the Minimalist Program (Chomsky 1993), whereby movement is motivated by the need for elements to check their own Case and agreement features against those of the relevant functional head rather than vice versa.[11] In order to satisfy the condition imposed on syntactic structures in (13), elements may move to the governing domain of Tense/Mood, but this movement may be *altruistic* if the element is already in a case-assigning position. This is exactly the situation in clauses where no external argument is licensed and coindexed with AGR. An analysis for these constructions is proposed in section 4.7.

The hypothesis that nominative case is assigned by a bi-unique case assigner is also consistent with intuitions about core grammatical functions. The requirement that a functional category associated with finiteness must assign nominative case at S-structure ensures that in every finite clause one element is licensed to be highest on the GF hierarchy relative to the GFs licensed by the verb. In transitive clauses this GF corresponds to Dixon's (1968) *A* function, i.e. agent of a transitive clause, whereas in unergative and unaccusative sentences the highest GF will pattern as S, a category not linked with a specific theta-role. The property of bi-uniqueness in the nominative case-assigning node thus provides a structural mechanism consistent with Maling's (1993) Case in Tiers approach for Finnish, where grammatical case is mapped onto a sentence from left to right according to a GF hierarchy, and where nominative is always assigned to the highest available GF in a given clause. It should be noted, however, that although theoretical approaches to case assignment which link morphological case directly to grammatical function may explain 'quirky' case systems such as Icelandic,[12] if a unique mapping between nominative case and the highest GF is postulated, problems are encountered in accounting for Finnish sentences like (17-19):

17) Se-n arva-a.
    it-acc guess-3s
    'One guesses it'

18) Ystävyy-ttä   kest-i   vuode-n.
    friendship-part last-past/3s   year-acc
    'The friendship lasted a year'

19) Tuul-i   tunni-n.
    blow-past/3s   hour-acc
    '(The wind) blew for an hour'

In sentence (17), the verb is generic, and no nominative case is assigned; in (18), partitive case is assigned to the subject; and in (19), the weather verb assigns accusative case to its adverbial modifier but licenses no subject for nominative case assignment. Assuming that (16) holds for Finnish, a slightly more complex account of the mechanisms of case assignment in is required to be able to account for the data. Solutions are proposed in section 4.7.

In sum, the properties of Tense/Mood as a nominative case assigner are proposed as follows:

1. T/M^0 assigns nominative case
   a) under government (Koopman and Sportiche 1991) <u>or</u>
   b) via spec-head agreement
2. T/M^0 assigns case at S-structure
3. T/M^0 is a bi-unique case assigner.

4.5 OBJECTIVE CASE ASSIGNMENT

This section is devoted to a discussion of the mechanisms that underlie assignment of case to complements. First, the hypothesis that objective case is assigned external to VP is rejected: objective case is argued to be assigned under government by the verb rather than under spec-head agreement external to VP. The accusative-partitive case alternation is then discussed; the distribution of both objective cases has received some attention in the literature, and any account of grammatical case in Finnish must be able to account for the distribution of partitive as well as nominative and accusative cases. Both partitive and accusative cases are shown to be closely associated with a particular type of theta-role assigned at D-structure.

4.5.1 Objective case assignment: Spec-head agreement or government by head?

Following Chomsky (1993), there has been a recent trend within this framework toward restricting all structural case assignment to specifier positions, under spec-head agreement, as opposed to under government as previously assumed. One (tangential) theoretical aim of the Minimalist Program is to eliminate the structural asymmetry of case assignment inherent in the Principles and Parameters framework. In previous versions of Case Theory (e.g. Chomsky 1981), objective case is taken to be assigned to the right by the verb under government to a complement, but the assignment of nominative case to subjects is assigned leftwards under spec-head government to spec(IP). In Chomsky (1993) this asymmetrical government relation is recast as a specifier-head relation only, with elements required to move to higher specifier nodes in order to check features (case and ϕ-features) present in functional heads, especially TNS and AGR. In addition to subject agreement (AGR_S), previously assumed to project as a single functional head (Pollock 1989), object agreement (AGR_O) is also taken to project in the syntax. The two agreement nodes assign nominative and accusative case under spec-head agreement. The Case Filter is subsumed within Checking, an interface condition "that all morphological features must be checked somewhere, for convergence" (Chomsky 1993:41) rather than acting as a filter at S-structure as in previous models. Although he does not specifically claim that AGR_O is part of a universal template, Chomsky suggests that in a language like English where both subject and object agreement features are weak, movement to AGR_O by the object occurs at LF so that case assignment occurs under checking of weak agreement features under spec-head agreement. Because this movement occurs post-Spell-Out, it is nonovert. Consistent with the proposal for nominative case assignment to subjects, where nominative case is associated with the incorporation of Tense into AGR_S, accusative case is technically assigned only after the verb has undergone head movement to AGR_O.

Analyses following Chomsky (1993) have focussed on the case-assigning properties of AGR_S and AGR_O in syntactic accounts of ergativity. Following observations relating to the distribution of object agreement in ergative languages (e.g. Moravcsik 1978), Chomsky (1993:13) accounts for the two language types as an instance of parametric variation reducible to the relative strength of features in AGR_S and AGR_O. Assuming that absolutive and accusative case are both assigned by the lower AGR node, while ergative and nominative case are both assigned by the upper AGR node, he argues that in Nominative-Accusative languages, NPs in intransitives pattern as subjects of transitive clauses because AGR_S is "active" and case-assigning but AGR_O is inert or missing, while the reverse holds true in Ergative-Absolutive languages: AGR_O assigns absolutive case to the single argument. Chomsky concludes that "the distinction between the two language types reduces to a trivial question of morphology" (1993:13). However, given the fact that "no language has thus far been reported that is fully ergative, at both morphological and syntactic levels" (Dixon 1994:14), Chomsky's hypothesis requires more fine-grained testing in order to predict why one or the other of the two case-assigning nodes in a given language might be active or inactive, resulting in an ergative split. For instance in Basque, a syntactically ergative language, a split-S pattern also occurs in intransitive sentences. Arguments in unaccusative sentences are marked with absolutive case, and those in unergative clauses receive ergative case (Laka 1993:151-2):

20) emakumeak emakumea ikusi du
    woman-the-erg woman-the-abs seen has
    'The woman saw the woman'

21) emakumea erori da
    woman-the-abs fallen is
    'The woman has fallen'

22) emakumeak barre egin du
    woman-the-erg laugh done has
    'The woman has laughed'

Laka (1993) notes that this pattern in unergatives does not conform to that predicted by Minimalist accounts: the single argument of an intransitive sentence in an ergative language should receive absolutive case regardless of the grammatical function of the argument. Laka's explanation of the data for Basque depends in part on the morphological status of unergative verbs, which in Basque include unincorporated nouns and light verbs. The fact that unergatives in Basque are not the result of incorporation allows an analysis wherein the noun within the VP has the status of an argument, and the sentence is syntactically transitive with both AGR nodes active and case-assigning. Unaccusatives in Basque, Laka argues, are truly monadic, and absolutive case is assigned by AGR_O as predicted. Unfortunately Laka's analysis cannot be extended to Finnish, since unergatives and unaccusatives are not distinguishable by differences in verbal morphology.

Models which assume VP-internal subjects *and* VP-external accusative case assignment encounter technical problems when all elements within VP raise to higher functional projections, in the case of V to incorporate inflectional features, and in the case of DPs to check features or get Case. Within the Minimalist Program, a transitive sentence is assumed to have the following structure by LF:

23)

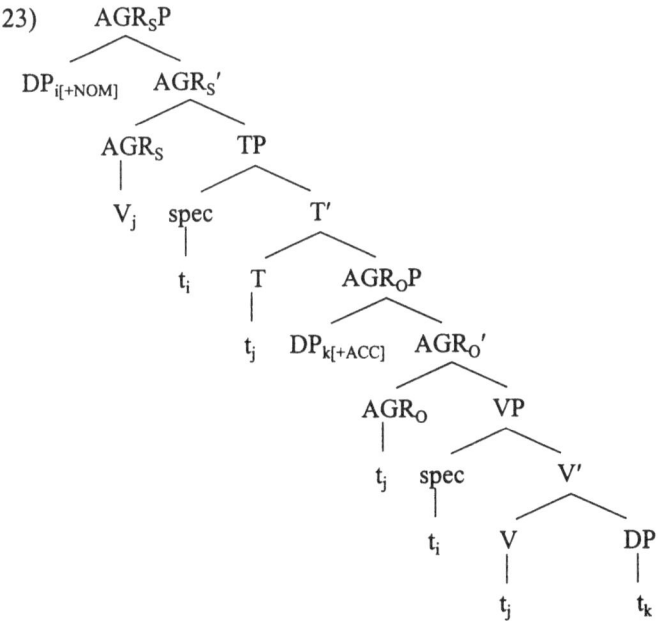

Within Principles & Parameters-based approaches, this model of case assignment encounters two main problems. Firstly, in an SVO language, surface case is the result of NP-movement of two arguments, one of which must cross the other on the way out of VP. The resulting structure, where the trace of the subject in spec(VP) intervenes between the antecedent object in spec(AGR$_S$) and its trace in V', is in violation of the ECP and Minimality.

Furthermore, if there are two functional heads where structural case can get assigned, there is nothing to rule out the subject moving to the (lower) accusative case-assigning position and the object raising to the (higher) nominative case-assigning position, as in (24) below:

24)
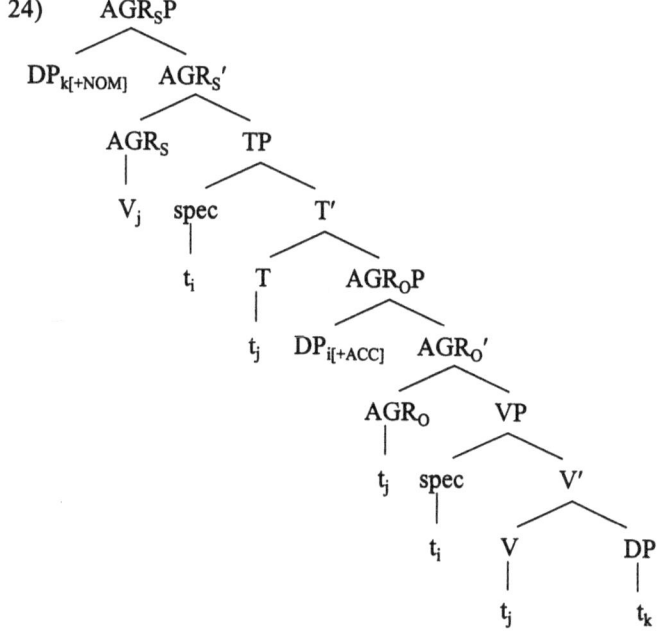

Within Principles & Parameters, movement is not motivated by feature-checking, so if two case-assigning functional heads are posited there is no way to rule out the possibility of elements raising to the 'wrong' position, as long as the Case Filter is satisfied.[13] In either case, one of the arguments must raise past a more local case-assigning specifier position on its way to get Case, presenting problems for Minimality.

Within the Minimalist Program, these two difficulties can be resolved with varying success. Firstly, movement of subjects and objects in the model is motivated by a need to check features against the appropriate node in the structure; case features emerge from the lexicon in both arguments and functional heads along with ϕ-features. A subject therefore cannot check its agreement and case features against the features in AGR_O, and similarly an object cannot check subject agreement features in AGR_S.[14] The model thus ensures that the correct argument must move to the correct AGR node.

The problem of 'crossing' paths is more difficult to reconcile, since movement is supposed to be as economical as possible. Chomsky (1993) recognizes the difficulties caused by this and is forced to stipulate that the subject raises to spec(AGR_SP) to check features *prior* to Spell-Out, when the positions of spec(AGR_OP) and spec(TP) have not yet been projected. This allows movement without violating Shortest Move, a constraint related to Relativized Minimality (Rizzi 1990). The object raises to spec(AGR_OP) to check features *after* Spell-Out, when the relevant positions have projected. Furthermore, Chomsky must redefine the notion of 'distance' so that the object may move directly to spec(AGR_O) without passing through spec(VP), which would otherwise violate Shortest Move. The derivational nature of the Minimalist Program allows such appeals to cyclicity, but inelegant stipulations must still be made. Due to such technical problems, in recent unpublished work Chomsky suggests that AGR_O does not project universally. In sum, both the Minimalist Program and representational approaches broadly subsumed within the Principles and Parameters framework encounter a number of technical problems when both VP-internal subjects and VP-external accusative case assignment are assumed.

The second type of problem encountered by the postulation of an accusative case assigning functional head external to VP involves morphology and morphological licensing. As mentioned previously, within the Minimalist Program it is assumed that object agreement features are present on all verbs, but that these features may be 'strong' or 'weak.' This approach again brings to light a problematic discrepancy between feature specification and the realization of those features in the morphology. There is no evidence from the morphology of English (or indeed the majority of languages) for the syntactic projection of object agreement features as a head, yet in the Minimalist Program object agreement features are suggested as being present (at LF, at least) in all languages. Conversely, as we have seen, in Finnish a third person singular overt agreement morph does not necessarily host subject agreement features coindexed with an external argument; in this case a head might be morphologically licensed but empty of features. It is also unclear whether individual φ-features such as gender and number may project independently as functional heads (Shlonsky 1989). To posit a functional head which hosts a given inflectional feature has wide-ranging ramifications for syntactic theory, in that another position is created as a landing site for A or A' movement and case assignment under spec-head agreement.

One much-needed theoretical constraint on the postulation of functional heads is provided by the PF-Licensing Principle given in (2) above. The PFLP restricts the acquistion and representation of elements in the syntax to those which are licensed by phonological material at PF. This entails that a projection of agreement (subject or object) in a given language crucially depends on its realization in the phonology (and by extension, the morphology) of that language. Under this hypothesis, functional head templates are strictly language-specific; a putative AGR projection in English or Chinese is thus ruled out by the morphology, in part because insufficient phonological or morphological evidence is available to allow an acquirer of English or Chinese to posit such a projection. Since AGR_O in these languages cannot project or be acquired under the PFLP, it cannot assign accusative case cross-linguistically.

Data from French passive participles is often cited as evidence in favour of a universally-projecting AGR_O. However, there is clear evidence that AGR_O is not morphologically licensed in Finnish. The Finnish data is interesting in this respect: although active participles agree in number with subjects, passive participles fail to agree with the derived subject (25 and 26):

25) a. Nainen   on   korja-nnut   viemäri-n.
       woman(nom) be/3s repair-pcp/sg drain-acc
       'The woman has repaired the drain'

   b. Naise-t   ovat   korja-nneet   viemäri-n.
       woman-nom/pl be/3p repair-pcp/pl drain-acc
       'The women have repaired the drain'

26) a. Astia   on   tiska-ttu.
       dish(nom) be/3s wash-pcp/pass
       'The dish has been washed'

   b. Astia-t   on   tiska-ttu.
       dish-nom/pl be/3s wash-pcp/pass
       'The dishes have been washed'

The data from Finnish passive participles show that passivized elements do not pass through a lower agreement projection, or if they do, that they fail to trigger agreement as a result. Since a putative projection of AGR_O would be lacking in φ-features in all sentence types, an acquirer of Finnish would have little evidence on which to postulate a projection.

Despite the indications that AGR_O is not licensed in Finnish, it might be possible to postulate another functional head as being responsible for licensing accusative case. Several recent analyses have posited Aspect as a functional head involved in accusative case assignment. For example, in Korean adjectives can appear marked for tense, aspect, and modality, behaving strongly like verbal predicates. However, only verbs (27b) can assign accusative case, while adjectives assign nominative case (27a) (Lee 1993:73):

27) a. Minho-ka   holangi-ka /*lul   mwusepta
       Minho-nom tiger-nom /*acc   be afraid of
       'Minho is afraid of a tiger'

   b. Minho-ka   Mary-lul /*ka   anta
       Minho-nom Mary-acc /*nom know
       'Minho knows Mary'

In Korean, nominative objects alternate with accusative objects depending on aspectual information encoded in the predicate. Based on this data as well as data from gerundive constructions similar to Finnish temporal clauses, Lee (1993) concludes that accusative case in gerunds gets licensed as the result of V incorporating an aspect morpheme, which projects as a functional head Aspect. Furthermore, an aspectual feature [-STATIVE] must be present for finite verbs to assign accusative case. Lee contrasts her analysis to that of Miyagawa (1991), who suggests that accusative case in Japanese is assigned at S-structure under spec-head government by the functional head Aspect. Both works attempt to unify case assignment rules with analyses of scrambling.

Arguments have been made in support of a functional head associated with Aspect in Finnish and other Finno-Ugric languages (Mitchell 1991b postulates a functional head ASP for Finnish; Julien 1994[15] analyses ASP as analagous to AGR_O in Saami). As discussed in Chapter 1, there is evidence from Finnish morphology that Perfect tense projects as a functional head immediately dominating VP in active sentences, consistent with models of case assignment wherein AGR_O is still within the maximal projection of V (e.g. Koopman and Sportiche 1991, Ramchand 1995). Since sentential semantics seem to play such a crucial role in the assignment of objective case in Finnish, especially in the partitive-accusative case alternation, PERF might be a viable candidate for VP-external accusative or objective case assignment.

However, the complex nature of the Finnish tense/aspect system makes such a postulation difficult. The participles licensing PERF encode features for perfect and pluperfect tense, but most aspectual distinctions in Finnish are signalled by the partitive-accusative case alternation, independent from perfect tense:

28) Hanna   ol-i   rakenta-nut talo-n
    Hanna(nom) be-past/3s   build-pcp   house-acc
    'Hanna had built a house'

29) Hanna   ol-i   rakenta-nut talo-a
    Hanna(nom) be-past/3s   build-pcp   house-part
    'Hanna had been building a house'

Mechanisms of Case Assignment

Moreover, the Perfect functional head in Finnish is licensed only by participial affixes that appear on verbs when Tense/Mood and AGR are hosted by an auxiliary:

30) Aili   ol-i   men-nyt kauppa-an.
    Aili(nom) be-past/3s   go-pcp   shop-to
    'Aili had gone to the shop'

In the absence of perfect and pluperfect tense, no participle appears:

31) Aili   men-i   kauppa-an.
    Aili(nom) go-past/3s   shop-to
    'Aili went to the shop'

Given the 'Minimal IP' hypothesis adopted earlier in the chapter, the fact that PERF is not licensed by the morphology in all sentences suggests that it is not involved in objective case assignment.

Finally, a problem with word order emerges in sentences such as (30) and (31) above if either accusative or partitive is assumed to be assigned exclusively under spec-head agreement in PERF. Since the trace of AUX prevents head movement of the verbal complex V+PERF higher than PERF, the object would have to occur preverbally in order to get assigned case, yielding a surface SOV word order (32):

32)

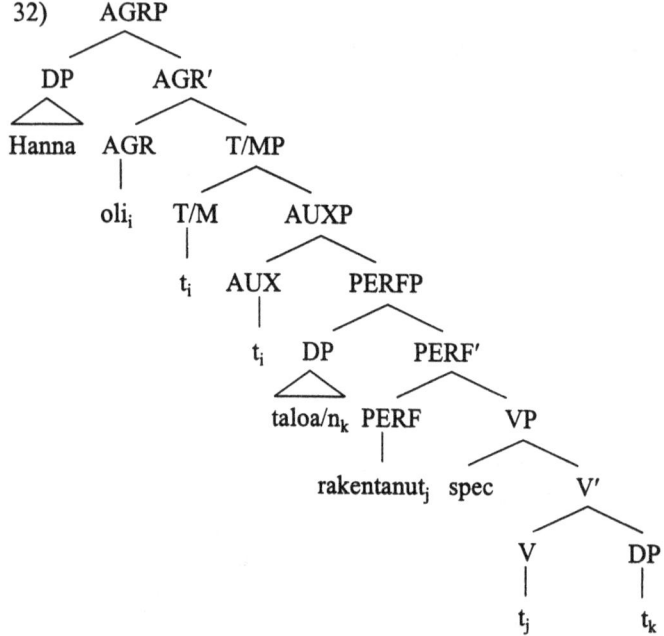

Unlike e.g. Scottish Gaelic (Ramchand 1995; Adger 1994), no word order effects are visible which correlate with the aspectual distinction signalled by the partitive/accusative case alternation. For these reasons PERF will not be posited as a VP-external objective case assigner that assigns under spec-head agreement.

Because of the difficulties in accounting for objective case assignment external to VP, it is proposed here that objective case (both accusative and partitive) is assigned under government by a verb to its complement, consistent with previous accounts of Case assignment within the Principles and Parameters framework and as assumed in earlier analyses of case in Finnish (van Nes-Felius 1983; Milsark 1985; and Reime 1989; 1993). Specific mechanisms of assignment for partitive and accusative objective cases are discussed in greater detail in section 4.5.2 where it is argued that objective partitive and accusative case is associated with the assignment of aspectual theta-roles by the verb.

4.5.2 The partitive-accusative case alternation

In the previous section, the verb is taken to be the objective case assigner for Finnish. This hypothesis does not, however, explain the alternation of partitive and accusative objective case: if V both governs and theta-marks its complement, then one objective case may be inherent and one structural. Recall from Chapter 2 that the partitive/accusative alternation in Finnish signals a variety of aspectual oppositions, including boundedness, telicity, and resultativity, and is assigned under Negation:

33) a. Mikko   sö-i   kakku-a.
    Mikko(nom) eat-past 3s cake-part
    'Mikko ate some of the cake' or 'Mikko was eating the cake'

   b. Mikko   sö-i   kaku-n.
      Mikko(nom) eat-past 3s cake-acc
      'Mikko ate the entire cake'

34) a. Mikko   e-i   syö-nut   kakku-a.
    Mikko(nom) neg-3s eat-pcp/past cake-part
    'Mikko didn't eat some of the cake' or 'Mikko wasn't eating the cake'

   b. *Mikko   e-i   syö-nut   kaku-n
      Mikko(nom) neg-3s eat-pcp/past cake-acc

Based on previous observations that the partitive has the "widest functional distribution" of the objective case forms in Finnish (Yli-Vakkuri 1987:203) and that the partitive is unmarked in the partitive/accusative opposition (Heinämäki 1984), it is argued by Vainikka (1989, 1990, 1993) and Vainikka and Maling (1996) that the case system of Finnish utilizes a structural default mechanism for grammatical case assignment. According to this approach, all NPs in complement position (of V, P, and A) receive partitive rather than accusative case by structural default. Accusative case, posited as the marked objective case, is assigned as the result of a single aspectual feature [+COMPLETED] under government by V. However, positing partitive as an objective structural case (i.e. assigned at S-structure) cannot account for the fact that partitive case may appear on DPs in subject position:

35) Kalakukko-a e-i syö-da.
    fish pie-part neg-3s eat-pass
    'The fish pie will not be eaten.'

To account for this, Vainikka argues that partitive case is assigned at D-structure. Accusative case in her analysis (Vainikka 1989c) is assigned or realized at various stages of the derivation, depending on the type of argument receiving case; pronouns and plurals receive their case affix -*t* before 'genitive percolation,' the process by which the full DP accusative morph -*n* affixes to DPs. The latter process can occur only after subjects have raised to IP and left 'stranded' their genitive -*n* case feature.

Following work by Perlmutter (1978) and Burzio (1986), Belletti (1988) seeks to refine the Unaccusative Hypothesis by arguing that unaccusative verbs lose their ability to assign accusative case, but may still assign inherent partitive case. Examining data from Romance, English and Finnish, she accounts for the Definiteness Effect by suggesting that partitive is a universally-occurring inherent case linked with an 'existential theta-role,' assigned by unaccusative verbs. According to Belletti, partitive-marked DPs may only receive an indefinite reading. However, as noted by Vainikka and Maling (1996) and Ramchand (1995), this prediction is simply not borne out by the Finnish data; an object in the partitive may be interpreted as definite:

36) Anna kirjoitt-i kirja-a.
    Anna(nom) write-past/3s book-part
    'Anna was writing the book'

Moreover, there are problems with Belletti's proposed universal link between partitive case and the assignment of an 'existential' theta-role, given that partitive is invariably assigned under negation in Finnish (37):

37) a. Minä   tapa-si-n   miehe-n.
    I(nom) meet-past-1s man-acc
    'I met a/the man'

b. Minä   e-n   tava-nnut   mies-tä.
   I-nom neg-1s   meet-pcp/past   man-part

c. *Minä   e-n   tava-nnut   miehe-n.
   I-nom   neg-1s   meet-pcp/past   man-acc

Vainikka and Maling (1996), in an answer to Belletti, conclude that partitive is structural, and therefore not linked to a particular theta-role. By reducing accusative case assignment to the presence of a verbal feature [+COMPLETED], the alternation between the two objective cases is skewed toward the partitive as a structural default, with the accusative dependent on the presence of a *verbal* feature. The appearance of the partitive case is not seen as having a bearing on the interpretation of the argument as definite or indefinite, or on the interpretation of the predicate as a whole. One problem with this approach is that it fails to account for the appearance of accusative case in possessive (stative) predicates:

38) Sinu-lla   on   minu-t.
    you-adess   be/3s   me-acc
    'You have me'

Vainikka and Maling's analysis wrongly predicts (38) to be ungrammatical, because the copular verb denotes an imperfective stative rather than a [+COMPLETED] event.

Rigler (1992) strongly rejects the viability of formal syntactic accounts of the partitive-accusative alternation in Finnish. She argues that the alternation is closely associated with the aspectual notion of boundedness, which is neutral in telicity and durativity. She notes that there is no direct correlation between the boundedness of the verb and the case form of its complement, so that a verb or sentence with an aspectual feature such as [+/- COMPLETED] could not predict the occurrence of a partitive object. She concludes that the partitive-accusative alternation is accountable only in purely semantic terms, determined at the phrasal level, and that neither case could be structurally assigned.

One syntactic account of objective case in Finnish which does take into account the interplay between the lexical semantics of a verb on the one hand, and the properties of the object on the other, is given in de Hoop (1992). This analysis links morphological partitive case in Finnish with 'weak' structural case, which is assigned as a default at S-structure and induces a weak interpretation. Weak structural case is assigned as the result of a particular *relation* of an argument to a predicate, and contrasts with strong structural case in accusative DPs. To account for certain scrambling effects in Dutch, de Hoop must stipulate that elements assigned Weak Structural Case must occur in their D-structure positions at S-structure. Although Finnish data such as (35) are problematic for such an analysis, the effects of argument type and predicate type on the eventual interpretation of the sentence is an important step forward.

Ramchand (1995) adopts de Hoop's notion of Weak and Strong structural case, and incorporates them into an account of aspect and argument structure primarily for Scottish Gaelic. In Scottish Gaelic, word order varies between VSO and SVO, depending on the presence of an aspectual particle *ag* associated with the aspectual feature [-BOUND] (Ramchand 1995:17):

39) a. Dh'òl   Calum   leann.
    drink-past Calum-dir beer
    'Calum drank beer'

b. Bha   Calum ag òl   leann.
    be-past Calum asp drink-vnoun beer
    'Calum drank/was drinking beer'

In (39a) above, the object appears sentence-finally. In (39b), specification for tense appears on an auxiliary, while the verb appears as a verbal noun. The object appears post-verbally. Ramchand posits a projection of Aspect (ASP) headed by *ag* as part of the extended projection of the verb in Scottish Gaelic and in other languages.

Moreover, count nouns in Scottish Gaelic may be interpreted as definite or indefinite depending on their structural position (and case-marking), regardless of the resultativity or irresultativity of the predicate (Ramchand 1995:65):

40) a. Bha   Calum a'gearradh   chraobhan.
    be-past Calum ag cut-vnoun trees-gen
    'Calum was cutting trees'

   b. Gheàrr Calum chraobhan.
      cut-past Calum trees-dir
      'Calum cut some particular trees'

41) a. Bha   Calum a'faicinn   chraobhan.
    be-past Calum ag see-vnoun trees-gen
    'Calum saw trees'

   b. Chunnaic Calum chraobhan.
      see-past Calum trees-dir
      'Calum saw some particular trees'

Ramchand argues that boundedness is a property specified by the aspectual head dominating V, and that Strong and Weak structural cases are assigned to two separate positions, spec(VP) and complement of V, depending on where the argument is base-generated. Arguments may be governed by V as complements, while arguments in spec(VP) are properly governed by ASP. The assignment of strong and weak structural case is not simply determined by which element governs it, however. In an attempt to better formalize poorly-defined roles within Theta Theory (AGENT, PATIENT, etc.), and following recent work in the syntax of aspect, Ramchand links Strong structural case with the assignment of certain aspectual theta-roles by the verbal predicate at D-structure. These roles are (Ramchand 1995:103):

42) (1) Patient₌, assigned with creation/consumption verbs, in which the property of quantizedness has an effect on the interpretation of boundedness (e.g. *Calum has eaten the apple*);
(2) Patient→, assigned with verbs of motion, in which the quantizedness of the object does not affect the interpretation of boundedness, and to which the addition of a goal phrase makes the interpretation telic (e.g. *Calum has pushed the car*);
(3) Patient₊/₋, assigned by change-of-state verbs in which the quantizedness of the object does not affect the interpretation of boundedness, and to which the addition of a resultative phrase makes the interpretation telic (e.g. *Calum has broken the window*);
(4) Mod, assigned by statives and which specifies that no bounded interpretation is possible in otherwise aspectually underdetermined predications. This role is not assigned by Aspect (e.g. *The sea looks black*).

Ramchand argues that these roles cannot be specified at the lexical level; only in D-structure configuration, i.e. postlexically, can these theta-roles be assigned by a predicate, under government by an aspectual head. This approach contradicts standard Theta Theory, which assumes that thematic roles can be specified by a verb at the lexical level. The evidence from Gaelic, however, suggests that only at the syntactic level can these roles be assigned, when the relevant functional categories related to Aspect govern V at D-structure.

In her model of case assignment, strong structural case is assigned under government by Aspect in conjunction with the assignment of an aspectual theta-role (i.e. all roles except θ_{mod}) while weak structural case is assigned by V, which cannot assign aspectual theta-roles itself. In this framework, the whole division between inherent and structural case begins to unravel: structural case is linked with particular theta-roles *and* with particular positions. Moreover, Ramchand assumes that no case-driven movement takes place between D-and S-structure; elements are base-generated *in situ*, and no NP-movement takes place. This effectively renders the D-/S-structure distinction between inherent and structural case invalid.

Can these proposals account for the partitive-accusative case alternation in Finnish? Ramchand discusses the Finnish data, using them as an example of a language which signals Weak structural case by morphological means (partitive). Although the data from Scottish Gaelic clearly support a projection of Aspect, we have seen that positing the same projection for Finnish is more problematic, since verbal morphology is independent from the case alternations which encode aspect (data in (43) given previously as (28) and (29)):

43) a. Hanna   ol-i   rakenta-nut talo-a.
    Hanna(nom) be-past/3s build-pcp   house-part
    'Hanna had been building a house'

   b. Hanna   ol-i   rakenta-nut talo-n.
      Hanna(nom) be-past/3s build-pcp   house-acc
      'Hanna had built a house'

In Finnish, there is no morphological evidence for an independent projection of Aspect, and this is problematic for Ramchand's analysis. Moreover, there are no word-order effects to suggest that partitive is assigned in a different structural position from accusative case. The aspectual theta-roles she discusses, however, do correlate with the distribution of accusative case in Finnish, and her θ_{mod} does pattern with partitive (or Weak structural) case.

The problem remains as to how Ramchand's notion of configurationally-determined aspectual theta-roles can be adopted to account for the partitive/accusative alternation in Finnish, despite the lack of evidence for a functional projection of Aspect. To a certain extent it is possible to skirt the issue here. Whether aspect (and therefore the assignment of aspectual theta-roles) is determined lexically or at D-structure, by D-structure these roles have been assigned, since the extended projection of V (Grimshaw 1991) includes shared features for all aspects of verbal semantics associated with tense and aspect. Also at D- and S-structure, the semantic operator Negation governs V and blocks the interpretation of the predicate as bounded. Since the partitive/accusative alternation correlates with the assignment of these aspectual roles, objective case assignment may be directly associated with them. The following case-assigning rules are proposed:

44) a. Associate accusative case with assignment of aspectual theta-role.
b. Associate partitive case with assignment of θ$_{mod}$ role.[16]

Assuming that V assigns case under government rather than via an external functional projection as argued in section 4.5.1, V emerges as the assigner of both aspectual theta-roles and objective case, and the alternation between accusative and partitive case is accounted for.

Since one of the other functions of accusative case is to signal definiteness, given (44) the question arises as to what happens when an definite object receives a non-aspectual theta-role, and partitive case. De Hoop (1992) describes partitive case in Finnish as a Weak Structural case, and notes that the argument is interpreted as definite:

45) Maija   korja-si   ove-a.
Maija(nom) repair-past/3s door-part
'Maija was repairing the door'

In other words, the fact that the partitive case signals indefiniteness is superseded by the irresultative aspect of the sentence, because the relationship between the argument and predicate is more relevant to the assignment of Weak structural case than the individual properties of the argument (e.g. definiteness). De Hoop's observations run counter to the claim made by Belletti (1988) that partitive case is inherently assigned by verbs licensing an existential theta-role associated with *in*definiteness.

In the current work, both accusative and partitive case are linked with the assignment of aspectual and non-aspectual theta-roles. If aspectual theta-roles are assigned at D-structure, at what level is objective case assigned by V? One possible analysis of objective case in Finnish is that accusative and/or partitive are assigned inherently. The definition of inherent case is subsumed under the Uniformity Condition on Case Marking, given in Chomsky (1986a:194):

46) If α is an inherent Case-marker, then α Case-marks NP if and only if α theta-marks the chain headed by NP.

Inherent Case is assumed to be assigned at D-structure associated with theta-role assignment but checked at S-structure (Haegeman

1991:315); this entails that an element may move out of VP and still be assigned case, for example, dative subjects of passives in German. However, the structural/inherent case distinction cannot easily account for 'quirky' subjects in Icelandic and certain passivized verbs in German (Webelhuth 1995:56-59).

Moreover, the assumption that structural accusative case is assigned at S-structure is problematic. If accusative case assignment under V is structural rather than inherent, and therefore assigned at S-structure, how can a verb assign case to its complement if it has undergone head-movement into higher functional projections (see 48c below) by S-structure? If structural accusative case can be assigned by a head-chain (as opposed to *to* an NP-chain) then structural case assignment by verbs must also hold at D-structure.

For objective case assignment by verbs, then, the inherent/structural case distinction is not particularly clear-cut. Moreover, it has been argued that a reformulation of theta-roles to involve aspectual semantics better accounts for the Finnish data. These roles are assigned at D-structure rather than specified in the lexicon, which entails that theta-role assignment is linked to structural configuration in a different way than previously supposed. In light of these factors, the notion of inherent objective case is rejected for Finnish, and partitive and accusative case are both analysed as structural cases.

4.6 CASE ASSIGNMENT IN TRANSITIVE SENTENCES

So far, grammatical case has been argued to be assigned in the following two ways (47):

47) 1. (a) Tense/Mood (T/M) is a bi-unique assigner of nominative case, either under spec-head agreement or under government.
(b) Nominative case is assigned at S-structure.

2. (a) Accusative case is associated with the assignment of aspectual theta-roles; partitive case is associated with assignment of θ_{mod} role.
(b) Objective cases are assigned by V under government at D-structure.

Given these mechanisms, case assignment in transitive sentences can be accounted for. The examples are transitive sentences with a nominative subject and a partitive or accusative object reflecting a resultative/irresultative aspectual distinction:

48) a. Mikko   silitt-i   paida-n.
    Mikko(nom) iron-past/3s   shirt-acc
    'Mikko ironed the shirt'

 b. Mikko   silitt-i   paita-a.
    Mikko(nom) iron-past/3s   shirt-part
    'Mikko was ironing the shirt'/ 'Mikko ironed part of the shirt'

The sentences above share the same S-structure representation, given below as (48c):

Mechanisms of Case Assignment

48) c.

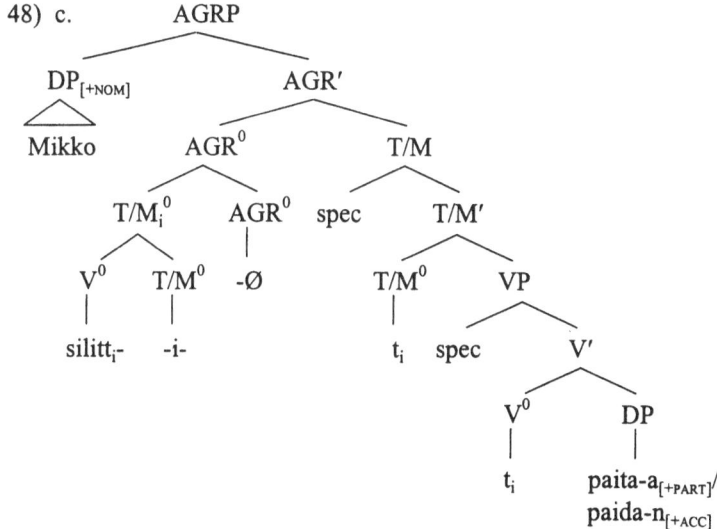

The external argument of V is base-generated in spec(AGRP), where it is coindexed with φ-features there. V undergoes head movement to Tense/Mood and AGR to incorporate inflectional affixes and thus avoid a violation of the Stray Affix Filter. Since T/M is incorporated into AGR at S-structure, nominative case can be assigned to the subject DP in its specifier position, and the bi-unique case-assigning property of T/M is satisfied. The internal argument of V is assigned case *in situ* under government by the coindexed trace of V, by virtue of the GTC (Baker 1988) given in (5): in the resultative sentence, an aspectual theta-role is assigned, and the verb assigns accusative case, while in the irresultative sentence, no aspectual theta-role is assigned and the object surfaces in partitive case.

In an unergative sentence such as (49a) below, V does not L-mark a complement. The verb undergoes head movement to AGR via Tense/Mood (49b), while the external argument remains *in situ* in spec(AGRP):

49) a. Mies   nauro-i
       man(nom)   laugh-past/3s
       'The man laughed'

b.

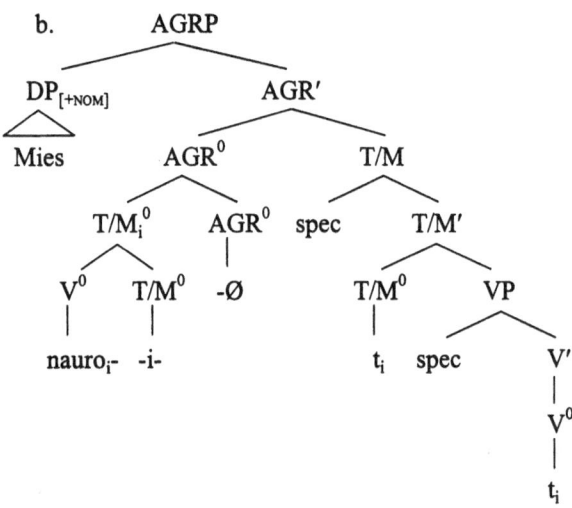

No internal argument is licensed and the external argument is coindexed with AGR. Nominative case is assigned under government to *mies* by the head Tense/Mood.[17]

4.7 DOUBLE CASE MARKING: AN ACCOUNT FOR SPLIT-S ERGATIVITY

In transitive sentences, V assigns accusative or partitive case to its complement at D-structure and T/M assigns nominative case to the external argument in spec(AGRP). The external argument is coindexed with agreement features in AGR^0. Case assigment to arguments in this configuration satisfies both the requirements of the Case Filter and the requirement that Tense/Mood assign a nominative case feature given in (16). In this section it is proposed that when an argument is base-generated internal to V' and is assigned objective case at D-structure, it may also receive a nominative case feature if there is no external argument available to receive nominative case at S-structure. Recall the following sentence pair given in Chapter 2 (ex. 30):

50) Laukku   tuo-tiin   asema-lta.
    bag(nom) bring-pass/past   station-from
    'The bag was brought home from the station'

51) Heidä-t   tuo-tiin   asema-lta.
    they-acc bring-pass/past   station-from
    'They (animate) were brought home from the station'

As discussed in Chapter 3, contrary to standard analyses of passives and contrary to Burzio's Generalization, accusative case marking on the animate pronoun in (51) signals that the verb does not lose its ability to assign accusative case as a result of impersonal passive morphology. In sum, the Finnish data are difficult to account for within purely syntactic accounts in which certain verbs lose their ability to assign accusative case. Cross-linguistic data from other languages in which passivized elements remain in accusative case (e.g. Spanish) are equally problematic in light of Case Theory (Jaeggli 1986). Belletti (1988) and Lasnik (1992) dispute the idea that passive morphology removes the verb's ability to assign structural Case, arguing instead that both passive verbs and copulae can be inherent case assigners.

In his analysis of the double object construction in English, Larson (1988:360-1) suggests that V assigns both inherent and structural case simultaneously to its complement: inherent objective case is assigned by V (presumably at D-structure), while the complex INFL+V assigns both structural nominative and accusative case. Objects of transitive verbs are thus doubly case-marked [+ACC, +OBJ]. Ditransitives, on the other hand, 'separate out' the two types of case, so that one internal argument receives structural accusative while the other receives inherent objective case. One of the syntactic effects of passivization, he argues, is to suppress structural *or* inherent case assignment by V. Jaeggli (1986) also presents an analysis in which more than one abstract case can be assigned to an argument simultaneously.

Earlier in this chapter it is proposed that Finnish assigns both accusative and partitive case, and that T/M must assign a nominative case feature at S-structure. Following the proposals by Larson and Jaeggli, the case split in pronouns and full DPs in Finnish is taken to emerge as the result of double case assignment of two abstract case features simultaneously to a single argument. Double case marking occurs when the verb fails to license an external argument coindexed with AGR. If no external argument is available in spec(AGRP) to receive the nominative case feature within the governing domain of T/M, movement of an argument to a position where it can be assigned nominative case is motivated by this requirement. If the only argument available is internal to VP and already case-marked with the assignment of aspectual roles at D-structure, then that element will be assigned structural case twice.

Suppose that, for one of the reasons discussed in Chapter 3, a verb α has the following argument structure:

52) α (x)

In the case of passives, the verb takes two arguments, but the external argument has been internalized, yielding the argument structure given in (52). In the case of unaccusatives and raising verbs, no external argument is licensed in the lexicon, i.e. the verb is a one-place predicate. In Chapter 3, it was proposed that external arguments are base-generated local to AGR if coindexed with it. With raising verbs and unaccusatives, no external argument is base-generated at all; in passives, the external argument is absorbed by the passive morphology and not realized at D-structure; and in imperatives, the external argument is rendered syntactically inactive by the presence of imperative mood.

In finite transitive or unergative sentences where external arguments are base-generated in spec(AGRP), T/M governs the subject in spec(AGRP) and assigns its nominative case feature under government. If Tense/Mood projects in the structure but no element is base-generated in spec(AGRP), then an element must move into the governing domain of Tense/Mood to be assigned nominative case. According to the definitions of government and i-command given previously, T/M or one of its coindexed traces formed by head movement governs the following positions: spec(AGRP), spec(T/MP), or spec(VP),[18] so nominative case may be assigned to any of these

Mechanisms of Case Assignment

positions. If the only available element is the internal argument β, it must raise to a position governed by Tense/Mood (53):

53)
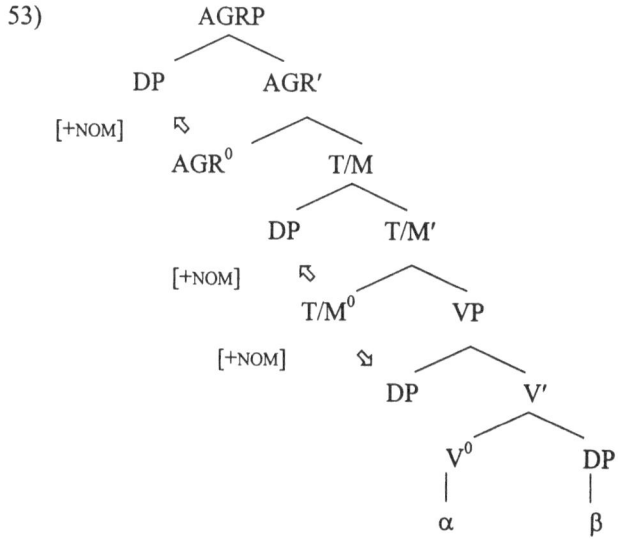

However, if β moves from where it is base-generated as complement of V, its trace is still governed by the trace of V at S-structure. The argument will end up with two case features, one assigned by V associated with aspectual roles assigned at D-structure (accusative), and the other assigned by Tense/Mood at S-structure (nominative).

Given that elements in all positions governed by Tense/Mood may be assigned nominative case, how is it possible to rule out a structure in a transitive sentence like (54), where the internal argument DP_i is doubly case-assigned in spec(VP)?:

54)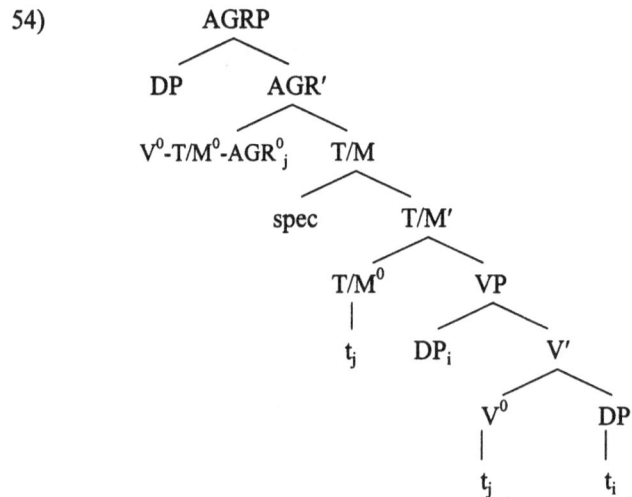

The structure above turns out to be disallowed by the case-assigning properties of Tense/Mood. Recall the bi-uniqueness condition in (16) imposed by Tense/Mood: one argument must be assigned nominative case, but there is only one case feature to assign. If that feature is assigned to the internal argument rather than the external argument in a transitive sentence, than the external argument will violate the Case Filter and the derivation will fail, ruling out (54).

4.7.1 Lexical case assignment

The idea that elements may receive two case features simultaneously is a powerful hypothesis. In particular, lexical case assignment must be taken into account in the model proposed here. Certain verbs in Finnish assign lexical case to their complements, e.g. *erikoistua*, 'to specialize in,' which assigns illative case:

55) Isoäiti erikoistu-i kirjallisuute-en.
grandmother(nom) specialize-past/3s literature-ill
'Grandmother specialized in literature'

In a passive sentence, where Tense/Mood does project, the illative complement must be able to satisfy the relevant case-assigning requirement:

56) Kirjallisuut-en   erikoistu-taan.
    literature-ill   specialize-pass
    'Literature is being specialized in' or 'They are specializing in literature'

In cases where an element receives both structural nominative and lexical case, lexical case assignment does not block the assignment of the nominative case feature, but overrides it in the morphology. This is accounted for by the postulation of morphological realization rules for case assignment, described in the next section.

The question arises as to whether or not double case assignment is a freely-occurring process in the syntax. The grammaticality of (56) predicts that any additional complements governed by a verb such as *erikoistua* will not require nominative case, since the lexically case-marked element will have both case features, [+ILL] and [+NOM]. The data do not, however, bear out this generalization. Adverbial modifiers of duration, manner and measure in Finnish may receive case as (quasi-)arguments (these are discussed in section 4.8). A duration adverbial modifying a sentence sentence such as (56) appears in nominative, rather than accusative, case (57):

57) a. Kirjallisuute-en   erikoistu-ttiin   vuosi.
       literature-ill   specialize-pass/past   year(nom)
       'Literature was specialized in for a year'

    b. *Kirjallisuute-en   erikoistu-ttiin   vuode-n.
        literature-ill   specialize-pass/past   year-acc

To account for such data, Maling (1993) proposes a Case-Tier, a hierarchy of cases that are mapped onto caseless elements in a sentence according to ranked grammatical function. The ILLATIVE element does not participate in the Case Tier since it is assigned case lexically. The next element in the GF hierarchy is the adverbial modifier, which receives the highest case in the Tier, [+NOM].

The current analysis as given so far does not rule out (57b), because the lexically case-marked element in (56) is assigned two case features and this should be possible in (57b). However, within the current model for case assignment, either the lexically-assigned argument *or* the adverbial modifier must be doubly case-marked, since no external argument is licensed to receive nominative case. In order to rule out (57b), it is necessary to postulate a generalized constraint for Finnish under which the assignment of two *grammatical* case features is preferred to the assignment of a lexical plus a grammatical case feature:

58) Assign second case feature to structurally case-marked elements before lexically case-marked elements.

In fact, such a rule falls out of Maling's Case-Tier described in section 4.8 (Maling 1993:60):

59) a. NOM is assigned before ACC
    b. only one XP can get assigned NOM, any remaining NPs get ACC
    c. which XP gets NOM reflects the hierarchy of GFs, where
       SUBJ > OBJ > MEASURE > DUR > FREQ

In Maling's model, lexically or semantically case-marked elements do not participate in the Case-Tier, so the Tier only accounts for the distribution of grammatical cases. However, given the requirement assumed in the current analysis that one nominative case feature must be assigned per finite sentence, operation of a Tier generates the correct results if lexically-assigned oblique roles are added to the bottom of the hierarchy:

59) d. SUBJ > OBJ > MEASURE > DUR > FREQ > OBL

An element assigned an oblique role will therefore receive a nominative case feature only if no GFs higher in the hierarchy are available. Implementation of the hierarchy thus resolves possible conflicts as to which element receives nominative case, and by extension double case-marking, in a sentence where no external argument is coindexed with AGR. In Chapter 6 this modified case

Mechanisms of Case Assignment 159

hierarchy is extended to necessive constructions to account for case in sentences with genitive subjects.

4.7.2 Morphological rules for case assignment

In the syntactic framework adopted here, verbal inflectional affixes such as tense/mood and agreement project as functional heads in the syntax and combine according to the rules of X-bar theory. Moreover, inflectional affixes acquired as part of the functional lexicon have their own lexical entries encoding particular properties such as case-assignment and c-selectional requirements for building IP structure. This approach presupposes that inflectional morphemes behave similarly to contentives in the syntax, and are stored in a similar fashion in the lexicon.

These assumptions raise issues relating to inflectional morphology as a whole, in particular as to whether nominal inflectional morphology operates in the same way. Since Finnish is an agglutinating language it might be possible to treat Finnish cases as heads, each with its own lexical entry and selectional requirements. Although related suggestions have been made for the semantic cases (Nikanne 1989; 1991 and 1993 links semantic cases (or Kases) with a nonovert prepositional head), it would be more difficult to posit lexical entries for the grammatical cases because nominative case is phonetically unrealized. Instead, it is assumed broadly following Zwicky's (1986) approach that case affixation is realized as the result of morphological rules that operate postlexically and postsyntactically, rather than as the result of word-formation processes within the lexicon. Such rules include featural specification for person, number and case, and yield surface forms such as (60):

60) a. N^0
        [-pl]   → $/N^0/$
        [+/- pron]
        [+NOM]

    b. N^0
        [+pl]   → $/N^0\text{+-}t/$
        [+/- pron]
        [+NOM]

    c. N^0
        [+pl]   → $/N^0\text{+-ITEN}/$
        [- pron]
        [+GEN]

The phonological rules given above condition the realization of surface case forms. In (60a) the nominative case form is zero for singular full DPs and prounouns in transitives and unergatives, where a single [+NOM] feature is assigned; (60b) the nominative plural form is /-t/ for both pronouns and full DPs; and in (60c) the plural genitive case form is realized as /-ITEN/. However, these rules do not yield the correct forms for accusative pronouns, zero-accusatives or partitive DPs. Milsark (1985) mentions the difficulty of positing a morphological case realization rule to generate the -*n*/zero alternation for full DPs which is sensitive to the presence or absence of a syntactic subject.

The syntactic analysis posited earlier in this section provides a solution for morphological case realization: syntactic environments lacking a syntactic subject are also those in which two case features get assigned to the internal argument. In order to account for the surface forms of doubly case-marked elements, additional morphological rules are posited which incorporate *two* case features. Two rules for pronouns and full DPs yield the accusative-zero case alternation (61):

61) a. N^0
         [+/-pl]
         [+ animate pron]
         [+ACC]
         [+NOM]   → /N^0+t/

    b. N^0
         [-pl]
         [- animate pron]
         [+ACC]
         [+NOM]   → /N^0/

The rules in (61) ensure that doubly case-marked nominative and accusative animate pronouns are realized with the /-t/ case morph, while singular full DPs and inanimate pronouns with the same case features are zero-marked. A separate rule accounts for surface partitive case in elements doubly case-marked for both nominative and partitive:

62) N^0
         [+/-pl]
         [+/-pron]
         [+NOM]
         [+PART]   → /N^0+TA/

Rule (62) above ensures that the partitive case feature will 'override' a nominative case feature present in both DPs and pronouns.

Finally, a set of case realization rules yield surface oblique case where a lexically case-marked oblique element simultaneously receives a nominative feature. One rule must be specified per oblique case, for example the inessive:

63) N^0
         [+/-pron]
         [+NOM]
         [+INESS]   → /N^0+SSA/

In the literature on Finnish there has been some disagreement as to the properties of the case/number affix -*t*, which appears on plurals in nominative and accusative case and on pronouns in accusative (and double ACC+NOM case in this model). In some previous work (e.g. the case assignment schema adopted by van Nes-Felius 1983 and Renault 1984; see (56) in Chapter 2) it is assumed that the -*t* morph is triggered by a single feature which encompasses both animate pronouns and plurals. Vainikka (1989c) and Reime (1989; 1993) both distinguish between the two homophonous -*t* affixes. The former argues that pronominal -*t* is assigned lexically (presumably as the result of a combination of lexical pronominal and accusative case features) while the plural -*t* represents the nominative (unmarked/caseless) form in all contexts.[19] Reime assumes that plural and pronominal -*t*, while homophonous, are distinct in their feature composition. This debate brings to light the issue of the level of redundancy expressed by morphological case realization rules.

Since the -*t* form for plurals has syncretized in the nominative and accusative but not in the other cases, it is assumed following Reime that pronouns and plurals do not share a single lexical feature that yields the -*t* affix. Instead, each morphological case realization rule is assigned to carry binary feature values for [+/-PRON] and [+/-PL] as well as features for grammatical case assignment. Two of the rules which produce affixation with -*t* are given in (60b) and (61a). These rules are repeated below as (64a) and (64b). The third rule required is given below as (64c):

64) a. N^0
[+pl]
[+/-animate pron]
[+NOM] → /N^0+t/

b. N^0
[+/-pl]
[+animate pron]
[+ACC]
[+NOM] → /N^0+t/

c. N^0
[+pl]
[-animate pron]
[+ACC] → /N^0+t/

These rules yield /-t/ forms for (64a) plural nominative DPs, (64b) doubly case-marked accusative pronouns, and (64c) plural accusative DPs.[20]

4.7.3 Case, ergativity and animacy hierarchies

One interesting question which remains is, do the surface case forms for doubly case-marked full DPs and pronouns simply reflect lexical idiosyncracy, or is this pattern predicted by animacy hierarchies for split case systems? Such a hierarchy has been proposed to account for ergative splits by Silverstein (1976):

65) 1&2 > 3 > proper nouns > human > animate > inanimate ...
    pronouns   common nouns
    Accusative →   ←Ergative

This well-attested implicational hierarchy predicts that the higher the animacy of the element being case-marked, the more likely it is to be interpreted as being higher on the scale of grammatical functions. Dixon (1979), following Silverstein, notes that personal pronouns are higher in animacy that ordinary DPs, so that when split-ergativity occurs, the prediction is that full DPs should appear marked for accusative case rather than pronouns because they are conceptualized as less "agential". In a split-S system, 'subjects' of unaccusative and related verbs which are assigned objective case may be seen as patterning within an ergative subsystem:

66)   Split-S in Finnish

(unergatives)	S_A	S_O	(unaccusatives)
nominative			accusative pronouns
	A	O	

However, the situation in Finnish appears to be the reverse of that predicted by Dixon: personal pronouns receive accusative case marking rather than full DPs, despite the fact that they are higher in animacy. An explanation for this within the context of the animacy hierarchy may be related to morphological markedness. In an ergative language, DPs receiving ergative case are morphologically marked, while absolutive DPs are unmarked. In a Nominative-Accusative language, nominative DPs are unmarked, while accusative DPs are marked. A split-S subsystem within a Nominative-Accusative language might therefore employ the more marked case form to signal the S_O function, in this case the accusative.[21]

The distribution of the partitive case versus the accusative and nominative in Finnish has been argued to conform to a split-S or 'active' system by Moravcsik (1978) and Itkonen (1979). In section 4.5.2 an account for the accusative-partitive case alternation was proposed which linked the distribution of the two objective cases with the assignment of aspectual theta-roles at D-structure. This aspectually-based split-S pattern closely resembles similar case systems noted by Mithun (1991), in particular for Mohawk, where subjects of intransitive sentences are case-marked as subjects or objects based on a distinction between state and event or activity/achievement (*Aktionsart*) (67a), or alternately, based on relative affectedness (67b) (Mithun 1991:532-3):

67) a. kahtΛtye?s   I (AGENT CASE) go away (often)
       ΛkahtΛ:ti?   I (AGENT CASE) will go away
       wakahtΛtyu   I (PATIENT CASE) have gone away

    b. tkayé:ri   It's (AGENT CASE) right, correct
       kará:kΛ   It's (AGENT CASE) white

       yóhteru   It's (PATIENT CASE) dangerous
       yokà:rute?   It (PATIENT CASE) has a hole

The analysis proposed here for Finnish, then, may be extended to capture the data from languages like Mohawk: in unaccusative predicates, the internal argument is assigned an aspectual theta-role (or non-aspectual role) at D-structure; if no external argument is present, the argument is forced to raise to a higher functional projection associated with finite Tense, where it is assigned two case features simultaneously. The resulting surface case forms are realized via a distinct set of morphological rules for doubly case-marked elements, which capture the relationship between syntactic environment (i.e. lack of a syntactic subject) and event structure in these languages.

In this section, case splits in Finnish are accounted for as the result of the simultaneous assignment of two grammatical case features (either [NOM+PART] or [NOM+ACC]) to a single internal argument. Double case assignment is forced in sentences lacking an external argument by the requirement of Tense/Mood to assign a single nominative case feature. In the next sections, particular constructions are analysed where this phenomenon occurs.

4.7.4 Impersonal passives

Given the proposed mechanism for double case assignment, the case alternation between full DPs and animate pronouns can now be accounted for in various constructions where no external argument is coindexed with AGR. The first construction to be analysed is the impersonal passive.

Following observations by Perlmutter (1978) and Marantz (1984), impersonal passives are taken to lack an external argument, so Tense/Mood is unable to assign its nominative case feature to a subject in spec(AGRP). Evidence from the morphology of Finnish impersonal passives suggests that AGR hosts a default third person singular marker. As discussed previously, impersonal passives in Finnish are formed with an affix -TAAN, which shows a past/nonpast Tense distinction via infixation:[22]

68) a. Kirje   ava-taan
    letter(nom) open-pass/np
    'The letter will be opened'

   b. Kirje   ava-ttiin
    letter(nom) open-pass/past
    'The letter was opened'

Under negation or when marked with a Mood affix, the morpheme -TAAN is clearly composed of two subparts, -TT(A) and -Vn:

69) a. Kirje   ava-tta-isi-in.
       letter(nom) open-pass-cond-Vn
       'The letter would be read'

   b. Kirje-ttä e-i   ava-ta.
      letter-part neg-3s open-pass
      'The letter is not being opened'

In section 1.2.2 the *-Vn* affix in the impersonal passive was discussed as being diachronically derived from a third person possessive affix (Px). Unlike Px agreement in most nonfinite clauses, however, *-Vn* in impersonal passives does not signal agreement between the verb and one of its arguments; thus a plural DP fails to trigger any change in agreement morphology on the impersonal passive verbal stem:

70) Kirjee-t   ava-taan.
    letter-nom/pl open-pass/np
    'The letters are being opened'

Given the lack of an external argument coindexed with agreement, the following D-structure representation (71) is proposed for impersonal passives as in (70):

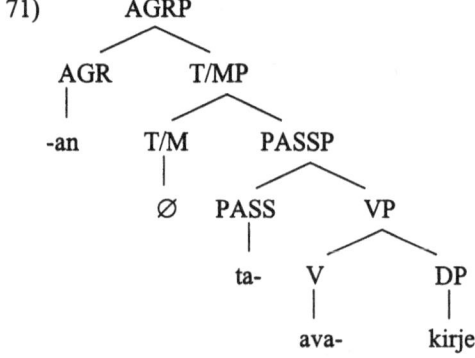

This structure yields spec(AGRP), spec(T/MP) and spec(PASSP) as positions governed or i-commanded by T/M, and therefore available landing sites for the internal argument. Doubly case-marked elements in impersonal passives may occur preverbally or postverbally, reflecting the possible landing sites:

72) a. Kalakukko-a²³ syö-dään.
fish pie-part eat-pass
'Fish pie is being eaten'

b. Syö-dään kalakukko-a.
eat-pass fish pie-part
'Fish pie is being eaten'

73) a. Näh-tiin häne-t/ mies.
see-pass/past him/her-acc man(nom)
'S/he / the man was seen'

b. Häne-t/ mies näh-tiin
him/her-acc man(nom) see-pass/past
'S/he / the man was seen'

The S-structure representation for (73b) is given below (74):

74)
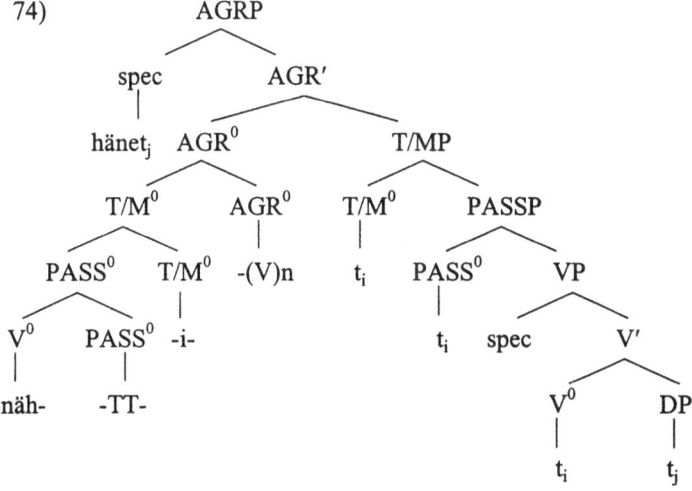

In this sentence, the verb moves into PASS, T/M, and AGR to collect inflectional affixes. No subject is base-generated in AGR because the passive morphology has absorbed the external argument. In order for nominative case to be assigned, the internal argument is forced to move into a position where it can be governed by T/M,[24] in this case, spec(AGRP). Because it receives an aspectual theta-role from V, it is assigned accusative case. In spec(AGRP), the coindexed trace of the internal argument is still governed by the trace of the verb, and is interpreted as having an aspectual role. *Hänet* receives two case features, +NOM and +ACC, which are realized as accusative /-t/ by the appropriate morphological realization rule.

From examples such as (70) it is clear that no agreement is triggered to signal coindexation between AGR and the raised internal argument. The explanation for this lies in the feature specification of the head AGR. AGR in impersonal passives is 'weak,' devoid of φ-features [-φ]. Coindexation with an element specified for φ-features will result in a disjoint index, [+φ, -φ]. Since no entry in the agreement paradigm corresponds to such an index, the agreement morphology continues to reflect the default specification, which is homophonous to third person singular AGR.

4.7.5 Unaccusatives

In section 2.2.2.2 unaccusatives (or 'existentials') were argued to license a single argument, which is base-generated internal to VP, and no agreement morphology is present:

75) Äidi-lle   synty-i   kaksose-t.[25]
     mother-to   born-past/3s   twins-nom/pl
     'To the mother were born twins'

In unaccusatives, as in impersonal passives, AGR is [-φ] which accounts for the lack of coindexed agreement morphology in (75). At D-structure, the single argument of an unaccusative verb is assumed to be base-generated internal to VP, with no external argument being licensed. Internal arguments of unaccusatives are assigned an aspectual theta-role at D-structure, yielding either a partitive or zero-accusative DP postverbally after double case assignment.[26]

Note that because the notion of i-command is being adopted, spec(VP) is a nominative case-marked position under T/M. Internal arguments of unaccusatives (75) may move to this position, and receive double case-marking as in (74) above:

76)
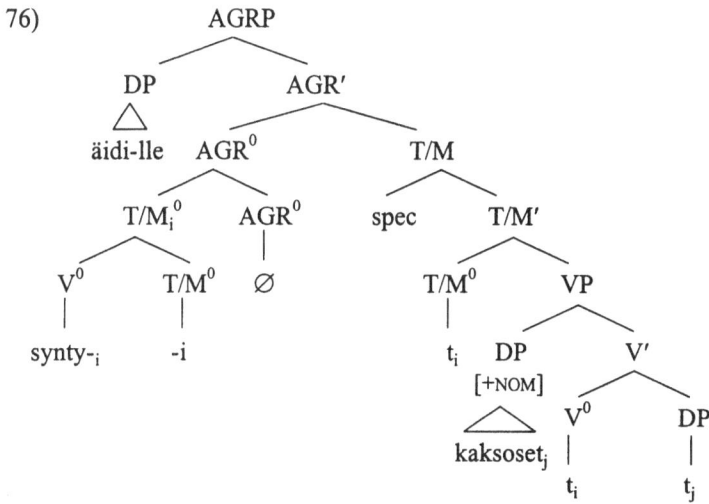

If internal arguments are taken to receive nominative case marking within VP, there is no need to account for postverbal nominative case assignment as an instance of case-transmission via coindexation of the internal argument with AGR (or an empty pronoun coindexed with AGR) as suggested in Chomsky (1981) and Burzio (1986). This approach allows an analysis that is more consistent with the Unaccusative Hypothesis: if a verb fails to license an external argument, then AGR lacks φ-features as a result and cannot have the status of an argument. Instead, nominative case assignment to the internal argument is an indirect result of V failing to license an external argument.

4.7.6 Copular constructions

Consider the following sentences involving locative phrases with copulae (data previously given in Chapter 3):

77) a. Koulu-ssa on uude-t opettaja-t.
    school-in be/3s new-nom/pl teacher-nom/pl
    'The school has new teachers'

　　b. Uude-t opettaja-t ovat koulu-ssa.
    new-nom/pl teacher-nom/pl be/3p school-in
    'The new teachers are at the school'

　　c. *Koulu-ssa on sinä / sinu-t
    school-in be/3s you(nom) / you-acc

78) a. Minu-lla on kynä.
    I-adess be/3s pen(nom)
    'I have a pen'

　　b. Minu-lla on sinu-t.
    I-adess be/3s you-acc
    'I have you'

Freeze (1992) argues that copular existentials (77a above) and possessive constructions (78) share identical structures. Moreover, he links the features [+/- HUMAN] of the possessor with alienable versus inalienable possession; although it is not explicitly stated, this is presumably what results in the suspension of the Definiteness Effect in (78b). Freeze's hypothesis is adopted here for Finnish, though the details of his analysis are modified slightly. Following Belletti (1988) and Lasnik (1992), copulae, along with unaccusatives, are analysed as case-assigning verbs. Classifying possessive constructions with existentials is, however, problematic for Belletti's analysis: unaccusative and copular verbs are posited as partitive (inherent), but not accusative, case assigners, so (78b) should be ruled out. This is not a problem for the current analysis, however, since no real distinction is being made between inherent partitive and structural accusative case.

Mechanisms of Case Assignment

Assuming that copular verbs in such constructions fail to license an external argument, it is also not surprising that agreement and word order effects surface in copular predicates similar to those in unaccusatives (75). Both types of copular predicate are analysed as sharing the same structure as unaccusatives; the internal argument is also assumed to receive double case-marking by similar mechanisms.

4.7.7 Imperatives

As described in previous sections of this dissertation, imperatives occur with a special form for most inflectional affixes, including NEG (*äl-*), T/M (*-ko*), AUX (*ol-*), and AGR. Despite having a distinct paradigm of agreement markers, however, first and second person imperatives show split patterns of case along with verbs lacking external arguments. In section 3.4, the argument structure of imperatives was discussed. It was suggested that in first and second person, imperative mood in Finnish, like impersonal passive morphology, removes the external argument from the syntax.[27]

Morphophonological evidence from imperative 'agreement' markers suggests that they do not show the same properties as inflectional AGR in other moods. A noticeable feature of the imperative agreement paradigm is the failure of these elements to trigger consonant gradation in the preceding syllable:

79) From *ottaa*, 'to take':

1s: (no form)
2s: Ota (sinä) se!   'Take (sg. addressee) it!'
3s: Otta-koon (hän) sen!   'Let him/her take it!'
1p: Otta-kaamme (me) se!   'Let us take it!'
2p: Otta-kaa (te) se!   'Take (pl. addressee) it!
3p: Otta-koot (he) sen!   'Let them take it!'

Consonant gradation is noted as one of the diagnostic features which distinguish Finnish inflectional affixes from clitics (Pierrehumbert 1980; Nevis 1984, 1986, and 1987; and Kanerva 1987). According to these analyses, the paradigm of imperative 'agreement' markers shares other features with clitics: they would violate no phonological rules of

Finnish if they appeared as free morphs, and they fail to affix to stem forms of lexical items. Given the ambiguous status of these elements as clitics or inflectional affixes, it is proposed here that these elements may be pronominal reflexes of external arguments but cannot head a projection of AGR; instead, they occur in specifier positions as non-heads. This notion is explored in greater detail in Chapter 5, where it is argued that possessive affixes (Pxes) also occur as specifiers rather than heads. Like Pxes, imperative 'agreement' markers are assumed to be category AGR, but are restricted in their distribution to specifier positions. In Chapter 5, a mechanism is outlined by which AGR in specifier positions unifies with the verbal compound. An analysis of case assignment in imperatives is given in (80):

80) a. Otta-kaa   se!
    take-imp/2p   it(nom)
    'Take (pl. addressee) it!

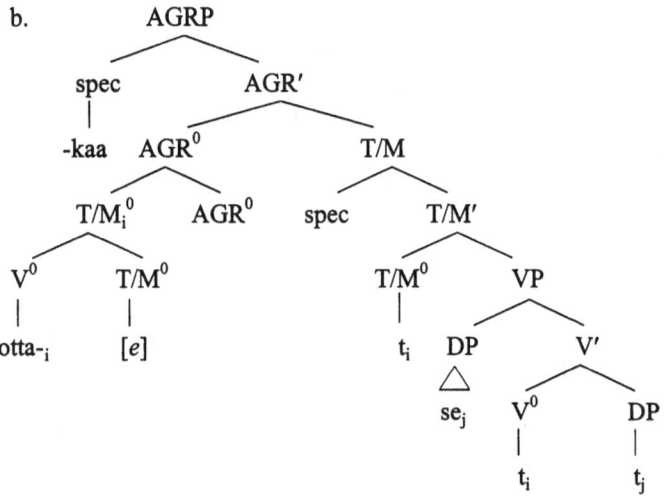

In the representation above, the internal argument is assigned an aspectual or non-aspectual role within VP at D-structure. The AGR node is licensed by the agreement morph *-kaa* in its specifier position, but it is not coindexed with an overt external argument. Since *-kaa* is a bound morph, it must affix itself to a host or violate the Stray Affix filter, but once it has become attached to the verbal stem it is no longer available to receive the nominative case feature from T/M.[28] The internal argument must move to the governing domain of T/M get assigned the case feature; the surface case of the doubly case-marked internal argument is realized via the relevant morphological rule.

Several apparent problems arise from the structure proposed here which are clarified in the next chapter. Firstly, according to the PFLP, the AGR head must be phonetically licensed at PF; following Cann (1993), phonetically overt material in the specifier position of a head may also license the head. By a process which is more fully described in Chapter 5, the agreement element *-kaa* cliticizes onto the host verb from spec(ASPP). This is possible because *-kaa* and ASP are coindexed via spec-head agreement.

The structure in (80b) above accounts for the word order restrictions involving overt subjects in imperatives, which may only occur postverbally (81):

81) a. Ota   sinä   laukku!
    take(imp) you(nom) bag(nom)
    '*You* take the bag!'

   b. *Sinä   ota   laukku!
     you(nom) take(imp) bag(nom)

Assuming that the second person singular form in the imperative agreement paradigm is phonetically empty but paradigmatically licensed, the only available position for an overt subject is postverbally at S-structure within a lower functional projection, because both spec(AGRP) and AGR are filled by morphological material. The assignment of nominative case to overt subject pronouns, however, remains unexplained in this account.

The most problematic construction for this analysis is the third person imperative (optative), the only imperative construction that can introduce an R-expression. Third person imperative verbs assign accusative, rather than nominative, case to their objects (82):

82) Anta-koon   Jorma   kirjee-n   äidi-lle!
    give-imp/3s Jorma(nom) letter-acc   mother-to
    'Let Jorma give the letter to mother!'

An analysis for this construction as a variety of transitive sentence is possible, given the differences in verbal semantics and argument structure between third person and other imperative forms. Third person imperatives actually signal optative rather than imperative Tense/Mood, and they may introduce an R-expression, unlike first and second person pronominal imperatives. However, the agreement morpheme in this construction is part of the same paradigm as the other imperative referent markers; it also fails to trigger consonant gradation. The current analysis predicts that the optative subject will be unavailable to receive the nominative case feature, forcing the internal argument to be doubly case assigned and surface in zero-accusative case. The grammaticality of (82) is therefore not predicted, which is problematic for the current analysis as well as other analyses of case in Finnish.

4.8 CASE ASSIGNMENT AND MEASURE PHRASES

Consider the following English sentences:

83) a. Louise weighed 50 kilos.

    b. *Louise weighed.

84) a. The rain lasted an hour.

    b. *The rain lasted.

That the measure phrases in these examples are arguments rather than adverbial modifiers is evident from the ungrammaticality of the examples in (83b) and (84b). In many languages, measure phrases in such sentences do not receive case, but are clearly part of the verb's theta-grid (perhaps receiving the role of quasi-argument). Adger (1994), based on data from Scottish Gaelic, argues that measure phrases are licensed by the Theta Criterion and coindexation with Tense/Aspect but not necessarily via the assignment of structural case.

In some languages, however, measure phrases show case-related effects similar to other arguments, and appear to be assigned structural case. Maling (1993) shows that in Finnish, as in Korean, measure phrases participate in the same case phenomena as full DP arguments, and are sensitive to a case hierarchy. Where the verb has a measure phrase as an internal argument, the measure phrase will receive accusative case as a singular DP:

85) Se   kest-i   vuode-n
    it(nom) last-past/3s   year-acc
    'It lasted a year'

Measure phrases may also appear as optional adverbial modifiers of duration, manner, and frequency. Unlike in e.g. Scots Gaelic, measure phrases in Finnish appear to passivize, surfacing in nominative case in impersonal passives:

86) Juo-daan   koko   yö!
    drink-pass whole   night(nom)
    'Let's drink the whole night!'

Measure phrases surface in zero-accusative case in all expected sentence types, including imperatives and necessive constructions:

87) Laula   tunti!
    sing(imp) hour(nom)
    'Sing for an hour!'

88) Sinu-n   pitäisi   kirjoitta-a   kokonainen   viikko.
    you-gen   should/3s   write-TA   whole   week(nom)
    'You should write the whole week'

However, interesting effects surface when an adverbial modifier co-occurs with a DP internal argument. Depending on the aspectual properties of the predicate, an accusative adverb may co-occur with an accusative object (Maling 1993:57):

89) Liisa muist-i matka-n vuode-n.
    Liisa(nom) remember-past/3s trip-acc year-acc
    'Liisa remembered the trip for a year'

But if no external argument is licensed by the main verb, the DP object appears in nominative case and the measure phrase in accusative case:

90) a. Muista matka vuode-n!
       remember-imp trip(nom) year-acc
       'Remember the trip for a year!'

   b. Liisa-n täyty-y muista-a matka vuode-n.
      Liisa-gen must-3s remember-TA trip(nom) year-acc
      'Liisa must remember the trip for a year'

When adverbials co-occur with DP arguments or with other adverbial modifiers, Maling shows that elements receive case-marking according to a GF hierarchy, formalized as a Case-Tier (given previously as 58). This system predicts that the highest element in the hierarchy receives nominative case, while all others appear in accusative case. For instance, in an impersonal passive sentence where a duration adverbial co-occurs with a frequency phrase, the duration adverbial gets nominative case, regardless of word order (Maling 1993:59):

91) a. Kekkose-en luote-ttiin yksi vuosi yhde-n kerran.
       Kekkonen-ill trust-pass/past one(nom) year(nom) one-acc time
       'Kekkonen was trusted for one year once'

   b. Kekkose-en luote-ttiin yhde-n kerran yksi vuosi.
      Kekkonen-ill trust-pass/past one-acc time one(nom) year(nom)
      'Kekkonen was trusted for one year once'

The data bear out some important generalizations made earlier in this dissertation. Firstly, they provide additional evidence that Burzio's Generalization does not hold for Finnish, and that impersonal passives and other verbs lacking an external argument remain assigners of accusative case to elements within their governing domain. Secondly, they are predicted by the case-assigning property of Tense/Mood proposed in section 4.4.2:

Mechanisms of Case Assignment

92) Tense/Mood is a bi-unique case-assigner.

This requirement of T/M ensures that a single nominative case feature is assigned to some element in every finite clause. The data from adverbial modifiers support this hypothesis: as long as the requirement is minimally satsified, all other elements can remain *in situ* within VP and receive accusative case under government. Maling's hierarchy is adopted as a constraint on this principle.

Several problems remain for the current analysis. Evidence from adverbial modifiers shows that verbs can assign two aspectual theta-roles simultaneously and independently of each other:

93) Jorma   rakast-i   Tanja-a   toise-n   kerra-n.
    Jorma(nom) love-past/3s Tanja-part second-acc time-acc
    'Jorma loved Tanja for the second time'

Assuming the adverbial modifier to be adjoined to VP somewhere within its governing domain, the question remains as to exactly how case gets assigned in such sentences.[29]

Also difficult to account for within both the current analysis and Maling's (1993) analysis is case assignment to adverbial modifiers of weather verbs. Since weather verbs are assumed to lack an external theta-role (Chomsky 1981:324 ff.), adverbial modifiers of these verbs are predicted to occur in nominative case (or double NOM+ACC). Contrary to the prediction, adverbial modifiers of weather verbs appear in accusative case:

94) Tuul-i   tunni-n.
    wind-past/3s hour-acc
    'The wind blew for an hour'

These facts are accounted for if weather verbs license pro rather than PRO. This hypothesis entails that third person singular agreement morphology in weather verbs contains ɸ-features and that an 'ambient' external theta-role is licensed. The data from adverbial modifiers can therefore mostly, but not completely, be accounted for by appealing to the mechanism of double case assignment.

4.9 CONCLUSION

In this chapter, the distribution of accusative, nominative, and partitive case is given a structural syntactic account. In particular, the case splits described in Chapter 3 between accusative pronouns and nominative full DPs, and between nominative and partitive object DPs, emerge as a morphological reflex of the syntactic phenomenon of double case assignment.

We have seen that a single lexically specified property of the functional head Tense/Mood motivates NP-movement in sentences where no external argument is available to receive this feature. Movement results in two case features being assigned to a single argument, objective case assigned by V in conjunction with aspectual theta-role assignment, and a structural case feature assigned at S-structure by Tense/Mood. One of the conclusions drawn in this analysis is that nominative and objective abstract case differ in the ways in which they license arguments. Nominative case assignment in Finnish is associated with grammatical function and licensing of syntactic positions that becomes relevant only at S-structure. Accusative and partitive case, on the other hand, are much more closely connected with theta-role assignment and predicate semantics. Movement of internal arguments to receive nominative case features has few overt syntactic consequences: in particular, word order effects are largely covert and agreement is not triggered as the result of an internal argument moving into the governing domain of T/M. AGR encodes ϕ-features of an external argument licensed at D-structure, and does not reflect spec-head relations resulting from movement later in the derivation. Returning to the issues raised by the discussion of mechanisms of case assignment within Case Theory in section 4.3, it is argued that in Finnish, nominative and objective case are not homogeneous abstract cases. Nominative case is assigned to heads of chains at S-structure, while objective case is assigned to chains at D-structure. However, both may be assigned *by* chains created by head movement of V into higher inflectional categories. This feature of case assignment allows nominative case to be assigned relatively freely within the structure.

Notes

1. Holmberg et al. (1993) assume a similar principle in their analysis of the Finnish IP, but do not formulate it as a linguistic universal.

2. One of the main motivations for the PFLP is to limit the number of functional projections posited which are headed by empty elements. Another motive behind the PFLP is to impose a theoretical constraint on the acquisition of elements, particularly functional, by limiting the available input to the learner to those elements which are phonetically overt. However, the principle as it is formulated above still allows for the acquisition of functional heads which are only ever licensed by traces of moved elements, and thus cannot rule out extended strings of functional heads which do not contain morphological material at D-structure. However, a more powerful version of the constraint, incorporating (a) and (b) but not (c), would rule out the acquisition of *all* phonetically null functional heads, including zero-morph inflection. One way around this problem might be to accept the notion of paradigms as a linguistic reality; phonetically unrealised elements may then be licensed by a paradigmatic alternation and not constitute a violation of the principle. Alternately, the PFLP might be seen as a requirement for labelling (Cann pers comm), such that elements lacking a phonetic signature require a strong syntactic or semantic label to trigger acquistion.

3. The terms 'maximal IP' and 'minimal IP' are used in the current discussion for convenience, but are not terms used by either Mitchell or Holmberg et al.

4. To be more precise, PERF and PASS can both derive participles that may take case inflection if occurring in an A-position. However, the process of deriving participles is assumed to take place in the lexicon rather than at D-structure, and results in a change of category from V to N.

5. For example, Iatridou (1990) gives strong evidence against Pollock's (1989) positing of AGR as a universally-occurring projection in French and English. Iatridou argues against AGRP not on morphological/acquisition grounds, but on syntactic grounds, demonstrating

that all the syntactic effects accounted for by Pollock can be equally well explained in other ways.

6. Ramchand does assume, however, that ASP projects within the maximal projection of V, so subjects originating in this node are technically VP-internal.

7. Koopman and Sportiche distinguish between VP, the phrasal projection of V, and V^{max}, the maximal projection of V. In their view, subjects are base-generated external to VP and external to putative AGR_O, but within the maximal projection of V and still below INFL; however, the authors disagree as to the exact nature of this site. In the current discussion this position is referred to as spec(VP).

8. Following Cann (1993) heads and specifiers are assumed to be necessarily coindexed and unify at D-structure. This coindexation relation may apply to external arguments and specifiers, and ensures that feature-sharing and categorial matching are maximally local. The mechanism for this unification becomes particularly relevant in Chapter 5, when the properties of nominal (Px) versus verbal AGR are discussed in detail.

9. Chomsky (1981) discusses this visibility condition in terms of theta-role assignment; however, since theta-role assignment is taken to occur at D-structure and case assignment at S-structure, the condition presumably assures that theta-roles can be *interpreted* at LF rather than assigned after D-structure.

10. Most such analyses require tense or finiteness features to be present in addition to subject agreement for nominative case to be assigned, because of ample cross-linguistic data from infinitives and nominalisations where nominal subject agreement is present but no nominative case is assigned.

11. In recent unpublished work, Chomsky reformulates the notion of Greed to include altruistic movement of an element to satisfy another element's requirements.

12. See Webelhuth 1995:56-59 and 1995:92, fn. 51 for a critical review of the literature relating to 'problematic' case systems.

13. Koopman and Sportiche (1991:244) discuss this problem and conclude that subjects must be base-generated external to AGR_O, in languages where AGR_O projects. As an example of morphologically overt object agreement they provide data from French passive participles, which might be argued to be within the maximal projection of V because of their argument-changing properties. Although this hypothesis is internally consistent with their proposals that subjects are base-generated external to VP, it remains unclear why a projection of object agreement should be construed as being within the maximal projection of V while Tense and other inflectional elements are not (cf. Grimshaw 1990 and the notion of Extended Projection), particularly for languages where object agreement morphology is not related to passive morphology.

14. Languages such as French which show object agreement in passive participles provide a counterexample, however: an internal argument checks features (and presumably gets assigned Case) in both spec(AGR_O) and spec(AGR_S).

15. In a manuscript. summarised by Anne Vainikka in Finnsyntax (August 7, 1994), a monthly electronic newsletter devoted to the generative syntax of Finnish.

16. Vainikka (1989c, 1993) and Vainikka and Maling (1996) argue that partitive case is a structural default case, while accusative is related to a semantic verbal feature [+COMPLETED]. In the current analysis, accusative case is linked with aspectual roles related to telicity and boundedness, and so resembles a more formal version of Vainikka and Maling's analysis. However, both accusative and partitive case are argued to be assigned at D-structure, since they are both assigned in association with particular theta-roles. Because the partitive case is associated with a nonaspectual role, it may be viewed as signalling an unmarked or default aspectual feature.

17. A problem arises at this point: in negated sentences, the functional head NEG intervenes between AGR and T/M. NEG raises to AGR and V raises to T/M, but T/M cannot raise to govern the spec(AGRP) position.

How can nominative case be assigned to the subject base-generated in spec(AGRP)? It may be the case that Negation has the status of a verb into which the verbal compound incorporates and shares features. Alternately, NEG may not project as a head at all, but adjoin to AGR or T/M. The fact that NEG projects between AGR and T/M in Finnish is equally problematic for an approach where nominative case is assigned by the complex formed when finite T/M moves into AGR (e.g. Chomsky 1993).

18. Larson (1988) also posits spec(VP) as a case-marked landing site for NP-movement in his analysis of English ditransitives; dative shift in his model occurs as the result of passive-like movement of one verbal complement from a non-Case-marked position internal to V' to the nearest Case-marked position, spec(VP). In the current model, spec(VP) is i-commanded (Koopman and Sportiche 1991) by Tense/Mood, and so is a nominative case-assigned position.

19. In Vainikka's model of case assignment, the genitive -*n* feature is assigned late in the derivation to the caseless nominative NP in complement position; if the nominative form is -*t* as a result of the plural feature, the -*n* affix is blocked.

20. One type of 'zero-accusative' case not accounted for within the present model is the unmarked objective case assigned to cardinal numerals, themselves assigners of partitive case:

    i. Söi-n   kuusi   kananmuna-a.
       ate-1s six(nom) egg-part
       'I ate six eggs'

According to the current analysis, the object DP receives an aspectual theta-role and therefore accusative case at D-structure, but the numeral itself appears in nominative case. Numerals in Finnish show unusual case-related effects in contrast to other determiners:

    ii. Söi-n   tämä-n   kananmuna-n.
        ate-1s that-acc egg-acc
        'I ate that egg'

This pattern of case assignment to numerals is problematic for this analysis; examples like (i) are left for further research.

21. Du Bois (1987), in the main functional account of ergativity and ergative splits, remains agnostic as to what animacy hierarchies can predict in split-S or 'active' systems. Further research in this interesting area will hopefully reveal testable predictions for languages like Finnish.

22. The precise mechanism of infixation of the past tense marker -*ii*- into PASS and AGR remains unresolved.

23. Note that this sentence violates the hypothesis given in Belletti (1988), since the verb does not assign an existential theta-role.

24. Since the verbal complex undergoes head movement to AGR by S-structure, it is ambiguous from the ordering of elements at PF whether the internal argument is in spec(TP) or spec(PASSP). To a certain extent the issue is irrelevant, since in both positions nominative case gets assigned.

25. Like Italian, Finnish also allows subject-verb inversion in unergatives as well as in transitive sentences. Vainikka (1989b:222-3) analyses this as rightward adjunction and notes that inverted subjects are stylistically marked.

26. As mentioned in section 2.2.2.1, partitive singular count nouns are unfelicitous in this sentence type. Vilkuna (1989) notes that subjects of existentials in Finnish are aspectually 'less informative' than transitive objects or impersonal passive objects, and associates existential predicates with resultative aspect.

27. Or perhaps more accurately, imperative subjects are so clearly recoverable from the discourse context that they are not subject to Visibility Conditions like other arguments.

28. The phonetically unrealized imperative morpheme in T/M is assumed to be an allomorph of the underspecified consonant in 2s imperatives, which triggers gradation on the verbal stem.

29. Even more problematic is the issue of double case-assignment in sentences with both an internal argument and an adverbial modifier (Maling 1993:58):

    i.   Muistele   matka-a vuosi!
          remember(imp) trip-part year(nom)
          'Remember the trip for a year!'

Even if such sentences were subject to a hierarchy whereby the adverbial modifier is assigned double case features before the verbal argument, there is no way to account for the surface word order, given that the modifier would have to raise to spec(VP) or higher to be within the governing domain of V. This problem will have to remain unresolved in the current analysis.

CHAPTER 5
The Morphosyntax of Possessive Affixes

5.1 INTRODUCTION

Possessive affixes (Pxes) in Finnish comprise a paradigm of morphemes (1) which raise a number of interesting issues in morphology: they resemble pronominal clitics in their distribution and function as subjects and possessors, yet phonologically and morphologically they behave as word-internal, bound affixes. Pxes occur affixed to nouns, adjectives, and many non-finite constructions, preceding a clear class of clitics but following inflectional affixes in the ordering of morphs. Pxes may be coindexed with pronouns (but not full DPs) in the genitive case, agreeing with oblique subjects of non-finite clauses. Like clitics, but unlike most inflectional affixes in Finnish, Pxes do not trigger consonant gradation in the preceding syllable. Furthermore, Pxes affix to the phrasal head only, without copying to mark modifiers; in this respect Pxes differ from inflectional morphemes.

1) The Px paradigm

   1s: minun auto-ni[1]   'my car'
   2s: sinun auto-si   'your (sg) car'
   3:   hänen/heidän auto-nsa[2] 'her/his/their car'
   1p: meidän auto-mme   'our car'
   2p: teidän auto-nne   'your (pl) car'

It is argued in this chapter that the morphologically ambiguous status of Pxes, which behave simultaneously like clitics and affixes, reflects distinctive properties at the syntactic level. In section 5.5.2 it is argued that both Pxes and verbal agreement affixes are part of the functional lexicon, specified as category AGR, and that their distinct selectional properties result in separate syntactic structures. Verbal agreement markers take Tense/Mood as a complement and function as heads, affixed to the verb via head movement in the usual way. Pxes, on the other hand, occur as specifiers of contentive heads, adjoining rather than affixing to the host. The licensing of Pxes is discussed in section 5.5.5.

5.2 THE DISTRIBUTION OF PXES[3]

The distribution of Pxes is perhaps best characterized relative to verbal agreement affixes: the two are in complementary distribution, verbal agreement dominating Tense and Px agreement occurring with N, P, and a range of non-finite verbal contexts. The most notable feature of the distribution of Pxes is that they are triggered by animate pronouns only; full genitive DPs do not co-occur with Pxes. In this respect they differ from verbal agreement markers, which may be coindexed with either pronouns or full NPs.

5.2.1 Pxes and nominal possession

Pxes may mark possession in DPs. The data in (2) illustrate binding properties of Pxes in the third, first and second persons, respectively:

The Morphosyntax of Possessive Affixes 187

2) a. Poika$_i$ my-i   marsu-nsa$_i$.
      boy(nom) sell-past/3s guinea pig-(acc^4)-Px3
      'The boy$_i$ sold his$_i$ guinea pig'/
      *'The boy$_i$ sold his$_j$ guinea pig'

   b. Poika$_i$ my-i   häne-n$_j$ marsu-nsa$_j$.
      boy(nom) sell-past/3s his/her-gen guinea pig-(acc)-Px3
      'The boy$_i$ sold his/her$_j$ guinea pig'

   c. Poika   my-i   marsu-ni.
      boy(nom) sell-past/3s guinea pig-(acc)-Px1s
      'The boy sold my guinea pig'

   d. Sijaa   vuotee-si!
      make-imp bed-Px2s
      'Make your bed!'

In (2a) above, the Px is an anaphor bound by a full DP antecedent; it cannot be interpreted as pronominal. In (2b) the third person Px is locally bound by a genitive pronominal antecedent. Examples (2c) and (2d) illustrate the pronominal status of first and second person Pxes: no antecedent is required to bind the Px.

First and second person Px agreement can occur doubled with a coindexed genitive pronoun for emphasis:

3) Poika   my-i   minu-n marsu-ni
   boy(nom) sell-past/3s I-gen   guinea pig-(acc)-Px1s
   'The boy sold *my* guinea pig'

Deverbal nouns can also host Px agreement, where the agent is expressed by a Px:

4) Minä   paheksu-n   juomis-ta-si
   I(nom) disapprove-1s drink-part-Px2s
   'I disapprove of your drinking'

Deverbal nouns such as *juomis* (from *juominen*) in (4) are assumed to be derived in the (contentive) lexicon, displaying all the syntactic characteristics of full DPs. Finnish does however have a large number of gerundive constructions which are more ambiguous in their categorial status. These are discussed below.

5.2.2 Pxes as modifiers of postpositions

Postpositions may occur with genitive modifiers, which can trigger Px agreement if pronominal (5b):

5) a. Me käv-i-mme ravintola-ssa Aili-n kanssa.
  we(nom) visit-past-1p restaurant-in Ail-gen with
  'We visited a restaurant with Aili.'

 b. Aili käv-i ravintola-ssa (meidä-n) kanssa-mme.
  Aili(nom) visit-past/3s restaurant-in (we-gen) with-Px1p
  'Aili visited a restaurant with us.'

Px binding in postpositional phrases mirrors patterns in possessive constructions described in section 5.2.1; third person Pxes are strictly anaphoric while first and second person Pxes may be pronominal.

5.2.3 Pxes and adjectives

Certain adjectives may host Px agreement:

6) Sinu-n velje-si on vastakohta-si.
  you(s)-gen brother-Px2s be/3s contrary-Px2s
  'Your brother is contrary to you.'

Nevis (1984) argues that adjectives ending in the suffix *-nen* may host Pxes, but notes that such adjectives are arguably more noun-like than other adjectives in that they must govern a preceding DP, which is typically marked for genitive case (Nevis 1984:183-4):

7) karhu-n-näköinen
  bear-gen-looking
  'looking like a bear'

In noun phrases Pxes normally occur affixed to the head noun, not to the modifying adjective:

8) a. sinipunainen talo-mme
   purple   house-Px1p
   'our purple house'

   b. *sinipunaise-mme talo
      purple-Px1p   house

Nevis (1984:185) notes that adverbial uses of *kaikki*, 'all,' can take Px agreement, but finds no other examples of lexical adverbs which share this ability to host.

5.2.4 Pxes in non-finite clauses

In certain non-finite clauses Pxes mark the agent or subject of the nominalized verb. Three clause types host Pxes: complement clauses are selected by a set of verbs of thinking, perception and speaking and alternate with finite clauses headed by the complementizer *että*, 'that.' Temporal and /-*kse*-/ clauses are adverbial adjuncts to a main clause. The constructions described below are also analysed in the chapter on non-finite clauses.

5.2.4.1 Complement clauses

Non-finite complement clauses are selected by a set of verbs involving thinking and perception. Pxes and genitive pronoun subjects in this construction may or may not agree with the matrix subject (9a and b). Full genitive DPs can also act as subjects of complement clauses, with no Px agreement (9c):

9) a. Tiedä-t   ole-va-si   oikeassa.
       know-2s be-pcp/np-Px2s right
       'You know that you are right'

   b. Matti   tietä-ä   sinu-n   ole-van   oikeassa.
      Matti(nom) know-3s you-gen be-pcp/np   right
      'Matti knows that you are right'

   c. Luul-i-n   Soili-n   syö-vän   kakku-a.
      suppose-past-1s Soili-gen eat-pcp/np   cake-part
      'I supposed Soili was eating the cake'

5.2.4.2 Adverbial adjunct clauses

Two types of adverbial adjunct clauses, temporal clauses formed with *-ttua/ttuä* and purpose clauses formed with *-kse*, can take pronominal Px agreement:

10) Tul-tua-an   koti-in   Maija   huoma-si   lahja-n.
    come-ttua-Px3   home-to   Maija(nom) notice-past/3s gift-acc
    'After coming home, Maija noticed the gift'

Pxes in temporal clauses can also be anaphoric. Purpose clauses, however, can take only pronominal Px agreement. A Px is required with the affix *-kse* (11a). This rules out full DP subjects in this construction, since they fail to trigger Px agreement (11b):

11) a. Minä   ost-i-n   jakoavaime-n   korja-ta-kse-ni   viemäri-n.
       I(nom) buy-past-1s wrench-acc   repair-TA-kse-Px1s   sink-acc
       'I bought a wrench in order to repair the sink'

    b. *Osti-n   ruoka-a   äidi-n   keittä-ä-ksi   keitto-a
        bought-1s   food-part   mother-gen   cook-TA-ksi   soup-part
        'I bought food in order for mother to cook soup'

5.2.5 Agreement in the third person

Third person agreement, signalled by both finite verb inflection and Pxes, behaves markedly different from agreement in the first and second person. Finnish is a pro-drop language in the first and second person. In the third person, however, a definite personal pronoun cannot be dropped (in written language). If the verb appears without a subject pronoun, the reading is for a generic subject (discussed in section 3.2):

12) a. Usko-n, että hän on oikeassa
    believe-1s that s/he(nom) be/3s right
    'I believe that he/she is right'

   b. Hän usko-o, että ...
    s/he(nom) believe-3s that ...
    'He/she believes that ... '

   c. Usko-o, että ...
    believe-3s that ...
    'One believes that ... '

As mentioned above, the Px system is closely associated with genitive pronouns. In formal and written Finnish, the first and second person Pxes can occur without an antecedent or genitive pronoun (13a). The third person Px, however, must be coindexed with an argument, either a clause-internal genitive DP or the nominative subject of the main clause (13b and c).[5]

13) a. (Minu-n) kissa-ni on sairas.
    I-gen cat-Px1s be/3s sick
    'My cat is sick.'

b. *Kissa-nsa on sairas.
    cat-Px3 be/3s sick
    'His/her cat is sick.'

c. Mikko$_i$ anto-i tytö-lle-en$_i$ lahja-n.
    Mikko(nom) give-past/3s daughter-to-Px3 gift-acc
    'Mikko$_i$ gave his$_i$ daughter a gift'

To avoid referential ambiguity in the third person, a local genitive antecedent is required if the Px does not agree with the subject noun:

14) Mikko$_i$ antoi häne-n$_j$ tytö-lle-en$_j$ lahja-n.
    Mikko(nom) give-past/3s s/he-gen daughter-to-Px3 gift-acc
    'Mikko$_i$ gave his/her$_j$ daughter a gift.'

Van Steenbergen (1990) accounts for the data by proposing that third person genitive pronouns are pronominal and third person Pxes are anaphoric.

5.3 PX MORPHOLOGY AND PHONOLOGY

The agglutinative morphology of Finnish is such that a fairly straightforward distinction can be made between stems and affixes. The set of 'affixes,' however, contains a class of inflectional suffixes (case, number, and agreement) and a class of clitics, both distinguishable by certain morphological and phonological properties described in this section. Pxes, however, are problematic for traditional morphological classification; they share properties of both clitics and inflectional affixes, and are not easily classifiable as either.

Finnish sentential clitics include *-han/-hän* and *-pa*, which convey various pragmatic overtones (15a and b); *-ko/-kö*, the question forming particle (15c); *-kin*, 'also; too' (15d); and *-kaan/-kään*, 'neither' (15e):

15) a. Hän-hän tul-i   huonee-seen.
       s/he-cl   come-past/3s room-into
       'S/he *did* come into the room'⁶

   b. Hän-pä   tul-i   huonee-seen.
      s/he-cl come-past/3s room-into
      'S/he came into the room (sarcastic tone)'

   c. Tule-t-ko   huonee-seen?
      come-2s-cl room-into
      'Are you coming into the room?'

   d. Minä-kin tul-i-n   huonee-seen.
      I(nom)-cl come-past-1s   room-into
      'I also came into the room'

   e. e-n   minä-kään
      neg-1s I(nom)-cl
      'me neither'

All clitics in Finnish with the exception of *-kin* and *-kaan/-kään* are are restricted to second (Wackernagel's) position (Wackernagel 1892). Finnish clitics attach to lexical forms rather than stems, and fail to trigger consonant gradation in the preceding syllable.

In contrast, inflectional affixes, including case inflection, number, and verbal agreement, attach to stems rather than to lexical forms (16a), trigger consonant gradation in the preceding syllable when the syllable is closed (depending on the initial consonant of the affix), and occur in a greater variety of syntactic positions than clitics (16c):

16) a. lapsi ~ lapse-t
    child   children (nom/acc)

   b. matkusta-a ~ matkusta-vat
      travel-inf   travel-3p
      'to travel' 'they travel'

   c. Lapse-t   matkusta-vat auto-lla
      child-pl/nom   travel-3p   car-adess
      'The children are travelling by car'

Finnish also has a set of clitic-like elements which more closely resemble words than affixes. This class of 'semi-clitics' includes unstressed conjunctions and adverbs, and the article *sitä* (Nevis 1987). From the phonological and morphological evidence it is clear that Pxes do not belong to this group, as they display strictly word-internal properties such as vowel harmony, a phenomenon common to both clitics[7] and inflectional affixes (17a and b) but which is not triggered by compounding and certain derivational processes (17c and d):

17) a. (case)   huonee-ssa   järve-ssä
                 room-iness   lake-iness
                 'in the room'   'in the lake'

    b. (clitic) huone-han   järvi-hän
                 room-cl   lake-cl
                 'room' (new information) 'lake' (new information)

    c. metsä-kauris
       forest goat
       'roe deer'

    d. epä-usko
       un-belief
       'unbelief'

The ordering of morphs further suggests that Pxes share properties of both clitics and inflectional affixes:

18) talo-ssa-ni-ko?
    house-iness-Px1s-qu
    'In my house?'

In (18) above, the Px occurs between -*ssa*, the inessive case marker, and -*ko*, the question-forming sentential clitic in Finnish. Pxes occupy an intermediate slot in the morphological template reflecting their status as elements which straddle the boundary between full inflection and clitics.

5.3.1 Clitic-like properties

Certain facts about the morphophonology of Pxes have led some authors (Pierrehumbert 1980 and Nevis 1984) to categorize them as clitics rather than affixes, in particular because of their failure to trigger consonant gradation.

5.3.1.1 Consonant gradation

Unlike fully inflectional elements in Finnish, Pxes do not trigger consonant gradation when they close the syllable:

19) a. pöytä   'table'

    b. pöydä-llä   'on the table'
       table-adess

    c. pöytä-kin   'the table, too'
       table-too (cl)

    d. pöytä-nsä   'his/her table'
       table-Px3

In (19b), /t/ in the nominal stem changes to /d/ as a result of case inflection affixed to the stem. In (19c) the sentential clitic -*kin*, 'too,' fails to cause gradation in the previous consonant. Example (19d) shows how Pxes also fail to trigger voicing of the stem consonant.

5.3.1.2 Affixation to head

Nominal inflection for case and number shows concord so that modifiers agree with their head (20a). Clitics, however, are hosted by the phrasal head only and are not copied to modifiers (20b). In this respect Pxes behave like clitics (20c). Copying of Pxes in strictly ungrammatical (20d):

20) a. iso-i-ssa valkois-i-ssa talo-i-ssa
       big-pl-in white-pl-in house-pl-in
       'In the big white houses'

   b. iso valkoinen talo-kin
      big white   house-too
      'The big white house too'

   c. iso valkoinen talo-ni
      big white   house-Px1s
      'my big white house'

   d. *iso-ni valkoise-ni talo-ni

This property of Pxes also highlights a parallel between Pxes and verbal AGR, since AGR marks only the verbal element in a clause and does not 'copy' to modifiers.

5.3.2 Affix-like properties

Kanerva (1987) argues that Pxes are best analysed as affixes rather than clitics, providing evidence that Pxes are word-internal, in contrast to sentential clitics.

5.3.2.1 Phonological evidence

Nevis (1984:174) notes that the consonant clusters which appear affix-initially within the Px paradigm cannot occur word-initially in Finnish. No words exist in Finnish beginning with *nn-*, *ns-*, or *mm-*. The consonant clusters which can appear affix-initially in inflectional elements cannot occur word-initially either; for example, a word cannot begin with *ll-* in Finnish, though the adessive case ending is *-lla/-llä*. In contrast, forms for true clitics (including *-kin*, *-ko*, and *-han/hän*) can and do appear word-intially, e.g *kinkku*, 'ham'; *koko*, 'whole'; and *hanhi*, 'goose.' Furthermore, stress in polysyllabic Finnish words may not fall on a word-final syllable; syllables which immediately precede both Pxes and clitics may receive secondary stress, indicating that Pxes are word-internal for the application of stress rules.

Kanerva (1987) also presents evidence that Pxes prevent word-final phonological rules from applying to the stem. A rule which raises *i* to *e* and another which lengthens *e* to *ee* word-finally in certain stem forms fails to operate under clitic attachment but operates with Px affixation (Kanerva 1987:503-4):

21) a. lapsi 'child'   b. herne 'pea'
    lapsi-kin 'the child, too'   herne-hän 'pea' + clitic
    lapse-ni 'my child'   hernee-si 'your pea'

One rule which applies mainly between words is the phenomenon of boundary gemination in Finnish, in which morphological elements trigger gemination in the following word- or clitic-initial consonant. Case affixes and Pxes fail to produce this effect, but clitics do trigger gemination (Kanerva 1987:504-5):

22) itse   'self'
    itse-näinen   'independent'
    itse-nä-än   'self'+essive case+Px3
    itse-ni   'myself' ('self'+Px1s)
    itse[k]-kin   'self' + clitic
    He itse[n] nauroivat 'they themselves laughed'

The facts from phonology, then, indicate that for the application of most rules Pxes are word-internal (i.e. affixal), with the notable exception of the rule of consonant gradation.

5.3.2.2 Affixation to stem

Unlike sentential clitics Pxes do not affix themselves to lexical forms, but require a stem form for affixation to take place:

23) a. perhonen   'butterfly'

     b. perhose-n   'butterfly's'
        butterfly-gen

     c. perhonen-kin   'the butterfly, too'
        butterfly-cl

     d. perhose-si   'your butterfly'
        butterfly-Px2s

In (23), the genitive case marker -*n* affixes to a stem form of the noun *perhonen*, while the clitic -*kin* cliticizes to the lexical (nominative) form of the noun. In this respect Pxes are subject to the same rules of affixation as inflectional affixes.

5.3.3 Diachronic evidence for the status of Pxes

Within the Uralic language group there are several possible orders for the affixation of grammatical case, semantic case, number, and possessive affixes (which in many cases are absent or vestigial). Comrie (1980) proposes that the original order for these elements in Common Uralic was [stem-]number-case-possessive affix, and that the varied order in the modern Uralic family is due to the separation of case suffixes and postpositions as well as phonological reductions of grammatical case leading to inflectional ambiguity. Written Finnish is perhaps the most conservative of all the Uralic languages in that it retains the full paradigm of possessive affixes and the old Uralic affix ordering.

     Several concepts form the theoretical core of Comrie's analysis. The first is that when a separate word is reduced to an affix, it will occupy the most peripheral 'slot' in the morphology; therefore the relative ordering of a series of affixes reflects the order that the affixes developed from separate words. The next principle involves the addition of new locative cases to the inflectional paradigm. If a language has a set of older cases which precede a paradigm of possessive affixes, and then acquires new cases (in the case of the Finno-Ugric languages the locative cases were often reduced forms of postpositions, added to the set of case affixes gradually over time), the new case affixes will either assume the most peripheral position in the affix sequence or be 'drawn' to the position of the old cases. In this sense locative cases do not necessarily reflect the order of addition to the semantic case system.

The third relevant principle is that of the phonological reduction of case affixes. If a case affix precedes a possessive affix which undergoes a phonetic change, the resulting consonant cluster may be phonologically unacceptable or awkward, e.g. the genitive/accusative *-n* affix in Finnish cannot occur before Pxes because of the illformedness of the resulting consonant cluster:

24) kirjee-*n-mme
    letter-acc/gen-Px1p
    'our letter (acc/gen)'

To accomodate this the case affix is deleted, resulting in a certain level of ambiguity. From these principles Comrie proposes that proto-Uralic acquired the Px paradigm as a set of reduced genitive pronouns at some very ancient period. They were acquired after a number morpheme was fixed in the morphology to follow the noun stem and after a set of 'old' cases affixed following the number marker. Finnish later acquired additional locative cases from reduced postpositions, which affixed themselves in the same position as the old (probably grammatical) cases. Thus Finnish retained the original ordering of number-case-Px while other Uralic languages developed other ordering systems according to the principles described above. Finnish also retained the entire paradigm of Pxes while in other languages, for example Saami and Estonian, Pxes have been restricted in use or lost altogether.

The relatively late acquisition of the possessive affixes into the system of 'inflectional' morphology, subsequent to genuine inflection, may provide an explanation for the unique syntactic and morphophonological nature of the Pxes and their linear position in the ordering of morphs, which appears to violate Baker's Mirror Principle (Spencer 1992).

5.4 PREVIOUS ANALYSES OF FINNISH PXES

Several points of view emerge from the existing literature on Finnish Pxes. While most if not all authors acknowledge that Pxes occupy an ambiguous position in Finnish morphology, most have argued either that Pxes are inflectional [i.e. agreement] affixes (Kanerva 1987), anaphoric reflexes of genitive pronouns (Nevis 1984, 1986 and 1987, van Steenbergen 1990, Vainikka 1989c), or independent syntactic units, effectively allomorphs of full pronouns which cliticize rather than affix to the host (Pierrehumbert 1980) and have status as arguments (Trosterud 1993). One of the main difficulties reflected in the literature in determining whether Pxes are anaphoric or pronominal is the paradigmatic split between third person Pxes, which are anaphoric according to most definitions of Binding, and first and second person Pxes, which may be pronominal.

Pierrehumbert (1980) explains the distribution of Pxes by positing them as clitic allomorphs of the reflexive pronoun *itse*, noting that Pxes and *itse* are in complementary distribution in specifier positions (Pierrehumbert 1980:609):

25) a. Hän on   ylpeä itse-stä-än.
       s/he be/3s proud self-ela-Px3
       'S/he is proud of him/herself'

    b. *Jorma   tul-i   itse-nsä auto-lla.
       Jorma(nom) come-past/3s self-Px3 car-by
       'Jorma came in his own car'

She suggests that an allomorphy rule operates in Finnish which generates a Px clitic as the weak form of a reflexive pronoun in specifier position, then posits additional rules which yield cliticization of the Px to the head noun as well as optional doubling of a Px with a genitive specifier.

Nevis (1984, 1986 and 1987) subsumes Pxes under a broad class of clitics, but distinguishes between Finnish particle clitics, which he classifies as bound words, and possessive affixes, which he categorizes as phrasal affixes. He demonstrates that Pxes are syntactic affixed units but not inflectional (i.e. agreement), and that they are anaphoric. To account for the syntactic properties of Pxes he assumes that Pxes are allomorphs of genitive pronouns (contra Pierrehumbert 1980) which cliticize onto the head noun from the specifier position of a node immediately dominating VP; in the case of third person Pxes he proposes movement of the Px allomorph, and to account for 'doubling' in the first and second person paradigm slot he suggests a copying rule whereby person and number features are copied from the genitive pronoun to the clitic in its specifier position. Nevis argues that these rules are ordered (copying then movement) to prevent the copying of coreferent third person pronouns. Finally, Nevis posits a final rule of 'free deletion' of first and second person genitive pronouns.

Vainikka (1989c) suggests that verbal agreement in Finnish is a type of anaphoric pronoun, and accounts for pro-drop patterns in terms of anaphoric binding, an analysis she extends to account for Px patterns. Van Steenbergen (1990) assumes that Pxes are strictly anaphoric agreement reflexes, positing a local empty genitive binder in cases where Pxes appear to be coreferential with elements outside the clause.

Disputing Nevis' hypothesis that Pxes are clitics in favour of an analysis as true inflectional affixes, Kanerva (1987) argues that to categorize Pxes as clitic pronouns, and therefore as word-external (syntactic) units, would be to undermine crucial notions of morphological integrity since Pxes show so many more features of word-internal elements than do clitics. These affix-like properties which form the core of Kanerva's arguments include evidence from the ordering of morphs in the structural template; Px affixation to stems rather than lexical forms; and phonological evidence that Pxes prevent word-final rules from applying to the preceding stem. He also argues that the failure to trigger consonant gradation is an insufficient criterion for clitichood. Furthermore he gives evidence of morphosyntactic dependencies involving Pxes; the reflexive pronoun *itse* requires pronominal Px agreement in all cases except the nominative.

Kanerva's position, that morphologically bound elements which are relevant to the syntax and simultaneously participate in word-internal processes should be analysed as inflectional suffixes, essentially presupposes the existence of an independent module for morphology, or at least assumes some version of the Lexicalist Hypothesis (Chomsky 1970). In the syntactic model adopted in the current work, inflectional morphology is taken to be a syntactic process, following Baker (1988) and subsequent work. In recent syntactic literature, the notion that inflectional morphemes such as agreement may be 'active in the syntax' (i.e. encode φ-features coindexed with a verbal argument) and still participate in morphological and phonological processes is no longer considered as problematic as it was.[8]

Trosterud (1993) acknowledges that Pxes have phonological and morphological characteristics of affixes rather than clitics, but argues that in determining whether Pxes are agreement markers or anaphoric pronouns the main issue is the status of Pxes as arguments. In determining the status of Finnish Pxes he assumes Borer's (1984) analysis, distinguishing between clitics and argument suffixes in languages such as Hebrew, which absorb Case assigned by the noun and require a dummy (genitive) case assigning element in doubled constructions, and inflectional affixes in Hungarian and Eskimo which do not get Case (since the doubled pronoun in these languages does not require an additional case assigner). Trosterud observes that the Finnish data is problematic from this perspective because both types of case-marking pattern are present. In the case of genitive full DPs with zero Px reflexes there is a single case-assignee, the genitive DP. In doubled constructions, when Pxes co-occur with genitive pronouns, there are two elements which require case. He concludes that Finnish is a language like Hebrew where possessive affixes are assigned case, i.e. have argument status, and that doubling in Finnish is an (unexplained) idiosyncrasy of personal pronouns. Trosterud further argues that Pxes are functional heads which select N as a complement. Given the following sentences (Trosterud 1993:231), he argues that the phrase structure representation of the two PPs are as illustrated in (27) below:

26) a. Osoita-n Maija-n$_i$ häne-lle itse-lle-nsä$_{i/*k}$
show-1s Maija-acc s/he-to self-to-Px3
'I show Maija to herself'

b. Osoita-n Maija-n$_i$ häne-n tädi-lle-nsä$_{i/k}$
show-1s Maija-acc s/he-gen aunt-to-Px3
'I show Maija to her aunt'

27) a. häne-lle itse-lle-nsä   b. hänen tädi-lle-nsä

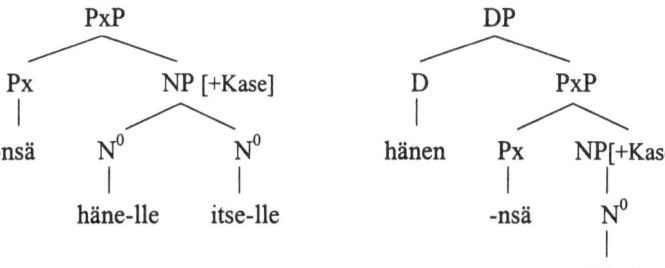

If a Px dominates the entire structure, then the phrase is anaphoric; if DP dominates, then the structure is pronominal and does not need to be bound with another element. The most relevant theme in Trosterud's analysis for the current work is that Pxes head NPs. It is argued in the next section that the distribution of Pxes is better accounted for by analysing them as specifiers.

5.5 THE SYNTAX OF PXES

Within the syntactic framework proposed by Tait and Cann (1990) and Cann (1993), an account of the mixed affix/clitic properties of Pxes is presented which subsumes both Pxes and verbal agreement markers under the functional category Agreement (AGR), the distribution of which is determined by differing selectional properties of the two functional heads. Notions of licensing and coindexation inherent in the theoretical framework adopted here make redundant to a certain extent the debate regarding the nature of Pxes as anaphoric pronouns or inflectional affixes. It is argued in this section that although Pxes have status as arguments and head their own maximal projections (PxPs), they are not functional heads in the extended projection of contentive elements because they do not select complements. Instead, it is proposed that they alternate with verbal agreement but are restricted to specifier positions only.

5.5.1 Pxes are category AGR

Pxes have been interpreted as an instantiation of syntactic AGR in previous work: Reime (1989; 1993) assumes that Pxes do not project independently in the syntax but are present as a feature [+AGR], associated with category N. Ouhalla (1991) suggests that in Hungarian and Turkish, possessive affixes project in the syntax as nominal AGR. Ouhalla argues that the functional head AGR is not specified for category, and accounts for the distribution of possessive affixes and verbal agreement in languages like Turkish and Hungarian by distinguishing between verbal AGR, which co-occurs with the element Tense, and nominal AGR, which does not. The major category of the structure headed by AGR is thus determined by the heads N (nominal) and TNS (verbal).

Ouhalla's hypothesis that AGR elements are underspecified for major category is adopted here on the strength of his arguments for Hungarian and Turkish. However, it will emerge that the two types of AGR in Finnish do not share structural properties to the extent that Ouhalla proposes.

Additional evidence that Pxes are a variation of verbal agreement can be gleaned from the morphology of the Px paradigm, the behavior of Pxes with regard to pro-drop, and finally, diachronic evidence involving impersonal passives. In each of these respects Pxes pattern closely with verbal AGR.

5.5.1.1 Paradigmatic parallels

Paradigmatically, Pxes and verbal agreement can be shown to have strong parallels. The first person singular forms are extremely similar, and the first person plural forms are identical.

28) Possessive affix (Px) paradigm (with genitive pronouns; -*Vn* represents a lengthening of stem vowel plus -*n*)

minu-n	-ni	1 singular
sinu-n	-si	2 singular
häne-n	-nsa, -nsä, -Vn	3 singular
meidä-n	-mme	1 plural
teidä-n	-nne	2 plural
heidä-n	-nsa, -nsä, -Vn	3 plural

29) Verbal AGR paradigm (with nominative pronouns; -*V* represents a lengthening of stem vowel)

minä	-n	1 singular
sinä	-t	2 singular
hän/se	-V	3 singular
me	-mme	1 plural
te	-tte	2 plural
he	-vat	3 plural

The paradigmatic similarities between Pxes and verbal agreement are to a certain extent predicted by the extreme likelihood that Pxes are reduced genitive pronouns (Comrie 1980). Both paradigms show a marked correlation in surface form between pronouns on the one hand and the corresponding agreement reflex on the other. In contrast, the affixes which mark person and number in the imperative mood (interpreted as verbal AGR in Mitchell 1991a) show no such obvious morphological correlations between agreement markers and pronouns:

30) Imperative "AGR"

(no form)		1 singular
sinä	*k/glottal stop	2 singular
hän	-koon/köön	3 singular
me	-kaamme/käämme	1 plural
te	-kaa/kää	2 plural
he	-koot/kööt	3 plural

With the exception of the first person plural, the imperative referent markers for person and number are not morphologically similar to nominative pronouns.

5.5.1.2 Pro-drop

There are interesting syntactic similarities between verbal AGR and Pxes in the third person. In finite sentences, personal pronouns can be omitted except for those in the third person, which can only be omitted for a generic, rather than pronominal, reading with certain verbs:

31) a. Voi-n   men-nä ulos.
       can-1s go-TA   out
       'I can go out'

    b. Voi   men-nä ulos.
       can/3s go-TA   out
       'One can go out'/
       *'He/she can go out'

    c. *Voi-vat mennä ulos.
       can-3p go-TA   out
       'They can go out'

Similarly, first and second person Pxes can occur as pronominal possessors (32):

32) Kissa-ni kuol-i
   cat-Px1s die-past/3s
   'My cat died'

But third person Pxes, at least, appear to be anaphoric, similar to third person verbal AGR:

33) a. Pekka   my-i   kissa-nsa.
       Pekka(nom) sell-past/3s cat-Px3
       'Pekka$_i$ sold his$_i$ cat'/
       *'Pekka$_i$ sold his/her$_j$ cat'

   b. *Kissa-nsa ol-i   sairas.
       cat-Px3   be-past/3s ill
       'His/her/their cat was ill'

   c. Asta   sano-i   ole-va-nsa   sairas.
      Asta(nom) say-past/3s be-pcp-Px3   ill
      'Asta$_i$ said that she$_i$ was ill'/
      *'Asta$_i$ said that he/she$_j$ was ill'

5.5.1.3 Pxes and negation

One more piece of evidence is available to suggest that Pxes and AGR share the same (functional) category. In Chapter 1 the following data was presented for the structure of the Finnish IP. In negated sentences, the agreement morpheme appears on the semi-verbal negation stem *e*- rather than on the verb:

34) a. Nuku-tte.
       sleep-2p
       'You're sleeping'

   b. E-tte   nuku.
      neg-2p sleep
      'You (pl) won't sleep'

A similar phemonenon occurs when impersonal passives are negated. A third person singular affix *-i* appears on the negation stem, while the final *-Vn* affix disappears from the impersonal passive verbal morphology:

35) a. Ikkuna ava-taan.
  window(nom) open-pass
  'The window is being opened'

 b. Ikkuna-a e-i ava-ta.
   window-part neg-3s open-pass
   'The window is not being opened'

Hakulinen (1946/1961:157) interprets the *-Vn* affix in impersonal passives as a Px. Although the morph is no longer productive, the fact that it does not occur in negated impersonal passives suggests that, diachronically at least, Pxes were equivalent to verbal AGR in syntactic negation.

5.5.2 AGR in the functional lexicon

Ouhalla (1991) proposes that functional heads (e.g. Tense, Aspect, Negation, Determiner and Agreement) determine key aspects of cross-linguistic variation. One of the interesting theoretical features of this approach is the categorial underspecification of the functional element AGR, which, it is argued, can co-occur with both nominal and verbal elements. This hypothesis, supported by copious cross-linguistic evidence, follows from general observations about the structural parallels between sentences and DPs. Furthermore, parameters are posited which account for the relative distribution of the functional heads TNS and (verbal) AGR on the one hand and DET and (nominal) AGR on the other. If Ouhalla's analysis were to be adopted here, Finnish NPs would share parameter settings with languages like Turkish. Turkish possessive affixes co-occur with determiners, unlike in English; this is taken to be the result of a cross-linguistic parameter which specifies that DET c-selects AGR (Ouhalla 1991:337). Finnish Pxes also co-occur with determiners; Finnish lacks articles, but evidence is available from demonstrative pronouns such as *tämä*, 'that':

36) tämä   talo-ni
    this   house-Px1s
    'This house of mine'

Furthermore, like Turkish, Finnish possessive affixes are associated with specifiers in genitive rather than nominative case, as in Hungarian. Ouhalla posits a case-assigning parameter of AGR to account for this.

In Ouhalla's model, AGR is a functional head in the binary branching structure of the noun phrase, c-selected by DET (as determined by parameter setting in languages like Finnish) and taking NP as a complement:

37)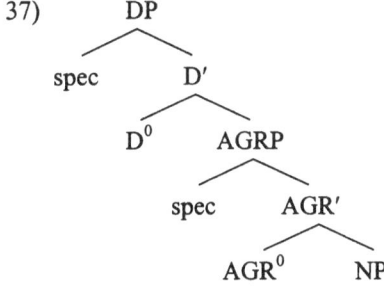

Trosterud (1993) also posits Px as a functional projection heading noun phrases, as illustrated in (27). However, there is strong evidence to suggest that although Pxes share (functional) categorial status with verbal AGR, the two variants do not share the same properties of headedness: while finite AGR with Tense is part of the extended projection of V, Px AGR may head its own projection but crucially does not head NP and PP in the same way that inflectional elements head V.

5.5.3 Pxes are non-heads

Cann (1993:6) discusses the various traditional criteria in determining the status as a head of a given constituent, summarizing them as listed in (38):

38) a. X^0 is obligatory.
  b. X^0 and X'' have the same general distribution.
  c. X^0 forms the morphosyntactic locus of X''.
  d. X^0 subcategorizes for and θ-marks its complements.
  e. X^0 does not subcategorize for, but may be in an agreement relation with, its specifier(s).

Pxes meet these basic criteria for headedness *within* the PxP itself; for example, property (e) expresses the relation of Pxes to genitive pronouns. However, if L-selection is indeed one of the most crucial properties of headedness (Cann 1993:68) then in this sense Pxes fail to behave like heads, either functional or contentive: as illustrated in section 5.2, Pxes co-occur with NPs, noun-like APs, nominalized VPs, and locatives (postpositions and locative Kase Phrases). Compared to functional heads such as verbal AGR, which selects for Tense, and Det, which selects for N, Pxes share few definitive characteristics of heads, appearing affixed to elements of varying category. Furthermore, Pxes are reflexes of pronouns in genitive case, a case strongly associated with specifier positions (Vainikka 1989c). In this work, then, Pxes are assumed to head their own maximal projections but do not form part of the extended projection of NPs, APs, PPs or any other phrases incorporating contentive elements. Instead, it is proposed that the distribution of Pxes is best accounted for as a result of their nonbranching structure in the functional lexicon.

5.5.4 AGR and syntactic structure

In the framework of Tait and Cann (1990) and Cann (1993), syntactic structure is generated according to the Radical Functional Projection Hypothesis. These principles are listed in (39) below:

The Morphosyntax of Possessive Affixes

39) The Radical Functional Projection Hypothesis:

a. Functional categories alone determine syntactic structure.
b. All functional categories project according to X-bar principles:

$$XP \rightarrow ... X' ...$$
$$X' \rightarrow ... X^0 ...$$

c. Lexically selected elements are projected from the lexicon as complements.
d. Complements are disjointly indexed with their governing functional heads.
e. Specifiers are necessarily co-indexed with their governing functional heads.
f. Co-indexed elements necessarily unify.

Selectional properties of both functional and contentive elements are taken to be encoded in the lexicon as trees (Tait 1991). Lexical entries can be of two basic types, as illustrated in (40); (40b) represents a lexical entry for affixes:

40)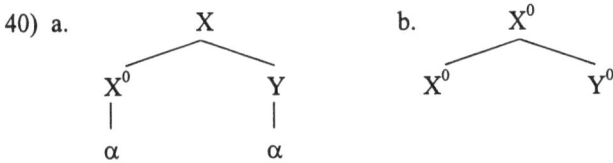

Argument structure is also encoded at the lexical level, with syntactic complements and theta-role assignment specified in the lexical entries of heads. In Cann and Tait's model, heads and specifiers must be categorially compatible. Structure is generated when lexical trees unify (in a manner similar to category unification in GPSG) according to the principles of X-bar, yielding maximal projections as in (41):

41)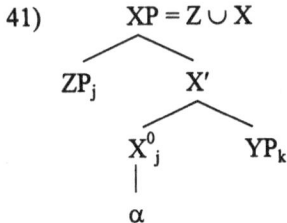
$XP = Z \cup X$

In such a structure, head and specifer unify only if categorially compatible, and once unified at D-structure are coindexed and share features (see Cann 1993 for a discussion of the mechanisms of unification and coindexation). Both coindexation and unification, then, depend on categorial compatibility.

Returning now to the data from Finnish as detailed in section 5.2, the distribution of verbal AGR versus Pxes can be summarized as follows: Pxes occur affixed to head nouns, certain adjectives, postpositions and nominalized clauses of ambiguous categorial status; verbal agreement is restricted in distribution to finite clauses. It is evident from this idiosyncratic distribution of Pxes that they do not select as functional heads, while the consistent co-occurrence of verbal agreement with tensed clauses suggests that selection is involved in the distribution of these elements.

Given the hypothesis that Pxes are a variant of verbal agreement and have the categorial status AGREEMENT, two separate reflexes under the same general category (AGR) can be posited, differing primarily in the binary feature [+/-FINITE]:

42) Category AGR <person, number>

AGR	AGR
[+FINITE]	[-FINITE]
(Verbal)	(Px)

Furthermore, the differing morphological status of the two types of agreement marker can be captured in the following generalization:

43) Affixal (functional) heads trigger consonant gradation.

(43) essentially states that consonant gradation is a phenomenon sensitive to syntactic structure, in that for it to be triggered in the syllable β preceding a given (consonant-initial) affix α, α must head β. As is demonstrated in the following sections, this morphological feature of the affix head AGR is a consequence of the type of movement involved in joining morphologically bound agreement elements to their hosts.

The distribution of verbal agreement in relation to finiteness, realized in Finnish as the functional head Tense/Mood,[9] is encoded in the f-lexical entry for verbal agreement as in (44), corresponding to (40b):

44)   Verbal AGR [+FINITE]:

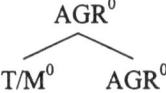

The principles of the Radical Functional Projection Hypothesis, outlined in (39), interacting with the Head Movement Constraint (Baker 1988), yield the following structure:

45)

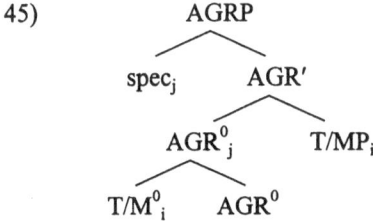

Given that Tense/Mood selects for V directly as a complement, the constituent structure of a finite clause (46a) is generated (46b):

46) a. Sinä   nä-i-t   minu-t.
       you(nom) see-past-2s me-acc
       'You saw me'

b.
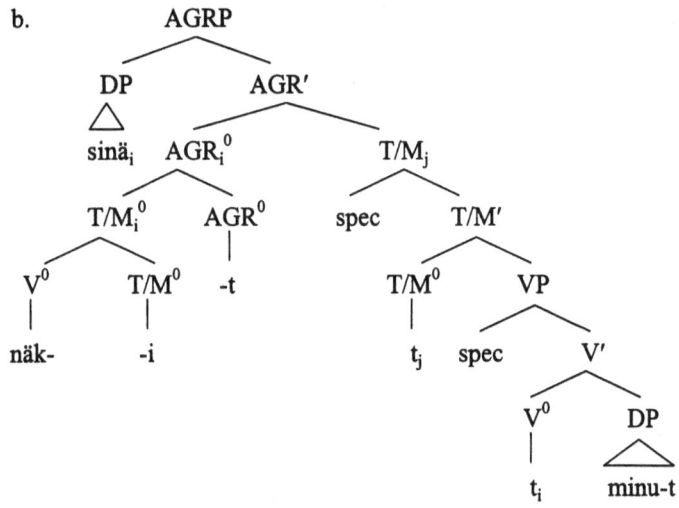

(46b) is the result of head movement in order to satisfy the PF-Licensing Principle (Tait and Cann 1990; Cann 1993). It is the only well-formed structure that satsifies the selectional properties of verbal AGR, which takes Tense/Mood as a complement and dominates the tree structure of finite clauses. Because verbal agreement is an affixed functional head, it may trigger consonant gradation in the preceding syllable. The distribution of verbal AGR is therefore constrained by its selectional properties as specified in the lexicon.

The lexical entry for Px agreement, on the other hand, does not involve selection for or by another element; its tree is nonbranching. It has been argued above that Pxes do not have status as heads in extended projections. Evidence for the lexical specification of Pxes is derived from their distribution across a variety of clause types: Pxes occur affixed to postpositions, certain adjectives, nouns and nominalized (gerund) clauses, indicating that they do not L-mark a complement. This hypothesis contradicts that of Trosterud (1993), who argues that Pxes are functional heads which select N as a complement.

The Morphosyntax of Possessive Affixes 215

His analysis, however, fails to predict the co-occurrence of Pxes with complements of other categories, particularly postpositions, adjectives and *kaikki*, 'all.'

The following nonbranching lexical tree is posited for Pxes under the category of AGR (47a). This structure projects in the syntax according to the principles of X-Bar Theory outlined above, yielding a specifier position coindexed with the Px head (47b):

47) a. Px AGR [-FINITE]:

AGR^0 [-FINITE]
|
Px

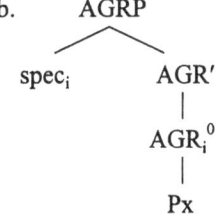

b. AGRP

spec$_i$ AGR'
            |
          AGR_i^0
            |
            Px

When licensed by the argument structure of the contentive head (as the subject of a nonfinite verb or possessor of a DP), Pxes attach to these non-tensed elements at the only available position, namely as specifiers (48):

48) a. häne-n   poika-nsa
       s/he-gen boy-Px3
       'his/her boy'

b.
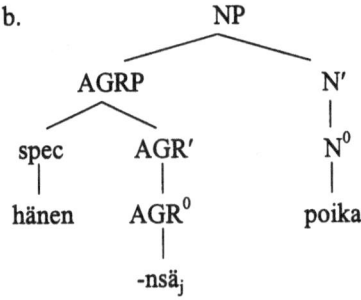

The structure represented in (48b) is not well-formed because head-movement of N^0 to the node AGR^0 in its specifier position is disallowed. Chomsky (1986:71) defines head movement as in (49):

49) Movement of a zero-level category β is restricted to the position of a head α that governs the maximal projection of γ of β, where α θ-governs or L-marks γ if $\alpha \neq C$.

AGR^0 does not theta-govern nor L-mark N^0 (because it fails to select N^0 as a complement), so head movement is not possible. However, a violation of the Stray Affix Filter can still be avoided. According to a revised definition of Head Movement (Cann 1993:14):

50) An expression immediately dominated by Y^0 may move into a position X^0 that governs its maximal projection, Y'''.

(50) predicts that the Px dominated by AGR^0 can move to adjoin to *poika*, since the landing site N^0 is not empty, ruling out substitution (51):

The Morphosyntax of Possessive Affixes 217

51)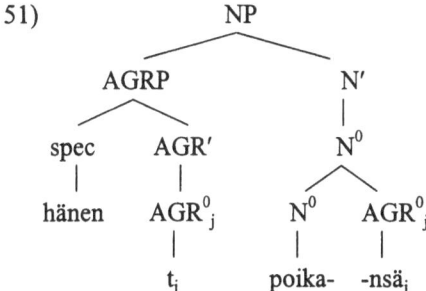

Further evidence for the adjunction, rather than proper affixation, of Px to its host is provided by the fact that the process does not trigger consonant gradation. The ambiguous phonological and morphological status of Pxes, which share aspects of both affix (inflectional) morphology and clitic morphology, is thus mirrored in the syntax.

Vainikka (1989c) presents a similar analysis, with Pxes occurring in specifier positions rather than as functional heads. However, she also proposes that Pxes are base-generated in specifier positions, consistent with the VP-internal subject hypothesis she adopts for finite clauses. In the current analysis Pxes are constrained in their distribution to specifier positions because they do not select complements. No site for base-generation of these elements needs to be stipulated, since their location on the morphology is determined in the lexicon.

In non-finite clauses where Pxes occur with locative case marking, Px agreement appears in the specifier position of the Kase Phrase as illustrated below in a D-structure representation (52):

52) a. pää-llä-ni
    head-adess-Px1s
    'on my head' or 'on top of me'

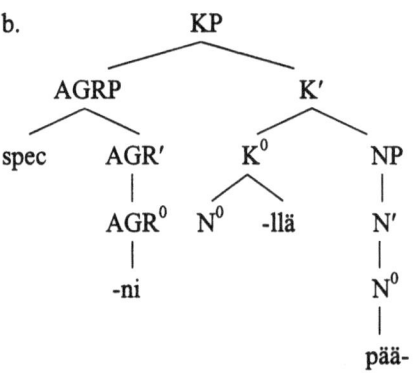

The noun *pää* raises to the locative Kase affix via head movement, and the Px adjoins to the noun-case complex to yield the surface form *päälläni*, with the surface order noun-case-Px.

As they are not selecting heads, Pxes project in specifier positions only.[10] This distributional requirement of Pxes extends to non-finite clauses in addition to NPs, APs and PPs. In Chapter 6, the structural properties of these clauses are discussed in greater detail. Assuming for the moment that non-finite clauses may be headed by the functional category ASP, it is proposed that these clauses have the structure in (53b):

53) a. tull-essa-ni
   come-ASP-Px1s
   'as I was coming ... '

b.

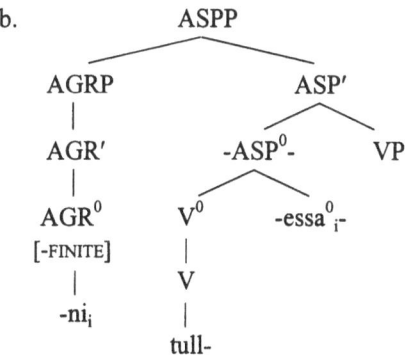

In the D-structure representation of a non-finite adjunct clause (53b), the PxP occurs in the specifier position of the projection headed by -*essa*, a temporal adjunct clause marker which signals a particular tense/aspect relation between main and subordinate clauses. The functional head ASP is necessarily co-indexed with its specifier according to the principles outlined in (39). The verb raises via head movement to ASP in the usual way, and the Px adjoins to -*essa* by the same processes outlined in the previous section. The adjunction of Pxes only to non-finite functional heads may be explained by positing (54):

54) AGR fails to unify with any verbal projection.

In the mechanism for unification described in (41) above, categorial compatibility was stated as the main prerequisite for unification of specifiers with heads. Verbal AGR, being a reflex of nominal φ-features coindexed with an external argument (if any), is nominal in category and is therefore unable unify in a spec-head relation with Tense/Mood or V, which are verbal categories. Elements like ASP, on the other hand, are categorially compatible with AGR and may unify.

Because the structure is untensed, i.e. nonfinite, well-formedness is dependent on AGR occurring as a specifier. If verbal (finite) AGR occurred in the specifier position of a gerundive clause, the structure would not be well-formed because AGR would fail to take Tense as a complement, as specified in the f-lexical entry for AGR[+FINITE]:

55) a. *tull-essa-n
   come-ASP-1s
   'as I was coming ... '

b.
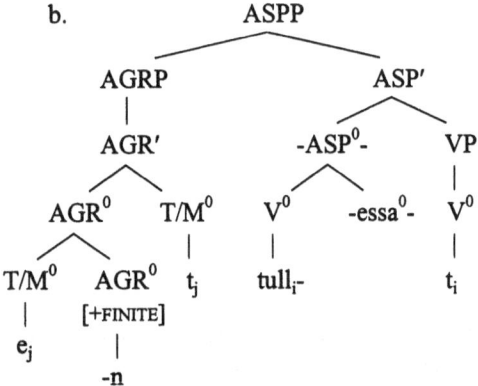

In the phrase structure representation above, the element selected as a complement by verbal AGR^0, T^0, is unfilled by morphological material; the only available elements are V and the nonfinite affix -*essa*, and neither can satisfy the selectional requirements encoded in the lexical entry for finite AGR^0. The derivation fails at PF because the PFLP is violated by the presence of an empty functional head.

The structure described above is ruled out because finite AGR selects T/M as a complement, and an empty head T/M would violate the PFLP. What then rules out a finite clause headed by AGRP in spec(ASPP), where the selectional requirements of all functional categories are satisfied, as in (56)?

56)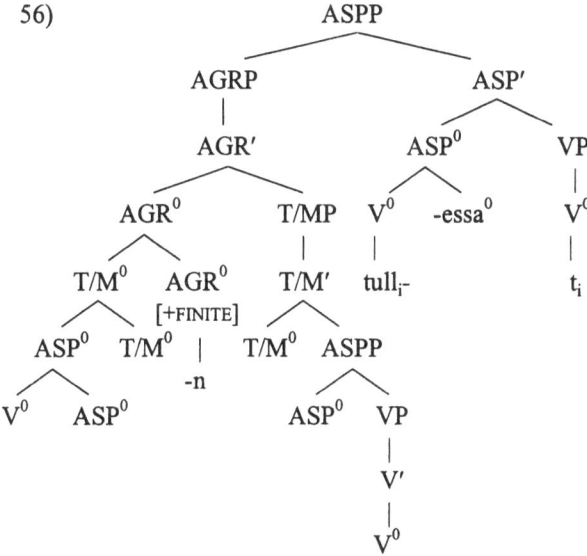

There are at least two reasons why the derivation in (56) fails. Firstly, because the finite AGR element in spec(ASPP) heads its own extended verbal projection, the external argument of the non-finite verb cannot be interpreted because AGR must be coindexed with the *finite* verb and its subject theta-role. Secondly, the structure violates the Stray Affix Filter because *-essa* occurs word finally, without a Px (phonetically overt or phonetically null; the licensing of zero Pxes is discussed in section 5.5.5 below). The distribution of agreement elements in specifier positions, though allowed within the syntactic model adopted here, is therefore constrained by general syntactic principles.

The selectional properties posited for the two types of AGR, which restrict the distribution of verbal agreement to tensed clauses and Px agreement to untensed clauses, also predicts that Px (-FINITE) agreement can never occur in tensed clauses, even with verbs which lexically select genitive subjects. Evidence from modal verbs taking genitive subjects shows that this is indeed the case, as no Px agreement is possible (57):

57) *Sinu-n   täyty-i-si   menn-ä koti-in
    you-gen   must-past-Px2s   go-TA   home-to
    'You had to go home'

The ungrammatical (57) has the following representation at D-structure:

58)
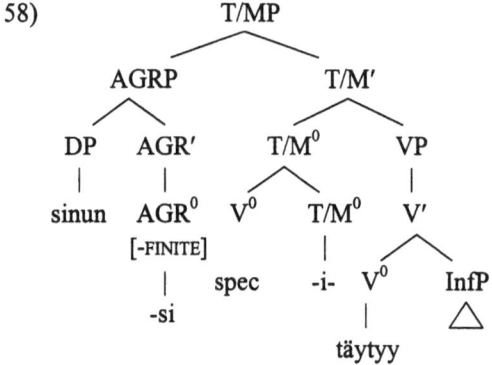

The D-structure derivation represented in (58) fails because, although the complement of Tense/Mood is available in the structure, the Px element -*si* cannot attach to the Tense infix -*i*- because it is incompatible with the feature [+FINITE] present in the element Tense/Mood. Thus the only well-formed structure in which a Px can occur is one in which the Px occupies a specifier position in an untensed environment; this is the result of the (lack of) selectional properties specified in the f-lexical entry for $AGR^0_{[-FINITE]}$.

5.5.5 The licensing of non-overt Pxes

It has been argued in the preceding sections that Px agreement heads its own projection but does not form part of the extended projection of contentive elements, and is restricted in distribution to specifier positions. The genitive pronouns which co-occur with Pxes are assumed to be specifiers of the head Px. However, Pxes themselves are not phonetically realized in all contexts. This appears to pose a problem for the PF Licensing Principle (as given in Cann and Tait 1989:9), described in Chapter 1 and repeated below in (59):

59) PF Licensing Principle:

α is PF-licensed iff.

a. the head of α contains phonologically realized material or
b. the head of α is bound by a PF-licensed position or
c. α binds a PF-licensed trace

Perhaps the most crucial role of the PFLP in a theory of syntax is to constrain the acquisition and representation of functional and contentive elements by requiring them to be phonetically realized in some way. Within the context of current syntactic theory one of the main motivations for this constraint is to curtail the proliferation of phonetically unlicensed, empty heads being posited, particularly functional elements. If Px affixes are not always phonetically realized, how can they license PxPs, given the restriction on empty heads placed on acquisition by the PFLP? And how can empty Pxes be acquired in these cases? Before an account of the licensing of these projections is given, the environments in which "empty" Pxes occur is reviewed.

The Px agreement paradigm, as mentioned in the introduction, is not triggered when locally bound by a genitive full DP (60).

60) Liisa-n   avaa-ma   kirje
    Lisa-gen   open-rel letter(nom)
    'The letter that Lisa opened'

Px affixes also fail to co-occur with inanimate genitive pronouns (61a) and the genitive interrogative pronoun *kenen* (61b):

61) a. se-n   jalka
      it-gen leg(nom)
      'its leg'

    b. Kene-n   kirja   se   on?
       who-gen book(nom)   it(nom) be/3s
       'Whose book is it?'

Px affixes in non-finite complement clauses cannot be locally bound. Firstly, 'doubling' with a genitive prounoun in disallowed throughout the paradigm; doubling with a first or second person Px for emphasis is ungrammatical (62a), and in the third person the genitive pronoun fails to trigger Px agreement (62b):[11]

62) a. *Minä kerro-i-n   minu-n ole-va-ni   oikeassa
       I(nom) say-past-1s   I-gen   be-pcp-Px1s   right
       'I said that I was right'

    b. Tanja   tietä-ä   häne-n   ole-van   oikeassa.
       Tanja(nom) know-3s   s/he-gen   be-pcp   right
       'Tanja$_i$ knows he/she$_j$ is right'/
       '*Tanja$_i$ knows she$_i$ is right'

In various contexts, then, a genitive pronoun can signal a referent when no Px agreement occurs.

The previous literature on the topic of Pxes focuses on their relationship to genitive pronouns. As described previously in section 5.2.5, the data is problematic because third person Pxes differ from first and second person Pxes in they are strictly anaphoric, and must be bound by an antecedent, either a genitive third person pronoun inside the clause or by a wider range of referential expressions outside the clause. Genitive DPs which are not animate pronouns fail to trigger overt Px agreement. Furthermore, first and second-person Pxes may be pronominal. These facts have led to a range of analyses. Some have argued (Kanerva 1987) that Pxes are purely inflectional affixes marking agreement with genitive pronouns. In this analysis a null genitive pronoun is posited when a Px is bound with an element outside the clause. Vainikka (1989c), van Steenbergen (1990), and Nevis (1984, 1986 and 1987) have suggested that Pxes are anaphoric, bound with overt or empty genitive pronouns. Others (Pierrehumbert 1980; Trosterud 1993) have interpreted them as being independent syntactic units with full status as arguments and genitive pronoun specifiers which cliticize onto the host. In Trosterud (1993) Pxes are also given status as functional elements which head noun phrases.

With recent developments in generative syntax whereby purely inflectional elements are interpreted as being as active in syntactic processes, if not more active than, contentive elements, the clitic versus affix issue has to a certain extent been resolved (though not without raising further theoretical issues). Furthermore, notions of licensing inherent in the syntactic framework adopted here allow for a shift of focus away from the relationship between Pxes and genitive pronouns, towards the issue of what licenses Px agreement in a given phrase. More important than the labelling of Pxes are their phonological and syntactic properties.

The PF-licensing Principle, given above in (59), places constraints on both acquisition and well-formedness in that all lexical elements must be licensed at PF. From these principles can be derived the notion that an element is PF-licensed if it is associated via coindexation with a PF-licensed element. Furthermore, the following relation between heads and specifiers is given in the Radical Functional Projection Hypothesis outlined in (39):

63) Specifiers are necessarily co-indexed with their governing functional heads.

It follows that an empty node α may be licensed if an element β in its specifier position has phonetic content (Tait 1991:193-4, Cann 1993:65), or at least the maximal projection of α will not constitute a violation of the PFLP. PxPs, then, can be licensed by genitive DP specifiers:

64) a.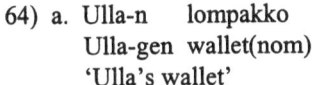
  Ulla-n   lompakko
  Ulla-gen wallet(nom)
  'Ulla's wallet'

b.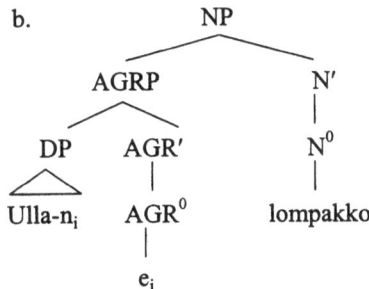

The empty node in (64) is PF-licensed through coindexation with the genitive DP *Ullan* in its specifier position;[12] the genitive DP binds and c-commands the head of the PxP, forming a coindexed chain. The projection of the 'empty' head Px is therefore licensed by overt phonetically realized material in its specfier position. Acquisition of phonetically unrealized nonfinite AGR^0 is unproblematic. To a certain extent, then, the status of Pxes as pronominal or anaphoric is irrelevant so long as the phrases they head are PF-licensed.[13]

5.6 CONCLUSION

In this Chapter an analysis of Possessive Affixes (Pxes) is posited which accounts for their distribution in all environments. It is proposed that both verbal AGR and Px agreement both share categorial specification for [AGR], but that the two agreement paradigms differ with respect to the feature FINITENESS. The syntactic structures in the f-lexical entries for finite versus non-finite agreement are structurally distinct: verbal AGR selects the functional head Tense/Mood as a complement, behaving as the syntactic head of the finite clause. The tree structure of Pxes is non-branching. Because Pxes fail to take complements they are restricted in distribution to specifier positions. Finally, it is proposed that Pxes and genitive DPs or pronouns may PF-license a projection of Px via spec-head coindexation.

Notes

1. The Px paradigm has two nonstandard Px allomorphs, *-in* which alternates with Px1s *-ni* and *-is*, which alternates with 2s *-si* (Nevis 1984:179).

2. Px3 *-Vn* (a lengthening of the stem vowel plus *-n*) alternates with *-nsa/-nsä*, and is preferred following a vowel-final case-affix (Kanerva 1987:508).

3. The given description of the distribution of Pxes throughout Finnish applies only to standard written Finnish. In spoken Finnish, Pxes are infrequent. Thus written Finnish (i) might occur as (ii) in spoken language:

   i. minu-n kissa-ni
      I-gen cat-Px1s
      'my cat'

   ii. mun kissa
       I(gen) kissa
       'my cat'

(*Mun* is a contracted form of *minun*, which occurs in many dialects of spoken Finnish.) Although Vainikka (1989c) accounts for these facts by developing a separate syntactic analysis for spoken Finnish, the current account is restricted in scope to the data from written Finnish only.

4. The affixation of Pxes to a stem already marked with genitive or accusative case causes truncation of the *-n* case affix due to phonological restrictions on certain consonant clusters (see Comrie 1980 for a discussion of the diachronic facts relating to this process of truncation). Where truncation of a case ending has occurred the case marking is glossed in parentheses.

5. Third person Pxes in nominalised clauses are not necessarily interpreted as bound with the local genitive DP antecedent (Leskinen 1969:432):

i. Hän₁ luul-i melu-n kuulu-van auto-sta-an₁.
S/he(nom) suppose-past/3s noise-gen be heard-pcp/np car-from-Px3
'S/he supposed the noise was coming from his/her car'

Leskinen (1969) notes that in sentences such as (i) above, the Px can be interpreted as being coreferent with the third person genitive main clause subject rather than with the more local genitive DP (i.e. the subject of the subordinate clause). This appears to be the result of an animacy effect; third person Pxes are interpreted as being bound to the highest available antecedent on the animacy hierarchy, if the context is otherwise ambiguous.

6. The English translations of (15a) and (15b) are context-dependent; one possible translation is given.

7. But not semi-clitics, which do not show vowel harmony (Nevis 1987).

8. Though some morphological data may be seen as evidence that Baker's Mirror Principle is not particularly robust (Spencer 1992).

9. A not uncontroversial assumption; Holmberg et al. 1993 posit a functional head Finiteness under which tense and agreement are both subsumed.

10. Given that finite AGR may be selected as a complement by another category, e.g. COMP, the question remains as to whether Px AGR may also be selected as a complement. Although nothing prevents this in theory, the distribution of Pxes suggests that it is not selected by any other category.

11. An account of these binding facts will be left for future research.

12. This analysis also accounts for the absence of Pxes in spoken Finnish, which appear instead as genitive pronouns exclusively.

13. The question of how third person Pxes are specified as [+anaphor], while first and second person Pxes are not, will be left open here, although it can be assumed that this is somehow specified in the lexicon.

CHAPTER 6
Complex Predicates and Non-finite Clauses

6.1 INTRODUCTION

In the previous chapters, data from simple finite clauses was analysed and a model for case assignment proposed which accounted for the alternation between accusative pronouns and nominative full DP internal arguments as the result of the assignment of two case features simultaneously. In Chapter 5 the status of Finnish possessive affixes (Pxes) was addressed, and it was argued that although category AGR, they are restricted to specifier positions in untensed structures. In this chapter these hypotheses are tested for nonfinite predicates.

6.2 CASE ASSIGNMENT AND COMPLEX PREDICATES

We have seen in previous sections that internal arguments of unaccusative, imperative, or impersonal passive verbs appear in zero-accusative, accusative or partitive case. The generalization drawn thus far is that a verb which fails to theta-mark an external argument or whose external argument is unavailable for case marking may assign double case features to its internal argument. This section addresses the issue of case in complex predicates in light of this hypothesis. This brief survey of the data brings to light relevant issues involving the link between argument structure and case assignment, but further research is required before a detailed account of case in all relevant non-finite constructions can be formulated.

6.2.1 +AGR raising verbs

A number of verbs in Finnish display patterns of case and agreement consistent with standard subject-to-subject raising in English. These verbs include *näkyä*, 'to seem,' *näyttää*, 'to appear,' 'to seem'; *kuulua*, 'to sound (like), to be heard (that)'; and *vaikuttaa*, 'to seem.' Both pronominal and full DP subjects of these verbs appear in nominative case, and the matrix verb shows agreement with the subject (data previously given in chapter 3):

1) a. Mauno näytt-i ole-van väsynyt.
  Mauno(nom) appear-past/3s be-pcp/np tired
  'Mauno appeared to be tired'

 b. *Mauno-n näytt-i ole-van väsynyt
  Mauno-acc appear-past/3s be-pcp/np tired

2) a. Sinä näytä-t ole-van väsynyt.
  you(nom) appear-2s be-pcp/np tired
  'You appear to be tired'

 b. *Sinu-t näytä-t ole-van väsynyt
  you-acc appear-2s be-pcp/np tired

The embedded constituent in this construction is a non-finite complement clause (discussed below in section 6.3.1). Objects of the lower clause, when it is transitive, are case-marked as in a basic finite transitive clause (3):

3) Te näytä-tte osta-van uude-n marsu-n.
  you(nom) seem-2p buy-pcp/np new-acc guinea-pig-acc
  'You (pl) seem to be buying a new guinea-pig'

These sentences may be given a straightforward raising analysis consistent with the current account of case assignment. The surface subject originates as a subject of the lower clause, which raises to the (tensed) main clause to receive the nominative case feature. Because it does not originate as an internal argument of the lower clause, and because verbs like *näyttää* fail to assign aspectual theta-roles as well as

Complex Predicates and Non-finite Clauses

objective case, the surface subject does not show the zero-accusative case split between full DPs and pronouns (1 and 2). The lower non-finite clause is untensed, so no nominative case feature is assigned within the clause.

6.2.2 Necessive verbs and -TA- infinitives

More interesting case-related phenomena are found in raising-type constructions where the surface subject does not receive nominative case. Consider the case of the lower clause object in the following sentences:

4) a. Sinu-n   pitä-isi   teh-dä se.
    you-gen should-cond/3s do-TA it(nom)
    'You should do it'

  b. Sinä   halua-t   teh-dä se-n.
    you(nom) want-2s do-TA it-acc
    'You want to do it'

It is noted in much of the previous literature on grammatical case in Finnish that infinitival complements appear to be 'transparent' to case assignment by the matrix verb. Sentences like (4a) and (4b) illustrate this generalization: in (4a), the matrix verb is a 'necessive' verb with a genitive subject that does not agree, and the form of the lower clause object is zero-accusative. In (4b), the matrix verb agrees with its subject, and accusative case is assigned to the internal argument in the lower clause.

Particularly relevant to the themes addressed in this dissertation are the properties of the matrix verb in (a). The verb *pitäisi* belongs to a class of 'necessive' modal verbs, which include *pitää*, 'should,' *täytyä*, 'must,' and *tarvita* 'need.' These verbs tend to share a certain semantic feature, namely that of obligation imposed on the speaker from an external source.[1] Unlike the [+AGR] raising verbs described in the previous section, necessive verbs license genitive case-marked subjects and an infinitival complement. Infinitives in Finnish are formed by affixation of two morphemes, -MA- and -TA-,[2] each of which may be lexically selected as a complement by certain matrix verbs. Necessive verbs (5) tend to select -TA- complements, while verbs like *innostua*, 'to get carried away (by),' select -MA- infinitival complements:

5) a. Maija-n   täyty-y   ava-ta   ovi.
Maijan-gen must-3s open-TA door(nom)
'Maija must open the door'

   b. *Maija-n   täyty-y   avaa-ma-an ovi.
Maijan-gen must-3s open-MA-ill door(nom)

6) a. Innostu-i-n   osta-ma-an kallii-n   koru-n.
get enthused-past-1s buy-MA-ill expensive-acc jewellry-acc
'I was carried away into buying expensive jewellry'

   b. *Innostu-i-n   osta-a kallii-n   koru-n.
get enthused-past-1s buy-TA expensive-acc jewellry-acc

Verbs selecting -MA- infinitives as complements, which assign nominative case to their subjects, are discussed in section 6.2.4 below. Subjects of necessive verbs appear in genitive case; nominative subjects are ungrammatical:

7) Sinu-n   pitä-isi   tuo-da heidä-t koti-in.
you-gen should-cond/3s bring-TA them-acc home-to
'You should bring them home'

8) *Sinä   pitä-isi   tuo-da heidä-t koti-in.
you(nom) should-cond/3s bring-TA them-acc home-to

Like AGR in impersonal passives, necessive verbal AGR is [-ϕ], failing to signal person and number features of the subject (9 and 10):

9) Häne-n   täyty-y teh-dä se.
s/he-gen must-3s do-TA it(nom)
'S/he must do it'

10) Heidä-n täyty-y   teh-dä   se.
    they-gen must-3s   do-TA   it(nom)
    'They must do it'

The question most relevant to the themes addressed in this dissertation is, do necessive verbs license an external argument? If they do not, and are basically unaccusative, then how do subjects get assigned genitive case, and how does nominative case get assigned to the lower clause complement? Several different hypotheses have been put forward in the literature. Vainikka (1989c) argues that necessive verbs do license a genitive subject as an external argument, base-generated in spec(VP). She suggests that genitive case in subjects of modal verbs such as *täytyä* appears as the result of the fact that no agreement features are base-generated in INFL, therefore the subject remains *in situ* in spec(VP) and retains genitive case features by structural default. Mitchell (1991b) posits a functional projection [+Obl] (for Obligation) as the site where genitive subjects of verbs of obligation are base-generated.

Marantz (1984) points out that VPs, being maximal projections, cannot lexically assign 'quirky' subject case, and argues that in languages like Icelandic, 'quirky' subjects originate as internal arguments. This analysis suggests that genitive subjects in Finnish are theta-marked as internal arguments of the necessive verb. In terms of animacy hierarchies, the semantic feature of obligation entails that the 'subject' of a necessive verb is low in volition and agency, which correlates with internal argumenthood and/or non(nom)inative case assignment in other environments (e.g. unaccusatives). Consistent with this observation, Laitinen and Vilkuna (1993) argue that genitive subjects of necessive verbs are *not* arguments of the necessive verb, but that necessive verbs are monadic predicates taking a clausal complement. Their analysis therefore suggests raising to subject from the *lower* infinitival clause. The question remains as to whether genitive is lexically or structurally assigned.

Within the current model for case assignment, a difficulty arises in postulating genitive as a structural case for subjects. If elements that move to spec(AGRP) get assigned structural nominative case via T/M, as proposed in Chapter 4, then the same position cannot be a locus for assigning structural genitive case. Necessive verbs are in fact tensed, so nominative case is the predicted structural case for subjects of these verbs. Vainikka (1989c and 1993), Maling (1993) and Vainikka and Maling (1996) solve this problem by adopting a general rule wherein genitive case is assigned by structural default to elements in specifier positions for both finite and non-finite clauses. If this includes derived subjects, however, it is unclear how this rule can disallow genitive case assignment to a derived subject in an impersonal passive, for example:

11) Kirja /*kirja-n   lue-ttiin.
    book(nom) /book-gen read-pass/past
    'The book was read'

The only way to rule out a genitive subject in (11) in Vainikka's and Maling's models is to stipulate that movement is not to spec(IP) (a position split into spec(T/MP) and spec(AGRP) in the current framework).

A possible analysis for these structures captures related data from a small set of semantically related verbs (*antaa*, 'to let'; *käskeä* 'to order, to tell'; *sallia* 'to allow, permit'; and *suoda* 'to grant'), which also select a -TA- infinitival complement. Subjects of the lower clause selected by these verbs take genitive subjects, regardless of the argument structure of the matrix verb:

12) a. Anna-n häne-n osta-a marsu-n.
       let-1s s/he-gen buy-TA guinea pig-acc
       'I'll let him/her buy the guinea pig'

    b. Anna   häne-n osta-a marsu!
       let(imp) s/he-gen buy-TA guinea pig(nom)
       'Let him/her buy the guinea pig!'

Objects in the lower clause complements in (12a) and (12b) show the familiar zero-accusative pattern sensitive to the argument structure of the matrix verb, but the *subject* of the lower clause in this construction invariably appears in genitive case. Following Laitinen and Vilkuna's (1993) proposal that genitive 'subjects' of necessive verbs are arguments of the lower clause predicate rather than the necessive verb, the data in (12) suggest that subjects of -TA- infinitival clauses, when not PRO, raise to object to be assigned lexical genitive case by certain verbs. This entails that genitive 'subjects' of necessive constructions are raised from the lower clause subject position via this lexical case-marked position, and then to surface subject position.[3]

Nominative case assignment to the lower clause object in (9), (10) and (12b) remains to be accounted for. Vainikka (1989c) assumes that -MA- and -TA- infinitives head their own projections but are not barriers to government from the matrix verb. If following Marantz (1984) and Baker (1988) complex predicates such as those described in this section merge into a single clause, then AGR and T/M govern both matrix verbs and their infinitival complements. By the same mechanism that assigns postverbal nominative case in impersonal passives and unaccusatives, T/M may assign nominative case under i-command to the object of a lower clause.

If the raised subject is assigned genitive case lexically (at D-Structure), then the question remains as to why the lower clause object gets assigned a nominative case feature instead of the genitive subject, if the subject raises to spec(AGRP). Similar phenomena have appeared in clauses involving lexical case assignment, as discussed in section 4.7.1:

13) a. Kirjallisuute-en   erikoistu-ttiin   vuosi.
       literature-ill   specialize-pass/past   year(nom)
       'Literature was specialized in for a year'

    b. *Kirjallisuute-en   erikoistu-ttiin   vuode-n.
       literature-ill   specialize-pass/past   year-acc

In (13a) above, the adverbial receives nominative case instead of the lexically case-marked element, even though lexically case-marked elements must be able to receive a nominative case feature when no adverbial is present. In Chapter 4 the following rule was proposed as (58), repeated below as (14a), which interacts with Maling's (1993:60) Case-Tier hierarchy (14b) to yield correct patterns of case assignment for doubly-marked elements:

14) a. Assign second case feature to structurally case-marked elements before lexically case marked elements.

    b. which XP gets NOM reflects the hierarchy of GFs, where
       SUBJ > OBJ > MEASURE > DUR > FREQ > OBL

If, given their low values for agentivity and volition, genitive subjects are assumed to be lexically-assigned obliques for the purposes of this hierarchy, this predicts that an argument functioning as an object in a necessive construction will receive nominative case before a genitive subject.

6.2.3 Experiencer verbs and -TA- infinitives

Another class of verbs appears in a similar construction to the necessive verbs described above. The surface subjects of experiencer verbs appear in partitive case rather than nominative or accusative, and also fail to agree with the verb. These verbs may take sentential complements (15):

15) a. Tanja-a   harmitt-i   teh-dä työ-tä   sunnuntai-na.
       Tanja-part annoy-past/3s do-TA work-part Sunday-on
       'It annoyed Tanja to work on a Sunday'

    b. *Tanja-n   harmitt-i   teh-dä työ-tä   sunnuntai-na.
       Tanja-acc annoy-past/3s do-TA work-part Sunday-on

    c. *Tanja   harmitt-i   teh-dä työ-tä   sunnuntai-na.
       Tanja(nom) annoy-past/3s do-TA work-part Sunday-on

Animate pronominal subjects also appear in partitive case:

16) a. Minu-a harmitt-i   teh-dä työ-tä   sunnuntai-na.
       I-part   annoy-past/3s do-TA work-part Sunday-on
       'It annoyed me to work on a Sunday'

    b. *Minu-t harmitt-i   teh-dä työ-tä   sunnuntai-na.
       I-acc   annoy-past/3s do-TA work-part Sunday-on

As in necessive constructions, the lower clause object appears in nominative or accusative case, depending on whether it is a full DP or a pronoun:

17) a. Minu-a pelotta-a ava-ta ovi.
   I-part fear-3s open-TA door(nom)
   'I'm afraid to open the door'

b. Minu-a pelotta-a näh-dä häne-t.
   I-part fear-3s see-TA s/he-acc
   'I'm afraid to see him/her'

Necessive verbs form a semantic class but are morphologically heterogeneous. Experiencer verbs are semantically related and share a morphological feature: affixed to the verb is a -*tt*- morph, which is listed in descriptive grammars (Sulkala and Karjalainen 1992:295) as the causative affix.[4] It is highly productive:

18) haluta 'to want' >> haluttaa   'to feel like'
     itkeä 'to cry' >> itkettää   'to feel like crying'
     nauraa 'to laugh' >> naurattaa   'to feel like laughing'
     pelätä 'to fear' >> pelottaa   'to be frightened by'

Following Baker (1988), causative morphology is taken to be a syntactic process that alters valency when the verbal stem incorporates the causative affix. However, partitive-subject Experiencer verbs lack a syntactically overt causer or agent. The morph -*tt*- in these verbs absorbs the external argument of the verb as in passivization, while promoting the internal argument to main clause subject.[5] Because of the stative semantics of Experiencer verbs, internal arguments are assigned a non-aspectual theta-role, and surface in partitive case. Since the matrix verb lacks a syntactic subject but still governs the (non-case-assigning) infinitival complement clause, the lower clause object is case marked as zero-accusative.

6.2.4 -MA- infinitives

Verbs that subcategorize for clausal arguments may select two types of infinitives, -MA- and -TA-. Verbs that select -TA- complements may lexically case-mark genitive subjects of the lower clause. Complex predicates formed with -MA- infinitives, on the other hand, assign structural rather than lexical case to arguments of the lower clause.

Complements of -MA- infinitives appear marked for objective case according to the argument structure of the matrix verb (example 19a previously given as 6a):

19) a. Innostu-i-n   osta-ma-a   kallii-n   koru-n.
get enthused-past-1s buy-MA-il expensive-acc jewellry-acc
'I was carried away into buying expensive jewellry'

    b. Innostu-ttiin   osta-ma-an kallis   koru.
get enthused-pass buy-MA-ill expensive(nom) jewellry(nom)
'(They) were carried away into buying expensive jewellry'

The data is further complicated by the facts noted by Vainikka (1989c) when overt subjects are present in the lower clause. A subset of verbs which select -MA- infinitival complements also allow overt subjects of the lower clause. Such verbs include *pakottaa*, 'to force,' *vaatia*, 'to demand,' *kehottaa*, 'to urge' and *estää*, 'to prevent.' These verbs belong to roughly the same semantic class as the four which take -TA- complements with subjects, and those that typically assign ECM in English. The case in which the lower clause subject appears, however, is also determined by the argument structure and agreement features of the matrix verb:

20) a. Hän   pakott-i   lapse-n   avaa-ma-an   ove-n.
s/he(nom) force-past/3s child-acc open-MA-ill door-acc
'S/he forced the child to open the door'

    b. Pakota   lapsi   avaa-ma-an   ovi!
force-imp child(nom) open-MA-ill door(nom)
'Force the child to open the door!'

Depending on the semantics of the two verbs involved, the lower clause subject and object may appear in mismatched objective cases:

21) Hän kehott-i   poikaystävä-ä-nsä   leikkaa-ma-an hiukse-nsa.
s/he urge-past/3s boyfriend-part-Px3 cut-MA-ill hair-(acc)-Px3
'S/he urged his/her boyfriend to cut his hair'

… Examples such as (21) provide evidence that both verbs may assign objective case independently of each other, and suggests that main clause verbs do not govern the complements of -MA- infinitives. Both the matrix verb and the lower clause verb headed by the infinitive -MA- retain an ability to assign aspectual theta-roles, and therefore objective case; the matrix verb assigns ECM to the lower clause subject, and the infinitive assigns objective case under government in the usual way.

However, assignment of nominative case in sentences like (20b) remains to be accounted for. In simple unaccusative and passive sentences, an internal argument may raise to a position following the verb where it is assigned nominative case. Since certain verbs take infinitives headed by -MA- as arguments, it follows that an entire infinitival clause headed by -MA- may undergo raising in a similar fashion to a position governed by T/M. The head -MA- is assigned nominative case, and the case feature percolates throughout the clause to all arguments. As we have seen, however, -MA- infinitives may assign aspectual (or non-aspectual) roles to their complements independent of the main clause, as in (21). Although the entire -MA- clause may raise to a position governed by T/M, and receive a nominative case feature, aspectual role assignment by -MA- may result in the assignment of double objective case. The morphological rules posited in Chapter 4 realize surface case in such examples.

6.2.5 Infinitives out of context

In Chapter 4 an analysis was presented to account for patterns of case assignment in Finnish which links nominative case assignment with the functional category Tense/Mood. A bi-unique case-assigning property of T/M was posited, which ensures that one nominative case feature is assigned per finite sentence. In other words, if T/M projects in a structure, then nominative case will be assigned. It should be pointed out, however, that the converse is not necessarily true; if lexical DPs occur out of clausal context, for instance in a bare infinitive, the zero-accusative case pattern is still evident, despite the absence of case-assigning T/M:

22) a. Jättä-ä   nyt   lapsi   /häne-t   yksin   koti-in!
       leave-TA now   child(nom)/ s/he-acc alone   home-at
       'To leave a child/ him/her at home!' (Goodness!)

   b. Luke-a   nyt kirja-a!
      read-TA now book-part
      'To read part of a book!' (What a waste!)

In (22) above, the object DP of the -TA- infinitive *lapsi* occurs in nominative case and alternates with an accusative pronoun in the same context. The partitive object in (22b) shows that aspectual roles do get assigned by the verb in this construction. It has been noted in previous sections that -TA- infinitivals appear 'transparent' to case assignment from the matrix verb, evidence that they themselves are non-case-assigning. The absence of either tense or agreement morphology in (22) makes any analysis linking finite verbal features with nominative and/or accusative case difficult. Proposals such as Reime's (1989; 1993), which links the assignment of accusative case directly to the presence of verbal agreement, do predict the 'zero-accusative' DP in (22) because the infinitive lacks agreement features, but are less successful in accounting for the accusative pronoun in the same environment.

Another construction which brings up related problems for the current account of nominative case assignment involves infinitival complements embedded within DPs:

23) Ole-t-ko   kuul-lut Miko-n   aikomukse-sta   osta-a talo?
    be-2s-qu hear-pcp Mikko-gen intention-ela   buy-TA house(nom)
    'Have you heard about Mikko's intention to buy a house?'

In (23) above, the main clause verb *kuulua* selects an elative case complement, which is realized on the nominal stem form of *aikomus*, 'intention.' *Mikko* occurs in genitive case as the possessor, while the lower clause complement of the -TA- infinitive remains in nominative case. Again, no T/M projects in the lower clause, which is embedded under a DP, so the current theory fails to predict the occurrence of nominative case on the object.

However, partitive case may be assigned in the same construction, signalling that aspectual and non-aspectual roles are assigned:

24) Ole-t-ko kuul-lut Miko-n aikomukse-sta kirjoitta-a kirje-ttä?
   be-2s-qu hear-pcp Mikko-gen intention-ela write-TA letter-part
   'Have you heard about Mikko's intention to write (some of) the letter?'

The strength of the current analysis is that by *not* associating subject agreement (or the licensing of a subject) with objective case, an infinitival verb out of clausal context is predicted to be able to assign accusative and partitive case at D-structure regardless of whether a syntactic subject or any finite inflectional morphology is present. Further research is necessary, however, before a model of case assignment can be developed which can account for all grammatical case assignment in these constructions.

6.3 GERUNDIVE CLAUSES

Finnish shares a common feature of the Uralic languages in that it allows for a large variety of nominalized gerundive clauses (*lauseenvastikkeet*), which have been the focus of traditional Finnish grammar studies for decades. Typical syntactic features of these constructions include categorial ambiguity, a more fixed word order than in finite clauses, and the presence in the morphology of one of several 'nominalising' elements. Wiik (1981) summarizes the consensus among Finnish linguists and defines *lauseenvastikkeet* as having overt subjects coindexed with Px agreement, and objects whose surface case form does not depend on properties of the matrix clause, thereby excluding -MA- and -TA- infinitivals. In modern Finnish *lauseenvastikkeet* are ubiquitous in formal written registers but infrequent in colloquial speech.

In the previous chapters several hypotheses are proposed to account for patterns of case and agreement that involve the functional projection Tense/Mood. In particular, nominative case in finite clauses is assigned by T/M and the distribution of verbal AGR is linked via c-selection with T/M. Given these properties of T/M, certain predictions can be made about transitive clause types in which T/M fails to project: nominative case will not be assigned, and external arguments (if any) will be coindexed with Px AGR rather than verbal AGR. The data from *lauseenvastikkeet* bear out these generalizations, and provide interesting data toward the study of nominalized constructions crosslinguistically. In this analysis, nominalizations are argued to be governed by ASP, a functional category unspecified for major category.

The definitive study of non-finite clauses in Finnish is Ikola (1974). Ikola describes a large number of constructions and provides transformational rules for the derivation of each. Only a small subset of Ikola's *lauseenvastikkeet* are analysed in this dissertation, comprising two major types: complement clauses, selected as clausal complements by verbs of perception and belief; and adverbial adjunct clauses, which specify temporal/aspectual information relative to the matrix clause.

6.3.1 Complement clauses

Complement clauses are by far the most thoroughly-studied *lauseenvastikke* in Finnish. An extensive body of literature in Finnish grammar exists which attempts to explain the mixed-category nature of the construction (e.g. Ikola 1974). These clauses are selected as complements by a restricted subset of Finnish verbs and share certain properties with DPs, yet their internal structures are extremely sentence-like. Similar constructions appear in many related Finno-Ugric languages and in Turkic.

A restricted subset of Finnish verbs take complement clauses as arguments (25a and 26a). All are verbs of direct perception and recounting (*verba sentiendi et dicendi*), such as *arvata* 'guess, expect,' *huuta* 'shout, cry,' *katsoa* 'watch' and *toivoa*, 'hope, wish.' Verbs that take complement clauses may alternately take a CP headed by the complementizer *että* (25b and 26b):

25) a. Aili odott-i   minu-n sano-va-n   vastaukse-n.
    Aili expect-past/3s I-gen say-pcp/np-*n* answer-acc
    'Aili(nom) expected me to say the answer'

  b. Aili   odotta-a, että minä   sano-i-n   vastaukse-n.
     Aili(nom) expect-3s that I(nom) say-past-1s answer-acc
     'Aili expected me to say the answer'

Complex Predicates and Non-finite Clauses 243

26) a. Leena   näk-i   ole-va-nsa   väärässä.
       Leena(nom) saw-3s   be-pcp/np-Px3   wrong
       'Leena saw that she was wrong'

    b. Leena   näk-i,   että hän   ol-i   väärässä.
       Leena(nom) saw-3s   that s/he(nom)   be-past/3s wrong
       'Leena saw that she had been wrong'

Complement clause morphology consists of a 'weak' verbal stem (i.e. a stem where consonant gradation has been triggered) plus a verbal participle, plus the morph -*n*, which may be truncated if Px agreement appears.[6] The participle can be active or passive and signals tense/aspect relative to the main clause event, as illustrated in (25a) and (26a) above.

The status of the -*n* morph affixed to the participle is the subject of some debate. Similar constructions in Turkish show accusative case on the gerund, evidence that complement clauses are nominalized, case-marked clausal arguments of certain verbs (Ouhalla 1991):

27)   Mary   John-un   elmalar-i   ser-me-dig-ni   soyle-di-O
      Mary   John-gen   apples-acc   like-neg-asp-acc-past   say-tns-agr
      'Mary said that John does not like apples'

In Finnish the situation is less clear-cut. If -*n* were accusative case, it should alternate with partitive case if the clause is negated. However, this fails to occur (28b and 28c):

28) a. Minä   sano-i-n   Aili-n   ole-va-n   kotona.
       I(nom)   say-past-1s   Aili-gen   be-pcp/np-*n*   at home
       'I said that Aili was at home'

    b. Minä   e-n   sano-nut   Aili-n   ole-va-n   kotona.
       I(nom)   neg-1s   say-pcp   Aili-gen   be-pcp/np-*n*   at home
       'I didn't say that Aili was at home'

    c. *Minä   e-n   sano-nut   Aili-n   ole-va-a   kotona
       I(nom)   neg-1s   say-pcp   Aili-gen   be-pcp-part   at home

Objects of negated verbs are invariably assigned partitive case, so the fact that (28c) above is ungrammatical indicates that -*n* is not a productive objective case marker.

Timberlake (1977) examines the history of this construction and finds evidence for syntactic reanalysis. In old Finnish texts, the same set of verbs assigned ECM (accusative or partitive) to the subject of the participial predicate, and the participle agreed in case and number as a modifier. When the genitive case and the accusative case forms in Finnish syncretized, Timberlake argues, accusative lower clause subjects were reanalysed as genitive, and began to appear with Px agreement. The agreeing participle remained in 'genitive' case.

The proposed constituent structure for complement clauses contains a VP dominated by a functional head which is category ASP. Recall that in finite clauses, PERF projects to host participles when Tense/Mood is supported by an auxiliary:

29) Hanna ol-i rakenta-nut talo-a
    Hanna be-past/3s build-pcp house-part
    'Hanna had built a house'

The same participial affixes which license PERF in finite clauses also appear in complement clauses, suggesting that they may be categorially related: participial forms in general are typically ambiguous with respect to major category. In (29) above, the participial verb is part of a verbal complex which assigns objective case to and theta-marks its internal argument. Alternately, a participle may function as a predicate in a copular construction, or as an adjective:

30) a. Talo on rakenne-ttu.
       house(nom) be/3s built-pcp/pass
       'The house was built'

    b. Rakenne-ttu talo on vihre-ä.
       built-pcp/pass house(nom) be/3s green-part
       'The built house (the house that has been built) is green'

In (30a), the fact that *talo* is not assigned accusative case signals that no aspectual theta-role is assigned to it by the participle. These facts suggest that *rakennettu* is not specified for major category; its case-assigning and agreement properties are determined by syntactic structure. Similar data from English gerunds has led to analyses by Milsark (1988) and Adger and Rhys (to appear) suggesting that 'nominal' and 'verbal' *-ing* in English share a single lexical entry which is underspecified for categorial features. The head ASP in Finnish is assumed to be similarly underspecified.[7] ASP is assumed to share a projection with the diachronically accusative *-n* affix. The suggested constituent structure for complement clauses is given below:

31) a. Arto   huus-i   löytä-nee-nsä   avaime-t.
      Arto(nom) shout-past/3s find-past/pcp-Px3 key-pl/acc
      'Arto shouted that he had found the keys'

b.

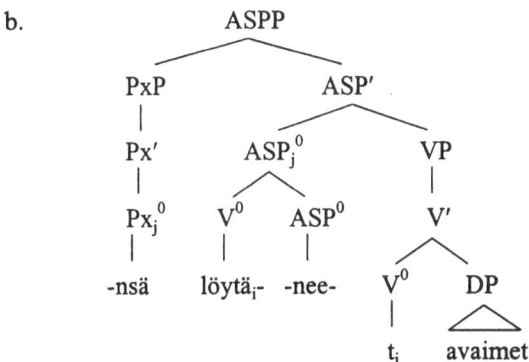

By postulating ASP as the head of the construction, several facts can be accounted for. Firstly, Px AGR rather than verbal AGR must encode φ-features coindexed with the lower clause external argument (in this case anaphoric pro), because as described in Chapter 5, for AGR to head this structure would violate the c-selectional properties encoded in its f-lexical entry. AGR c-selects T/M as a complement, which does not project in this structure. The external argument instead must be realized as a PxP in the specifier position of ASP. The head ASP and its specifier are coindexed, allowing the Px to cliticize onto the participial host.

The second consequence of ASP heading the structure is that no nominative case may be assigned; unlike raising verbs, the verbs that select ASPP complements do not assign ECM to the subject of the lower clause. Instead, regardless of the argument structure of the matrix verb, and whether or not raising of the lower clause subject occurs, no nominative case gets assigned within the ASPP:

36) Sinu-n   sano-taan   löytä-neen   avaime-n.
    you-gen   say-pass   find-pcp/past   key-acc
    'They say that you found the key'

The fact that these clauses are complements of rather than adjuncts to the matrix clause accounts for the fact that elements may undergo wh-extraction from the lower clause without violating the ECP:

37) a. Kene-t   Camilla   luul-i   näh-nee-nsä?
       who-acc   Camilla(nom)   suppose-past/3s   see-pcp/past-Px3
       'Who did Camilla suppose she saw?'

    b. Kene-n   hän   luul-i   näh-neen   Camilla-n?
       who-gen   s/he(nom)   suppose-past/3s   see-pcp/past   Camilla-acc
       'Who did s/he suppose saw Camilla?'

In section 6.4, similar extractions from another type of nominalized clause are shown to violate the ECP, consistent with a hypothesis that they are adjuncts rather than complements.

6.4 ADVERBIAL ADJUNCT CLAUSES

Two types of adjunct clause are analysed here, temporal clauses and purpose clauses. Both function as adverbial modifiers of the main clause predicate and both encode tense/aspect relative to the main clause. The morphology of adverbial adjunct clauses is similar to that of the complement clause, consisting of a non-finite ASP element signalling tense or aspect relative to the main clause plus an inactive case marker. As with the complement clause, the two component morphemes are analysed as being fused into a single functional head of category ASP.

6.4.1 Purpose clauses

34) Hän   men-i   Suome-en   oppi-a-kse-en   suome-a.
    s/he go-past/3s   Finland-to   learn-TA-kse-Px3   Finnish-part
    'S/he went to Finland in order to learn Finnish'

The morphology of this construction[8] is somewhat unusual in that the verbal 'stem' is formed from the -TA- infinitive, the same type of infinitive selected by necessive verbs. This is the only construction in Finnish where this morpheme functions as a non-finite stem for affixes, in this case the suffix -*kse*- which is identical to the translative case stem. Like all nominalized clauses in Finnish, agreement is signalled via Px AGR rather than verbal AGR.

The element -*kse*- is homophonous with the translative case stem. The translative case as it exists in modern Finnish is realized by the suffix -*ksi* and in most cases indicates 'transformation into':

35) Toukka   muuttu-u   perhose-ksi.
    caterpillar(nom)   change-3s   butterfly-tra
    'The caterpillar changes into a butterfly'

When the translative case co-occurs with another morpheme such as a Px, its stem form is -*kse*-:

36) Hän   rupe-si   opettaja-kse-ni.
    s/he(nom)   start-past/3s   teacher-tra-Px1s
    'S/he became my teacher'

Although diachronically derived from the translative case ending, two facts suggest that the case affix has become lexicalized along with the infinitival stem in this construction and is no longer active. First, the -TA- infinitive is not a productive stem for any other cases in Finnish or Px agreement. Secondly, if -*kse*- were the translative case, it should be possible for it to occur word-finally, as in (35) above. A purpose clause with a full DP genitive pronoun and a zero Px ought to be possible, but is ungrammatical (37):

37) *Tanja-n   osta-a-ksi   kirja-n
    Tanja-gen   buy-TA-ksi   book-acc
    'in order for Tanja to buy the book'

In fact, Px agreement in this construction has unusual binding properties; it must occur affixed to the -*kse*- infix in all cases and may be pronominal, but not anaphoric (i.e. subject to Principle A of the Binding Theory, which states that an anaphor must be bound in its governing category):

38) *Men-i-mme Helsinki-in osta-a-kse-ni   kirja-n
    go-past-1p Helsinki-to buy-TA-kse-Px1s book-acc
    'We went to Helsinki in order for me to buy the book'

It would appear, then, that in the purpose clause the translative case has become lexicalized as an infix that cannot occur word-finally.[9]

As is the case with all three types of adjunct clauses discussed in this section, wh-extraction out of the adjunct clause appears to result in an ECP violation:

39) *Suome-a-ko   men-i-t   Suome-en   oppi-a-kse-si?
    Finnish-part-qu go-past-2p   Finland-to study-TA-kse-Px2s
    'Was it Finnish you went to Finland in order to study?'

For these reasons Vilkuna (1989) categorizes both the final clause and the temporal clauses as 'non-splitting.'

6.4.2 Temporal clauses

The other two adverbial adjunct clauses denote events concurrent with (40) and preceding (41) the event of the main clause predicate:

40) Miko-n   tull-e-ssa   koti-in   ol-i-n   nukkumassa.
    Mikko-gen   come-e-ssa   home-to   be-past-1s   asleep
    'As Mikko came home I was sleeping'

41) Minä   lähd-i-n   sinu-n   tiska-ttu-a-si.
    I(nom) leave-past-1s you-gen wash up-ttu-a-Px2s
    'I left after you had washed up'

The first temporal clause construction is formed with the affix -essa/-essä, which can be further subdivided into two morphemes: the 'second infinitive' -e- and the inessive case -ssa/-ssä. The 'second infinitive' selects only two case forms in Finnish, the inessive and the instructive, and conveys a notion of simultaneity. The second temporal clause construction is composed of the past passive participial verb form -TTU plus an affix which was historically the partitive case ending -a/ä. Like several of the other nominalized constructions discussed in this chapter, the nonfinite affix and the case marker in both these constructions are analysed as syncretized morphs -essa/essä and -ttua/ttuä belonging to the functional category ASP.

As is the case in purpose clauses, extraction from the adjunct clause results in an ECP violation:

42) a. *Kene-n söi-t   päivällis-tä   tull-essa   kotiin?
       wh-gen ate-2s breakfast-part come-essa home-to?
       'Who$_i$ were you were eating breakfast while t$_i$ was coming home?'

    b. *Mi-stä söit   päivällis-tä   Miko-n   tull-essa
       wh-ela ate-2s breakfast-part Mikko-gen come-essa
       'From where$_i$ were you were eating breakfast while Mikko was coming t$_i$?'

WH-extraction may also license a projection of CP:

43) Kenen tull-essa   koti-in   söi-t   päivällistä?
    wh-gen come-essa home-to ate-2s breakfast-part
    'Who came home when you were eating breakfast?'

Note that in contrast to the purpose clauses in (34), temporal clauses do not require Px agreement (40).

6.4.3 Syntactic properties of adverbial adjuncts

All three of the constructions described in this section share certain syntactic properties: they do not allow negation, auxiliaries or nominative subjects; they take Px agreement; they are islands for extraction; and they all signal a particular tense/aspect relation to the main clause event. Although distinct in morphological composition and binding properties, Hakulinen and Karlsson (1979:388-91) categorize them together as non-finite temporal adverbial clauses. All of these facts suggest that T/M fails to project in these constructions but that ASP does project, and that their structural relation to the main clause is that of adjunction. The constituent structure of all three of these clauses is assumed to be identical to that of the complement clause analysed in (31b) above.[10]

6.5 CONCLUSION

The various complex predicates and nonfinite constructions briefly discussed in this chapter show a variety of case-related phenomena that are predicted by the hypotheses set out in the first five chapters in this dissertation. Data from complex predicates support the link between the lack of an external argument and the split-case pattern visible in simple predicates: finite matrix verbs that license an external argument govern the complement of the lower clause and assign accusative case, but if no external argument is licensed by the matrix, lower clause objects show the familiar alternation between nominative and and objective cases. However, data from infinitives out of clausal context proved difficult to account for within the current analysis of nominative case assignment. Certain facts about transitive nominalized clauses are shown to be predicted by the failure of Tense/Mood to project: no nominative case is assigned within the clause, and external arguments are coindexed with Pxes rather than verbal AGR. Nominalising morphology was shown to exhibit a tendency to incorporate an aspectual or infinitival element with an inactive case affix. These syncretized morphemes are analysed as projections of ASP, underspecified for major category and allowing Px agreement to occur in specifier positions.

Notes

1. These verbs may also get an epistemic modal reading.

2. The terminology used to described these infinitives is adopted from Vainikka (1989c).

3. Maling (1993:54, fn. 8), however, argues that genitive case in this construction is structural, since elements that appear to have raised to subject position after D-structure appear in genitive case. This analysis accounts for data from copular constructions governed by necessive verbs (ii) and idioms (i) (data in (i) from Maling 1993:54):

   i. a. John   potkais-i   tyhjä-ä   viime yönä
       John(nom) kick-past/3s empty-part last   night
       'John kicked the bucket last night'
    b. Johni-n   on täyty-nyt potkaista tyhjä-ä   viime yönä
       John-gen be must-pcp kick-TA   empty-part last   night
       'John must have kicked the bucket last night'

  ii. a. Soili-lla   pitäisi ol-la   avain.
       Soili-adess should be-TA key(nom)
       'Soili should have the key'
    b. Avaime-n pitäisi   ol-la   Soili-lla
       key-gen   should   be-TA   Soili-adess
       'The key should be with Soili'

According to the current analysis, the lower clause subject in i and ii(b) must be base-generated as the subject of the lower infinitival verb, then raised to surface subject via lower object position to receive genitive case. It is unclear, however, where *avaimen* in ii(b) is base-generated or how it is theta-marked.

4. Finnish also has causative verbs where the causer appears in nominative case and the agent in oblique case:

i. Minä pese-t-i-n   auto-n Peka-lla
I(nom) wash-caus-past-1s car-acc Pekka-adess
'I had the car washed by Pekka'

Unlike Experiencer verbs, causative verbs show agreement morphology and specify an agent. This is assumed to be a separate construction.

5. Vainikka (1989b:226) notes the following word order effects in experiencer constructions: experiencer verbs appear to take partitive complements, suggesting that the partitive 'subject' is an underlying complement. However, preposing an oblique modifier results in ungrammaticality:

i. Jukka-a   pelotta-a hammaslääkäri-llä.
   Jukka-part scare-3s   dentist-at
   'Jukka is afraid when at the dentist's'

ii. Hammaslääkäri pelotta-a Jukka-a.
    dentist(nom)   scare-3s   Jukka-part
    'The dentist scares Jukka'

iii. *Hammaslääkäri-llä pelotta-a Jukka-a.
     dentist-at   scare-3s   Jukka-part

Vainikka suggests that fronting of the partitive object may occur early in the derivation, an analysis consistent with the current analysis of causatives as merged predicates.

6. Complement clauses show very interesting binding effects, in that all Pxes must be anaphoric. Pronominal subjects (i.e. those not bound with the matrix subject) in complement clauses must be expressed by genitive pronouns. It is unclear how to formalise such a constraint on Px agreement, although it may be related to properties of the historically accusative *-n* affix.

Complex Predicates and Non-finite Clauses   253

7. If ASP is assumed to be underspecified for major category, then there is no need to analyse gerundive constructions in Finnish as involving a major category change from V to N in mid-derivation (as suggested by Baker 1985) or where N dominates V in the structure (Vainikka 1989c), violating Extended Projection.

8. Purpose clauses are identical in form to another construction which occurs with a small set of direct perception verbs:

    i. Muistaa-kse-ni   Pekka asu-u   Tamperee-lla
      remember-kse-Px1s Pekka(nom) live-3s tampere in
      'If I remember correctly Pekka lives in Tampere'

This construction shares the same distribution as adverbs of manner and is assumed to be a lexicalised adverb, since no internal arguments are allowed:

    ii. *Ymmärtä-ä-kse-ni asia-n Presidentti e-i   tie-dä mitään.
       understand-TA-kse-Px1s issue-acc pres. neg-3s know-TA nothing
       'As far as I understand the issue the president knows nothing'

9. The lexicalised adverbial adjunct clause described in fn. 8 also shows the same binding properties:

    i. *Peka-n   tietä-ä-ksi   sata-a tänään.
      Pekka-gen know-TA-ksi rain-3s today
      'As far as Pekka knows it will rain today'

10. Vilkuna (1989:222) also describes these constructions as being underspecified for major category, labelling them as category ADVERB.

Bibliography

Abney, S. (1987) *The English Noun Phrase in its Sentential Aspect.* PhD dissertation, MIT.
Adger, D. (1994) *Functional Heads and Interpretation.* PhD dissertation, University of Edinburgh.
Adger, D. and C.S. Rhys (to appear) Eliminating disjunction in lexical specification. In P. Coopmans, M. Everaert, and J. Grimshaw (eds) *Lexical Specification and Lexical Insertion: Selected Papers from a Workshop at the University of Utrecht.* Hillsdale, N.J.: Lawrence Erlbaum Associates.
Almqvist, I. (1989) Negation and object marking in Finnish. In J. Niemi (ed) 1993, pp. 16-25.
Andrews, A. (1986) The major functions of the noun phrase. In T. Shopen (ed) *Language Typology and Syntactic Description I.* Cambridge: Cambridge University Press, pp. 62-154.
Austerlitz, R. (1989) Uralic languages. In B. Comrie (ed) *The World's Major Languages.* London: Croom Helm, pp. 567-576.
Baker, M. (1985) Syntactic affixation and English gerunds. *West Coast Conference on Formal Linguistics* 4:1-11.
Baker, M. (1988) *Incorporation.* London: University of Chicago Press.
Belletti, A. (1988) The case of unaccusatives. *Linguistic Inquiry* 19(1):1-34.
Bobaljik, J. and C. Phillips (eds) (1993) *Papers on Case and Agreement I.* MIT Working Papers in Linguistics 18. Cambridge, MA.: MIT Press.
Borer, H. (1984) *Parametric Syntax: Case Studies in Semitic and Romance Languages.* Dordrecht: Foris.
Burzio, L. (1986) *Italian Syntax.* Dordrecht: Reidel.
Cann, R. (1993) Argument structure and syntactic projection. Ms., University of Edinburgh.

Cann, R. (1993) Patterns of headedness. In G.C. Corbett, N.M. Fraser and S. McGlashan (eds) *Heads in Grammatical Theory*. Cambridge: Cambridge University Press, pp. 44-72.

Cann, R. and M. Tait (1989) Free relatives revisited. Ms, University of Edinburgh.

Chomsky, N. (1970) Remarks on nominalization. In R.A. Jacobs and P.S. Rosenbaum (eds) *Readings in English Transformational Grammar*. Waltham, Mass.: Ginn and Co., pp. 185-221.

Chomsky, N. (1981) *Lectures on Government and Binding*. Dordrecht: Foris.

Chomsky, N. (1986a) *Knowledge of Language: Its Nature, Origin, and Use*. New York: Praeger.

Chomsky, N. (1986b) *Barriers*. Cambridge, MA.: MIT Press.

Chomsky, N. (1991) Some notes on economy of derivation and representation. In R. Freidin (ed) *Principles and Parameters in Comparative Grammar*. Cambridge, Mass: MIT Press, pp. 417-54.

Chomsky, N. (1993) A minimalist program for linguistic theory. In K. Hale and S.J. Keyser (eds) *The View From Building 20*. Cambridge, MA.: MIT Press, pp. 1-52.

Comrie, B. (1975) The antiergative: Finland's answer to Basque. *Chicago Linguistics Society* 11:112-21.

Comrie, B. (1980) The ordering of case and possessive suffixes in the Uralic languages: An approach to the comparative-historical problem. *Lingua Posnaniensis* 23:81-86.

Dixon, R.M.W. (1968) *The Dyirbal Language of North Queensland*. PhD dissertation, University of London.

Dixon, R.M.W. (1979) Ergativity. *Language* 55:59-138.

Dixon, R.M.W. (1994) *Ergativity*. Cambridge Studies in Linguistics 69. Cambridge: Cambridge University Press.

Du Bois, J. (1987) The discourse basis of ergativity. *Language* 63:808-55.

Eliot, C.N.E. (1890) *A Finnish Grammar*. Oxford: Clarendon.

Freeze, R. (1992) Existentials and other locatives. *Language* 68:553-595.

Grimshaw, J. (1990) *Argument Structure*. Cambridge, MA.: MIT Press.

Grimshaw, J. (1991) Extended projection. Ms., Brandeis University.

Haegeman, L. (1991) *Introduction to Government and Binding Theory*. Oxford: Basil Blackwell.

Hakulinen, A. (1973) Semanttisia huomioita lauseenvastikkeista. (Some observations on the semantics of clause substitutes) *Sananjalka* 15:38-68.

Hakulinen, A. and F. Karlsson (1979) *Nykysuomen lauseoppia* (*Modern Finnish Syntax*). Helsinki: SKS.

Bibliography

Hakulinen, A. and L. Karttunen (1973) Missing persons: on generic sentences in Finnish. In *Papers from the Ninth Regional Meeting of the Chicago Linguistic Society*, pp. 157-171.

Hakulinen, L. (1946/1961) *Suomen kielen rakenne ja kehitys*, Helsinki: SKS, translated as *The Structure and Development of the Finnish Language*. Ural and Altaic Series vol 3. Bloomington: Indiana University Press.

Hale, K. (1982) Some essential features of Walpiri verbal clauses. In S. Swartz (ed) *Papers in Walpiri Grammar in Honour of Lothar Jagst*. Darwin: SIL.

Hale, K. (1983) Walpiri and the grammar of non-configurational languages. *Natural Language and Linguistic Theory* 1:5-47.

Heinämäki, O. (1984) Aspect in Finnish. In C. de Groot and H. Tomola (eds) *Aspect Bound*. Dordrecht: Foris, pp. 153-177.

Holmberg, A. and U. Nikanne (eds) (1993) *Case and Other Functional Categories in Finnish Syntax*. Studies in Generative Grammar. Berlin: Mouton de Gruyter.

Holmberg, A. and U. Nikanne (1993) Introduction. In A. Holmberg and U. Nikanne (eds) 1993, pp. 1-20.

Holmberg, A., U. Nikanne, I. Oraviita, H. Reime, and T. Trosterud (1993) The structure of INFL and the finite clause in Finnish. In A. Holmberg and U. Nikanne (eds) 1993, pp. 177-206.

de Hoop, H. (1992) *Case Configuration and Noun Phrase Interpretation*. PhD dissertation, University of Groningen.

Ikola, O. (1974) *Lauseenvastikeoppia. (A Study of Clause Substitutes)*. Helsinki: SKS.

Itkonen, T. (1979) Subject and object marking in Finnish: an inverted ergative system and an "ideal" ergative sub-system. In F. Plank (ed) *Ergativity: Toward a Theory of Grammatical Relations*. London: Academic Press.

Jaeggli, O. (1986) Passives. *Linguistic Inquiry* 17:587-622.

Jakobson, R. (1936/90) Contribution to the general theory of case. Reprinted in translation in L. Waugh and M. Monville-Burston (eds) *On Language: Roman Jakobson*. London: Harvard University Press, pp. 332-385.

Jelinek, E. (1993) Ergative "splits" and argument type. In J. Bobaljik and C. Phillips (eds) 1993, pp. 15-42.

Julien, M. (1994) Clause structure in Northern Saami. Ms., University of Tromsø.

Kanerva, J. (1987) Morphological integrity and syntax. *Language* 63:498-521.

Koopman, H. (1987) On the absence of Case Chains in Bambara. Ms., UCLA.

Koopman, H. and D. Sportiche (1991) The position of subjects. *Lingua* 85:211-58.

Laitinen, L. and M. Vilkuna (1993) Case marking in necessive constructions and split intransitivity. In Holmberg & Nikanne (eds) 1993, pp. 23-48.

Laka, I. (1993) Unergatives that assign ergative, unaccusatives that assign accusative. In J. Bobaljik and C. Phillips (eds) 1993, pp. 149-172.

Larson, R. (1988) On the double object construction. *Linguistic Inquiry* 19:335-392.

Lasnik, H. (1992) Case and expletives: Notes toward a parametric account. *Linguistic Inquiry* 23:381-405.

Lee, Young-Suk (1993) *Scrambling as Case-Driven Obligatory Movement*. PhD dissertation, University of Pennsylvania.

Leskinen, H. (1969) Eräs 3. p:n possessiivisuffiksin viitaussuhde. (The third person possessive suffix referent). *Virittäjä* 73:432-4.

Maling, J. (1993) Of nominative and accusative: the hierarchical assignment of grammatical case in Finnish. In A. Holmberg and U. Nikanne (eds) 1993, pp. 49-74.

Marantz, A. (1984) *On the Nature of Grammatical Relations*. Cambridge, MA.: MIT Press.

Milsark, G. (1985) Case Theory and the grammar of Finnish. *Proceedings of New England Linguistics Society* XV:319-331.

Milsark, G. (1988) Singl-ing. *Linguistic Inquiry* 19:611-34.

Mitchell, E. (1991a) Evidence from Finnish for Pollock's theory of IP. *Linguistic Inquiry* 22:373-79.

Mitchell, E. (1991b) Case and the Finnish object. *Cornell Working Papers in Linguistics* 9:193-228.

Mithun, M. (1991) Active/agentive case marking and its motivations. *Language* 67: 510-546.

Miyagawa, S. (1991) Case realization and scrambling. To appear in the *Proceedings of the Tilburg workshop on Scrambling*, Holland.

Moravcsik, E. (1978) On the distribution of ergative and accusative patterns. *Lingua* 45: 233-79.

van Nes-Felius, J. (1983) *The Passive in Finnish*. Master's Thesis, Rijksuniversiteit de Groningen.

Nevis, J. (1984) Five morphemes in Finnish: possessive suffixes or anaphoric clitics? *Ohio State University Working Papers in Linguistics* 29:174-207.

Nevis, J. (1986) *Finnish Particle Clitics and General Clitic Theory*. Ohio State University Working Papers in Linguistics 33.

Nevis, J. (1987) Clitics and semi-clitics in Finnish. In P. Lilius and M. Saari (eds) *The Nordic Languages and Modern Linguistics*, pp. 251-263.

Bibliography

Niemi, J. (ed) (1989) *Papers from the Eleventh Scandinavian Conference in Linguistics* vol. 1, University of Joensuu.

Nikanne, U. (1989) On locative cases in Finnish. In J. Niemi (ed) 1989, pp. 147-164.

Nikanne, U. (1991) *Zones and Tiers: A Study of Thematic Structure*. Helsinki: SKS.

Nikanne, U. (1993) On assigning semantic cases in Finnish. In A. Holmberg and U. Nikanne (eds) 1993, pp. 75-88.

Ouhalla, J. (1991) *Functional Categories and Parametric Variation*. London: Routledge.

Perlmutter, D. (1978) Impersonal passives and the unaccusative hypothesis. In J. Jaeger et al. (eds) *Proceedings of the Fourth Annual Meeting of the Berkeley Linguistics Society, February 18-20, 1978*, pp. 157-89.

Pierrehumbert, J. (1980) The Finnish possessive suffixes. *Language* 56:603-21.

Pollock, J.-Y. (1989) Verb movement, universal grammar, and the structure of IP. *Linguistic Inquiry* 20:365-424.

Ramchand, G. (1995) Aspect and predication: The semantics of argument structure. Ms., Oxford University.

Reime, H. (1989) Accusative marking in Finnish. In J. Niemi (ed) 1989, pp. 177-200.

Reime, H. (1993) Accusative marking in Finnish. In A. Holmberg and U. Nikanne (eds) 1993, pp. 89-109.

Renault, R. (1984) Theorie des roles thematiques et case morphologique de l'objet en Finnois. *Recherches Linguistiques* no. 12. Paris: University of Paris VIII.

Rigler, E. (1992) Morphological, grammatical, and semantic cases in Finnish. Ms., University of Edinburgh.

Rizzi, L. (1990) *Relativized Minimality*. Cambridge, MA.: MIT Press.

Sadeniemi, M. (1950) Partisiipien ajanmerkityksestä. (On the significance of time in participles). *Virittäjä* 54:358-9.

Sadock, J.M. and A.M. Zwicky (1985) Speech act distinctions in syntax. In T. Shopen (ed) *Language Typology and Syntactic Description* I. Cambridge: Cambridge University Press, pp. 155-196.

Schmerling, S. (1982) How imperatives are special, and how they aren't. In R. Schneider, K. Tuite, and R. Chametzky (eds), *Papers from the Parasession on Nondeclaratives.* Chicago Linguistics Society, University of Chicago, pp. 202-218.

Setälä, E. N. (1891/1952) *Suomen kielen lauseoppi*. Helsinki: Otava.

Shlonsky, U. (1989) The hierarchical representation of subject-verb agreement. Ms., University of Haifa, Israel.

Shore, S. (1988) On the so-called Finnish passive. *Word* 39:151-76.

Spencer, A. (1992) Nominal inflection and the nature of functional categories. Ms., University of Essex.

van Steenbergen, M. (1990) Finnish: configurational or not? in L. Marácz and P. Muysken (eds) *Configurationality*. Dordrecht: Foris.

Sulkala, H. and M. Karjalainen (1992) *Finnish*. London: Routledge.

Tait, M. (1991) *The Syntactic Representation of Morphological Categories*. PhD dissertation, University of Edinburgh.

Tait, M. and R. Cann (1990) On empty subjects. In *Proceedings of the Workshop on Parametric Variation*, Centre for Cognitive Science, University of Edinburgh.

Taraldsen, T. (1986) On the distribution of nominative objects in Finnish. In P. Muysken and H. van Riemsdijk (eds) *Features and Projections*. Dordrecht: Foris, pp. 139-162.

Tauli, V. (1966) *Structural Tendencies in the Uralic Languages*. Indiana University Publications Uralic and Altaic Series vol. 17. The Hague: Mouton.

Timberlake, A. (1975) The nominative object in Finnish. *Lingua* 35:201-230.

Timberlake, A. (1977) Reanalysis and actualization in syntactic change. In C. Li (ed) *Mechanisms of Syntactic Change*. New York: Academic Press, pp. 141-177.

Toivainen, J. (1993) The nature of the accusative in Finnish. In A. Holmberg and U. Nikanne (eds) 1993, pp. 111-128.

Trosterud, T.(1993) Anaphors and binding domains in Finnish. In A. Holmberg and U. Nikanne (eds) 1993, pp. 225-243.

Vainikka, A. (1989a) Multidimensional case agreement. In J. Niemi (ed) 1989, pp. 101-110.

Vainikka, A. (1989b) Object fronting induced by subject movement. In J. Niemi (ed) 1989, pp. 216-227.

Vainikka, A. (1989c) *Deriving Syntactic Representations in Finnish*. PhD dissertation, U Mass Amherst.

Vainikka, A. (1993) The three structural cases in Finnish. In A. Holmberg and U. Nikanne (eds) 1993, pp. 129-162.

Vainikka, A. and J. Maling (1996) Is partitive case inherent or structural? In J. Hoeksma (ed) *Partitives. Studies on the Syntax and Semantics of Partitive and Related Constructions*. Berlin/New York: Mouton de Gruyter, pp. 179-208.

Vilkuna, M. (1989) *Free Word Order in Finnish: Its Syntax and Discourse Functions.* Helsinki: SKS.

Wackernagel, J. (1892) Über ein Gesetz der indogermanischen Wortstellung. *Indogermanische Forschungen* 1:333-436.

Webelhuth, G. (1995) X-bar theory and case theory. In G. Webelhuth (ed) 1995, pp. 17-95.

Webelhuth, G. (ed) (1995) *Government and Binding Theory and the Minimalist Program.* Oxford: Basil Blackwell.

Wiik, K. (1981) Mikä lauseenvastike on? (What is a clause substitute?) *Virittäjä* 85:21-39.

Williams, E. (1995) Theta theory. In G. Webelhuth (ed) 1995, pp. 96-124.

Yip, M., J. Maling, and R. Jackendoff (1987) Case in tiers. *Language* 63:217-250.

Yli-Vakkuri, V. (1987) Aspect and the affective attitude of the speaker. In M. Koski, E. Lähdemäki and K. Häkkinen (eds) *Fennistica Festiva in honorem Göran Karlsson septuagenarii.* Åbo: Åbo Akademis, pp. 189-205.

Zanuttini, R. (1991) *Syntactic Properties of Sentential Negation: A Comparative Study of Romance Languages.* PhD dissertation, University of Pennsylvania [Institute for Research in Cognitive Science Report No. 91-26].

Zwicky, A. (1986) The general case: basic form versus default form. *BLS* 12, 305-14.

Index

φ-features, 94, 95, 105, 115, 117, 125, 135, 136, 137, 151, 168, 169, 177, 178, 202, 219, 245

[+COMPLETED] feature, 45, 64, 67, 122, 141–3

absolutive case, 98, 99, 101, 105, 109, 123–4, 132–3, 164
active system. *See* split-S
adjectives, 9, 30, 137, 185, 188–9, 212, 214, 215, 244
adjuncts, 189, 190, 217, 219, 242, 246, 248–50
adverbials, 21, 44, 49, 68, 130, 157–8, 174–7, 189, 190, 194, 235, 242, 246, 248, 250
AGR (agreement)
 case and, 89–93, 131–40
 possessive affixes and, 204–22
 strength of features in, 93–5, 125, 135
Aktionsart, 42, 102, 164
alienable possession, 170

'ambient' theta-role, 177
anaphors, 13, 66, 92, 187, 188, 192, 200–3, 204, 207, 224, 226, 245, 248
animacy hierarchies, 163–5, 183, 228, 233
'antiergativity,' 100
A-position, 179
Arabic, 119, 123, 125–6
aspect. *See* *Aktionsart*, boundedness, resultativity, durativity, telicity
aspectual theta-roles, 111, 140, 145–9, 150, 151, 164, 168, 177, 178, 230, 237, 239, 244
auxiliary verbs, 3, 10, 11, 19, 23, 24, 26, 27, 28–9, 30, 31, 32, 54, 58, 114, 115, 139, 144, 244

Bambara, 120
Basque, 132–3
binding, 12–14, 56, 66, 77, 91, 113, 186–8, 200–3, 223, 226, 248, 250
bi-uniqueness, 128–30, 150, 151, 156, 177, 239

boundedness, 42–4, 46, 141, 143, 145–7, 181
Burzio's Generalization, 39, 52–3, 76, 78–89, 93, 95, 98, 103–5, 111, 153, 176

case absorption, 52, 202
Case Chain, 120–1
Case Filter, 52, 65–8, 75, 78, 90, 116, 118–21, 123, 125, 128, 131, 134, 152, 156
Case Theory, 39, 47, 66–8, 75, 111, 118–40, 153, 178
Case Tiers, 68–70, 129, 157, 158, 176, 235
case transmission, 124–5
'caseless' elements, 65–7, 70, 90, 117, 122, 157, 162, 182
Categorial Grammar, 16
checking, feature, 94, 117, 123, 129, 131, 133–5
Chinese, 119, 136
cliticization, 15, 27, 173, 198, 200, 201, 224, 245
clitics, 54, 59, 171, 185, 186, 192–8, 200–3, 217, 224, 228
comparative, 6
complement clauses, 189, 224, 230, 237, 242–6, 250, 252
complementizers, 4, 33, 81, 189, 242
conditional mood, 24, 32, 48
configurationality, 11–15, 56, 65, 66, 70, 76
consonant gradation, 4–6, 9, 30, 31, 35, 41, 48, 59, 73, 95, 96, 97, 171, 174, 185, 193, 195, 197, 201, 212–4, 217, 243
copular verbs, 29, 47, 50, 56–7, 82, 84–5, 101, 143, 153, 170–1
Crossover, 14
c-selection, 16, 113–4, 208–9, 241, 245

dative case, 149, 182
default agreement, 20–22, 54, 60, 61, 89–95, 165
default case, 9, 63–4, 67, 89, 181
definiteness, 45, 142–4, 148
Definiteness Effect, 142, 170
determiners, 34, 182, 208
deverbal nouns, 187
discourse, 11, 34, 45, 183
double case assignment, 71, 152–74, 177, 178, 235
durativity, 143

Eastern Pomo, 103–4
ECP (Empty Category Principle), 134, 246, 248–9
English, 8, 12, 19, 20, 47, 49–52, 54, 67, 73, 79, 88, 94, 99, 109, 110, 118, 119, 121, 125, 131, 136, 142, 153, 174, 179, 182, 208, 228, 230, 238, 245
ergative case, 98–101, 109, 110, 132, 164
ergative verbs. *See* unaccusative verbs
ergativity, 71, 98–105, 106, 109, 111, 131–3, 163–5, 183

ergativity, split, 71, 98, 105, 111, 132, 152, 163, 183. *See also* split-S
Eskimo, 110, 202
Estonian, 3, 199
Exceptional Case Marking (ECM), 119, 238–9, 244–6
exhortatives, 97
existential sentences, 55–6, 101–2, 168–71
'existential' theta-role, 142, 148
EXPERIENCER role, 61, 87
Experiencer verbs, 87, 236–7

Fennic, 3
φ-features, 131
Final 1 Law, 53
finite verb, 49, 138, 191, 221
finiteness, 19–21, 129, 213, 226, 228
Finno-Ugric, 3, 7, 138, 199, 242
focus, 34
French, 20, 31, 90, 121, 125, 136, 179, 181

Gaelic. *See* Scottish Gaelic
gemination, 5, 197
generic interpretation, 11, 91–3, 206
generic sentences, 90–3, 130
genitive case, 9, 13–14, 39, 40, 60–1, 62, 65, 67, 72, 73, 75, 85, 86, 89–90, 94, 97, 101, 108, 117, 122–3, 142, 159, 160, 182, 185–90, 191–2, 198, 199, 200–3, 205, 209, 210, 221–26, 227, 228, 231–37, 240, 244, 247, 251, 252
German, 149
gerunds, 138, 188, 214, 220, 241–6, 253
governing domain, 65, 119–21, 128, 154, 173, 176–8, 184
Government Transparency Corollary (GTC), 121, 151
GPSG, 16, 211
grammatical function (GF), 47, 63–4, 68–71, 98–100, 129, 132, 157–8, 176, 178
Greed, 129, 180

head movement, 15, 127, 131, 139, 151, 154, 178, 183, 186, 213–9
Head Movement Constraint (HMC), 213
Hebrew, 202
hierarchy, animacy. *See* animacy hierarchies
hierarchy, case, 70, 159, 175
hierarchy, GF, 68–70, 129, 157–9, 176–7, 235
Hindi, 100
Hungarian, 3, 202, 204, 209

Icelandic, 62, 103, 129, 149, 233
i-command, 119–20, 128, 154, 166, 169, 235
idioms, 14, 251
imperative, 21, 25–8, 30, 32, 37, 47, 52, 57–9, 63–5, 76, 87–9, 93, 95–7, 104, 105,

109–10, 154, 171–4, 175, 183, 205–6, 229
imperfective, 143
impersonal passive, 4, 30, 47–53, 56, 57, 64, 65, 69, 72, 76, 81–2, 83, 86–92, 97, 104, 107–8, 109, 126, 153, 165–8, 171, 175, 176, 183, 204, 208, 229, 232–5
incorporation, 121, 131–3, 151, 237
indefiniteness, 42, 46, 142–44, 148
individual-level predicate, 117
Indo-European, 50, 118
infinitives, 29, 35, 59–62, 73, 86, 117, 123, 126, 180, 231–41, 247–9, 250, 251
inherent case, 43, 119, 141–2, 146–9, 153, 170
INSTRUMENT role, 78
inverted constructions, 12, 54, 101, 124, 183
Irish, 125
Italian, 47, 54, 82, 94, 103, 124–6, 183

Karelian, 3
Khanty, 3
Komi, 3
Korean, 137, 138, 175

Lakhota, 103
Lapp. *See* Saami
lauseenvastikkeet, 241–2
lexical case, 156–9, 235, 237
lexical entry, 16, 159, 211–5, 220–2, 245
Lexicalist Hypothesis, 202

Livonian, 3
L-marking, 151, 214–6
locative case, 3, 199, 217, 258
Logical Form (LF), 107, 131, 133, 136, 180

Mansi, 3
Mari, 3
markedness, 110, 164
'Maximal IP,' 113–6
Mayan, 100
measure phrases, 174–6
'Minimal IP,' 113–6
Minimalist Program, 119, 129–36
Minimality, 134–5
Mirror Principle, 200, 228
modal verb, 22, 26–7, 93–4, 221, 231–6
modality, 137
  deontic, 60, 97
Mohawk, 164
monadic predicate, 86, 95, 233
mood, 10, 20–1, 23–8, 37, 48, 57–9, 61, 95–7, 154, 159, 171, 205
Mordvin, 3
Motor, 3
m-selection, 16

necessive predicate, 60–1, 85–7, 89, 94, 97, 108, 159, 175, 231–6, 247, 251
negation, 10, 21–2, 23, 25–30, 32, 42, 44–5, 48–9, 54–6, 72, 73, 101, 109, 114–5, 123, 127, 141–2, 147, 165, 181, 207–8, 243–4, 250

Index

nominalizations, 4, 9, 35, 126, 189, 210–22, 241–50
nominative objects. *See* zero-accusative case.
non-finite verb. *See* nominalizations, infinitives
nonovert pronouns. *See* pro, PRO
non-specific referents, 88, 91
numerals, 42, 46, 182

obligation, 18, 25–8, 30, 61, 97, 117, 231–4
oblique case, 67, 161
oblique role, 158
oblique subject, 51, 62, 185, 236
operator, 77–8, 115, 147
Ostyak. *See* Khanty

particle clitic, 200
passive, 4, 19, 22, 30, 31, 32, 47–53, 56, 65, 67, 69, 72, 79, 80, 81–2, 86–92, 97, 107–8, 109, 112, 114, 116, 118, 119, 126, 136–7, 153–4, 157, 165–8, 171, 176, 181, 182, 183, 208, 229, 232–5, 239, 243, 249
perfect tense, 19, 24, 26, 28–32, 35, 42, 114, 138–9
Permic, 3
PF- Licensing Principle (PFLP), 18, 36, 95, 112–6, 136, 173, 179, 214, 220, 222–6
Pidgin English, 19
pleonastic subjects, 4, 11–12, 125

pluperfect tense, 26, 28–32, 42, 112, 138–9
plural nouns, case in, 39, 41–2, 68, 76, 108, 142, 161–3, 166
polarity, 22
Portuguese, 117, 123
possessive constructions, 56–7, 84–5, 108, 170–1, 186–8
postlexical rule, 159
postpositions, 8–10, 188, 198–9, 210, 212, 214
potential mood, 24, 32, 37
Predication Phrase (PredP), 68
prepositions, 9
pro, 4, 11–14, 54, 91–3, 109, 125, 177, 191, 201, 204, 245
PRO, 52, 124–5, 177, 234
pro-drop, 4, 10–11, 94, 206–7
Projection Principle, 12, 77, 116
pronouns
 animate, 39, 41–2, 47–62, 64–6, 68, 70, 80–9, 100, 104–6, 122, 153, 160–5, 186, 224
 demonstrative, 34, 209
 inanimate, 4, 40, 161, 223
 interrogative, 223
 reflexive, 200–1
Proto-Uralic, 72, 199
purpose clauses, 190, 247–8, 249

quantifiers, 109
quasi-arguments, 39
quirky case, 62, 129, 149, 233

Radical Functional Projection Hypothesis, 210–3, 225
raising predicates, 12, 35, 79–82, 87, 93, 103, 117–8, 120, 154, 230–3, 239, 246
resultativity, 42, 141, 145
R-expressions, 173–4
Russian, 50, 73

Samoyed, 3
scope, 21, 56, 72, 101
Scottish Gaelic, 117, 140, 144–7, 174–5
semantic case, 7–8, 36, 159, 198–9
semi-clitics, 194, 228
Shortest Move, 135
Spanish, 50, 94, 153
Spell-Out, 94, 131, 135
split intransitives. *See* split-S (ergativity)
split ergativity. *See* ergativity, split
split-S (ergativity), 71, 77, 98–105, 110, 111, 132, 152–74, 183
stage-level predicates, 117
stative predicates, 102, 138, 143, 146, 237
Stray Affix Filter, 151, 216, 221
Strong Structural case, 45, 144–5
Sumerian, 100
superlative, 6
Swedish, 19

telicity, 42–3, 141, 143, 146, 181
tense. *See* finiteness, perfect, pluperfect
THEME role, 97, 203
Theta Criterion, 77, 175
Theta Theory, 78, 145–6
theta-grid, 174
theta-marking, 36, 52, 63, 76–89, 107, 116–8, 122, 229, 233, 251
theta-role, 45–53, 67, 71, 76, 77–89, 95, 105, 111, 117–9, 122, 129, 130, 140–51, 164, 168, 177, 178, 180, 181, 182, 183, 211, 221, 230, 237–9, 244
topic, 33–4
Turkic, 242
Turkish, 204, 208–9, 243

Udmurt, 3
Ugric, 3
Unaccusative Hypothesis, 47, 53–4, 83, 103, 125, 142, 169
unaccusative verbs, 12, 47, 53–6, 66, 73, 76–87, 97, 99, 101–2, 104, 107, 110, 122–6, 133, 142, 154, 163, 168–171, 233, 235
unergative verbs, 40, 47, 50, 53–4, 78, 83, 99, 102–5, 124, 129, 132–3, 151–2, 154, 160, 163–4, 183
Uniformity Condition, 148
Uralic, 3, 4, 8, 72, 198–9, 241

Veps, 3

Visibility, 68, 90, 118, 180, 183
Vogul. *See* Mansi
voice, 17, 30-2, 114
volition, 53-4, 102-3, 233, 236
Votic, 3
vowel harmony, 3-5, 30, 35, 41, 48, 73, 194, 228
VP-Internal Subject Hypothesis (VISH), 117, 125-6, 217

Weak Structural case, 45, 144-9
weather verbs, 12, 50, 130, 177
Welsh, 119, 125
wh-extraction, 246, 248-9
word order, 11-15, 22, 54, 66, 73, 81, 84, 96, 118-9, 124-6, 139-40, 144, 171, 173, 176, 178, 184, 241, 252
    SVO, 12, 54, 120, 125, 134, 144
    VSO, 120, 125, 144

X-bar structure, 12, 16, 77, 113, 114, 159, 211, 260

zero accusative case, 39
zero-accusative case, 20, 39, 47-71, 76, 80-9, 95, 96, 103-5, 111, 118, 122, 127, 138, 168, 174-5, 182, 229, 231, 234, 237, 239-40

For Product Safety Concerns and Information please contact our EU representative GPSR@taylorandfrancis.com
Taylor & Francis Verlag GmbH, Kaufingerstraße 24, 80331 München, Germany

www.ingramcontent.com/pod-product-compliance
Lightning Source LLC
Chambersburg PA
CBHW071348290426
44108CB00014B/1470